A Graceful Exit

Life and Death on Your Own Terms

A Graceful Exit

Life and Death on Your Own Terms

LOFTY L. BASTA, M. D.

with Carole Post, Ph. D.

Plenum Press • New York and London

Library of Congress Cataloging-in-Publication Data

Basta, Lofty L.
A graceful exit : life and death on your own terms / Lofty L. Basta with Carole Post.
p. cm.
Includes bibliographical references and index.
ISBN 0-306-45270-7
1. Right to die. 2. Terminal care--Moral and ethical aspects. I. Post, Carole, 1953- . II. Title.
R726.B325 1996
174'.24--dc20 96-1283
CIP

ISBN 0-306-45270-7

Insight Books is a Division of Plenum Publishing Corporation
233 Spring Street, New York, N.Y. 10013-1578

An Insight Book

10 9 8 7 6 5 4 3 2 1

Printed in the United States of America

To those who value life and dignity

"Getting out of this world gracefully is not an easy thing."

—Eugene A. Stead, Jr., M.D. (1968)

Foreword

The delicate and difficult subject of this excellently written book by my very good friend, Dr. Lofty Basta, is the love and care at or near the end of life. Every human being of sound mind strives at some point during his or her lifetime for a dignified, graceful, grateful, loving, peaceful, and thankful final farewell. Can such a goal be achieved realistically in the not too distant future given the documented serious problems that underlie the care of the terminally ill?

The twentieth century, which itself is quickly nearing its "graceful exit," will leave its mark in medical history not only for tremendous technological advances but also for the willingness of the medical, legal, paramedical, nonmedical, religious, and political communities and the public at large to deal with the medicolegal and ethical dilemmas from birth to death. In today's increasingly complex society in the United States, and indeed worldwide, there is greater insight into the field of "medical ethics," especially as it touches on such thorny issues as the economics of health care, patients' rights, conflicts of interest, and professional ethics. During the twentieth century, medical practice has changed radically in the United States through the combined impact of competition, prospective and capitated payments, managed care, and peer review. One of the reasons which has been advanced for the dramatic rise in health-care costs is the prevalence of unnecessary, inappropriate, and expensive medical procedures and interventional treatments. In medicine today, conservative medical treatment frequently is viewed as antiquated and suboptimal, and yet many patients, especially those receiving care at or near the end of life, are likely to exhibit the same or similar outcome when treated "conservatively"—noninvasively and nonsurgically. And, in general, "heroic" medical and surgical treatment of a terminally ill individual who has only a few days to live is at best futile, intrusive, and expensive, and may at times be categorized as inhumane.

Ethical, legal, and economic concerns arise when a number of nonclinical factors might be compelling a management approach that is medically futile and not in the patient's best interest. Ethical guidelines and legal standards are being developed and have positive implications for reinforcing patient trust and public regard. Presently, patients, physicians, hospitals, and the public at large are being required to rethink medical ethics and priorities, particularly health care at or near the end of life.

This superbly written and extensively referenced book by Dr. Basta tackles this intricate and sensitive subject—medical care of the terminally ill—and provides great insight from the standpoint of the compassionate, talented, scholarly, and honest physician who has practiced both the science and, more importantly, the art of medicine to the fullest. In addition, Dr. Basta's personal experiences with his own medical problems add immeasurably to his keen understanding of medical care at or near the end of life. He details the serious problems confronting the terminally ill and provides superb recommendations to resolve these situations, including the uniform living will.

This book offers something for every person who deals with the care of patients at or near the end of life. It emphasizes the need to fully inform the terminally ill patient, or his or her surrogate, about the medical options available. It also stresses allowing the patient or surrogate to be an active participant in the choices of care and to make the ultimate decisions before the final farewell by the patient to the loved ones.

It is an honor and a privilege for me to be asked to write this brief foreword.

S. SANDY SANBAR, M.D., PH.D., J.D., FCLM
Past President (1989–1990)
American College of Legal Medicine
Oklahoma City, Oklahoma

Preface

Dying: A Personal Note

Everyone can master a grief but he that has it.
—SHAKESPEARE (in *Much Ado about Nothing,* III; 21:28)

I am a physician specializing in the treatment of heart disease who has been afflicted with cancer. As a physician, I am bound by the Hippocratic oath to do everything I can to prolong the lives of my patients and alleviate their suffering. Over the years, steadily and imperceptibly, medical intervention to "alleviate suffering" has received a much diminished status compared to the prolongation of life in my practice of medicine and probably in most physicians' practices. Death became the prime enemy to be conquered; prolongation of life became the mission of my life. Toward this goal, I devoted my energies, talents, skills, and passions, all mediated by the powers of the new and exciting tools of high technology.

I have become conditioned to derive my "highs" from technological achievements. No joy approached that derived from opening a blocked blood vessel in a patient who had experienced a heart attack. No triumph came close to that of bringing a heart that ceased to beat in an orderly and effective manner back to its regular and orderly rhythm through a carefully administered jolt of electricity. And I felt the greatest ecstasy of all from bringing a person back from the abyss of death by prompting a heart that had stopped beating into beating again. I have loved my patients and my profession. It provided me with thrills, gratification, and a sense of accomplishment, as well as a good living.

The heady success experienced by many physicians can give them a feeling of immortality. I immodestly believed, "I might not be able to walk on water, but I am willing to try, and one day I shall succeed!"

One day in February 1987, that sense of immortality was shattered. That morning, I noticed some discomfort in my groin and the stream of my urine was weak. Reluctantly, I approached my friend, a urologist, Dr. Roger Haglund, and asked him to examine my prostate. After the examination, I knew the diagnosis when I looked at his face; his eyes declared the diagnosis. In a soft and kind voice he said, "You have a much enlarged prostate gland. There is a large and hard nodule in one of the lobes ... I believe it to be cancer."

My wife and I made the trip to M. D. Anderson Cancer Center in Houston and the diagnosis was confirmed. I was advised to undergo pelvic lymphadenectomy (surgical removal of small lymph nodes in my abdomen and pelvis) to assess the grade of cancer. This was to be followed by radiation therapy (the use of high-voltage X rays) to burn the tumor and the area around it, including the rectum and bladder.

The pundits of medical ethics preach the concepts of shared decision making between patient and physician, with the patient having ultimate autonomy to determine his or her treatment destiny. They caution against paternalization by the physician in medical decisions. Have these ethicists ever been patients themselves? The vulnerability of patients often leads them to forfeit this responsibility. Dr. Eugene Stead, a legendary physician who chaired the Department of Medicine at Duke University for 20 years, 1947–1967, was once quoted as saying:

> Two years in a hospital, night and day, are necessary to see how illness looks, to see what people behind the patient look like in all circumstances. I must confess that in this era of unprecedented technologic advance, it takes a doctor to experience disease firsthand to sensitize him to the human component of disease.

Well, I am a physician and now also a patient. Ask me about a heart problem, and I will answer you with confidence and authority. But, here I am, in a hospital bed, faced with death from a disease I know very little about. The expert made a recommendation. I trusted his professional opinion, and I trusted him as a person. My answer was, as expected, "Do what you think is best for me."

I recall the thousands of times my patients relinquished medical decision making to me with the pronouncement, "You're the doctor." In the practice of medicine, there is no substitute for a physician who earns his or her patient's trust. I wish we could keep it this way! This trust is the essence of that sacred and powerful bond between patient and physician called the doctor–patient relationship.

For the first time in my life, I had to experience what it is like to be a patient, to face major surgery and its sequelae, and to know what it is like to discover mortality.

It is one thing to be the valiant warrior armed with the powerful tools of high technology and well prepared to combat an enemy that you have been prepared and trained to face and conquer. It is another thing altogether when the enemy is within you. How vastly different when your own body becomes the battlefield. How different to witness the fight between a cancer expanding within you and the treatments promising to cure you, but also inevitably hurting you along the way. My experience with my illness brought into question, in my mind, traditional teaching about ethics in medical schools: Beneficence (doing good), nonmaleficence (abstaining from wrongdoing), justice, paternalism (forcing decision making), autonomy, and altruism are key players in basic philosophical ethics. But abstract ethics are remote from the drama of the human encounter with the confrontation of fear and hope, surrender and denial, acceptance and rejection, depression and defiance, hopelessness and anger.

My painful experience with my disease was also enlightening. I discovered that I am not afraid of death itself, but of how I might die. I dreaded a prolonged, painful existence. I realized that death is not an offense to nature but the realization of the completion of life. I know that if I were to choose, I would like to depart peacefully in my bed, without pain or suffering. I state this emphatically while I am enjoying life like never before. My disease has been in remission for several years. I am keenly cognizant of what brings meaning to life: love of family, genuine caring, and the immense pleasure of being surrounded by wonderful students and colleagues.

This book is a testament to my confrontation with the imminence of death. Although as a patient I have relinquished much medical decision making to my physician, I do not want to relinquish control over how I will die; I do not want to be "treated to death." I am writing this book to help others confront this issue and to help prepare them to make decisions that can control the final phase of their lives.

Contents

Introduction

Discussions about the need for health-care reform have intensified recently. A majority of Americans seem to agree that something needs to be done to curb the runaway costs of health care in America. However, there seems to be no consensus about the specifics of what needs to be accomplished, nor of how to go about it. Unless we have a proper diagnosis of what needs reform, the proposed treatment is unlikely to be effective. The prescription under consideration today will yield, at best, temporary symptomatic relief, and, at worst, may prove to be countertherapeutic and too costly.

Politicians delight in reminding us that, in the United States, we have the best medicine that man has ever known. And this is true. But the promise that we can offer more and better care to everyone all the time at a lower cost is implausible, naïve, preposterous, or outright deceitful. In order to control costs, we have to limit services, compromise quality, or implement a combination of the two. In a recent article in one of the leading medical journals, the *Annals of Internal Medicine*, a leading ethicist from the University of Pennsylvania, Arthur Caplan, Ph.D., contends: "[A]ttempting to sell the American public on a plan for reform that would rein in costs and expand coverage for the uninsured without acknowledging the necessity of some form of rationing was, at best, dishonest."[1]

It has been argued that the cost of medical care is excessively high in the United States in comparison to other Western nations, even when one allows for the fact that American medical services are the best in the world. Built into the cost of health-care services in the United States are needless administrative costs; an expensive medical liability system; an abundance of expensive, futile, or near futile care; and higher costs of pharmaceuticals and medical devices. Any national reform should address these problems. Unfortunately, other factors that serve to increase the cost of health care in America are more intractable and therefore difficult to address. These factors include social and behavioral problems, such as drug addiction, violence, and other examples of reckless behavior that have adverse effects on health. The urgent need to prevent, control, and treat AIDS has added an unanticipated financial burden on the world community and, particularly, on the United States.

An aging society with ever-increasing demands for more and better health care abetted by a breathtaking technological advance promising longer and healthier lives is at the core of the problem. Earlier in this century, it took 50 years to double all existing human knowledge. In the 1970s, 10 years were sufficient for an encore, and in 1985 it took only two years to double all that is known to man. Unfortunately, the promise of immortality and a technological fountain that grants eternal youth are as elusive as ever.

Futile medical care near the end of life, in part, stems from, and is intertwined with, fear of litigation. No doubt, "defensive medicine" constitutes a substantial portion of health-care expenditure in this country. It is true that an alert legal system contributes to the excellence of medical care standards in America. On the other hand, the ease of litigation and the size of punitive damages in some well-publicized cases have rendered the medical profession extremely cautious. Physicians worry constantly about the possibility of malpractice litigation with any unfavorable treatment outcome. Routinely, they seek high-tech interventions in order to prevent any remote possibility of being sued. This self-protective behavior from physicians, while justifiable, is self-perpetuating and very costly for the society at large. Some might argue, not groundlessly, that fear of litigation may not be the main reason for excessive terminal care, but it continues to be its main excuse.

How did we allow ourselves, as individuals and as a society, to get into this bottomless pit? Why do we allow people to be medically treated to death, without regard to the emotional and financial consequences for individuals, families, and society?

Physicians should have predicted that overtreatment could produce permanently disabled bodies connected to malfunctioning heads; they should have forewarned the public, but they wouldn't. Consequently, the public keeps demanding useless expensive care when it shouldn't. Legislators might have enacted the necessary laws to enable the establishment of priorities for the distribution of expensive and sparse resources, but they couldn't. And the courts (including the Supreme Court in the Cruzan case) have had the chance to guide our way through this nightmare, but they haven't.

In an era of increasingly shared medical information, medical practice is changing into a partnership between physicians and the public. Physicians no more command an absolute moral authority in deciding the troubling issues of whom to treat and whom to let die. Neither will user-friendly health data ever be sufficient for the lay public to answer these vexing questions. Medical ethicists would like to claim these issues as being within their domain. But ethics are not freestanding universal truths; they are merely logical deductions from ideological premises colored by our cultural, religious, and personal beliefs and biases.

One of the major dilemmas facing legislators is, no doubt, how to limit care without being accused of medical rationing. The latter is a no-no in political language. Rationing (the "R" word) is the equivalent to political cyanide. Given these facts, legislators have to discover a convoluted way by which they take us to the promised land of increased access to medical care at a lower cost, without the appearance of rationing care. They have relinquished this weighty issue to the mercy of market forces with their new schemes of managed care. I am fearful that, in order to accomplish their political objective, they will pit doctor against patient.

In the process, the one clear casualty will be that the sacred bond of doctor–patient relationship will be mortally sacrificed at the altar of cost containment. The traditional role of the physician as the patient's servant and advocate who provides the best care regardless of cost will likely be subject to political manipulation. Instead, in the new world of reform, the physician will be expected to act as the agent of the big new bureaucracy, a heartless business establishment whose relentless focus is on maximizing shareholder's profit. He is expected to limit and regulate health-care delivery on behalf of the big company (or the government). Should that happen, the American health-care system would sustain the worst self-inflicted damage in history. According to this scenario (which seems to be quite plausible), access to health care will be delivered (and rationed) according to guidelines set forth by bureaucrats. These guidelines will be formulated with the sole intention of limiting cost. Therefore, in a peculiar way, the legislators will have used noble slogans to cover less noble goals.

It behooves us as citizens of a society that upholds the highest ideals of equality and democracy to engage ourselves in formulating these guidelines that will set health-care priorities and conserve limited resources. Relinquishing this role to bureaucrats will prove to be a grave mistake.

In this book, I have addressed one component of the extremely complex problem of health care—medical care near the end of life. It is an attempt to explore the causes, the dilemmas, and the ethical and legal controversies, as well as the economic consequences of the excessive use of high technology and the exercise of futile medical care at the end of someone's life. This book is not intended to be a compendium of issues related to medical ethics or legal precedents relating to the care of the terminally ill. Rather, it is a search to find a common ground from which we can proceed toward establishing unified policies that guide treatment at the end of life.

I do this from the perspective of a practicing cardiologist who has been part of the medical revolution of the past four decades, and as a citizen who cares deeply about our country and its future generations. In so doing, I have drawn on my own vast clinical experience and on the wisdom of many others. All medical case histories included in this book are real. Most patients are referred to by fictitious names. When true names are mentioned, appropriate permission has been obtained from their families.

The book is written for common citizens who care deeply about preserving their dignity and sparing loved ones the agony and economic consequences inherent in life-and-death decisions. It should be a valuable guide for medical students and young physicians who have learned about manifestations of disordered body functions, damaged organs, and disturbed emotions. They need to know more about the fearful, hopeful, suffering, anxious human being behind the disease. Hospital ethics committees should be able to benefit from the case reviews and ethicolegal reviews.

As a physician, I have executed the "will" of thousands of patients regarding how they wish to die. As an author, I would like to help others exercise more control of the end-stage of their lives. This book is intended to educate all Americans about life-and-death issues. The topics I will address include the following:

- The inadequacies of existing living wills in the United States today.
- The need to adopt a new definition of *death* that is based on the "death of the person" rather than the death of an organ such as the heart or the brain. This information could equip all of us to better evaluate referendums on the right to die, health-care prioritizing, and other timely and controversial issues.
- The need to set up a commission comprised of both health-care professionals and laypeople to grapple with issues of life and death.
- The need to adopt a new, standardized living will. I am proposing an original document, the "Universal Living

Will" with a concomitant workbook section. This document could do much to ensure a death without suffering and with dignity for all.

Limited space and imperfect recollection prevent me from acknowledging the thousands of sources from which I have quoted freely, and the hundreds of persons who touched my life and influenced my thinking.

A few have contributed substantially to this effort, and I am deeply in debt to each of them. My associate, Dr. Robert Henning, has helped my perspective on the problems inherent in the present definition of death. Dr. Jeffrey Tauth provided valuable advice. Dr. Carole A. Post has been an integral partner in this effort. Judy Parker, R.N., has been my assistant for 12 years and helped with the project since its inception, and Marie Cheine, my present secretary, assisted with the last phase of the project.

Laila, my wife of 35 years, has been my mentor, advisor, and critic, and has made the journey of my life so worthwhile that I wouldn't have wanted to undertake it without her. Each of my three children, Victor, Steven, and Mona, has given me valuable suggestions and guidance. And my very special grandson, Max, makes me cherish every moment in life like never before.

NOTES

1. AL Caplan. "Straight Talk about Rationing," *Annals of Internal Medicine*, 122, 1995, 795–796.

Chapter 1

Quality of Death

An Ancient Perspective on a Contemporary Issue

The immortal Gods alone have neither age nor death. All other things almighty Time disquiets.

—SOPHOCLES (in *Oedipus at Colonus*, 406 B.C.:309)

AN ACT OF MISPLACED HEROICS

A few years ago, before I was diagnosed with cancer and forced to really ponder my own mortality, I was attending to a "routine" emergency at the hospital. Suddenly, a "code blue" was called. The familiar alarm declared that someone's heart had just stopped beating. Along with hordes of other health-care professionals, I hurried to the patient's room and took command of the resuscitation. The patient's heart resumed its beating and Mr. Jones, the patient, began breathing again.

There was a full moon that night. On the way to my car, I felt as if the moon and the stars were there to celebrate my triumph over death.

The next morning, the nurses informed me that Mr. Jones was fully recovered. He was alert and fully aware of himself, others, and the surroundings. I visited Mr. Jones in the intensive-care unit and congratulated him for his new lease on life. It was my first eye-to-eye contact with Mr. Jones. He stared at me and didn't utter a word. I wondered why. After a long moment of silence he said accusingly, "Why did you do this to me? You have taken away from me my one chance to leave this world in dignity." He went on to tell me that he had been made miserable by lung cancer, which had spread through his body. His pain was intolerable and no longer tractable to powerful pain-killing medicine. Bodily pain, as burdensome and demoralizing as it was, he could endure. But he could not abide the mental suffering that resulted from his total dependence, inability to care for himself, and the enormous drain on his life-savings from mounting medical bills. "Physical pain can be numbed with medicine, but mental suffering is not touched by any medicine," he said. He had been waiting for the moment of a peaceful, graceful exit. He concluded by saying, "I will never forgive you for what you have done to me." I wished at that moment that the ground could have opened up and swallowed me. I felt as if a shower of ice water had been poured on me. Tears overpowered me as I realized that the pinnacle of technological triumphs—the resuscitation of a life—and the nadir in human failures—the resuscitation of a miserable existence—can meet at one point in time, and that these two extremes can become one and the same act. My encounter with Mr. Jones taught me a valuable lesson: Bringing someone back from the darkness of death, someone yearning for a graceful exit, in order to subject him or her to myriad punishments is not a miracle reminiscent of the raising of Lazarus. It is a misguided insult to human dignity. It has nothing to do with the essence of medicine, the core of which is compassion for peoples' well-being.

Sooner or later I will face mortality. I want to make it perfectly clear that I do not want any health-care professional, knowingly or unknowingly, to treat me in the way that I treated Mr. Jones. I have not seen Mr. Jones since that encounter. I am sure he has long since departed this planet. But I would like to take this opportunity to say that I am eternally grateful for the lesson he taught me.

I know how I do not want to die. I do not want to die in a hospital bed, hooked up to a multitude of tubes that are connected to machines that breathe for me, produce urine on my behalf, or beat in place of my heart. I have had a great life, and I am enjoying the best years of my life. I want to preserve the remainder of it as long as I can, but not at any cost. This view is not just my own. It is shared by the vast majority of well-informed citizens. In a recent nursing conference, I asked this question of 200 nurses, many of whom work in intensive-care units. Not one nurse wished to die like most Americans. Instead, they wished to die at home in a clean, warm bed. Advances in medical technology have not diminished the truth of George Bernard Shaw's conclusion in his play, *The Doctor's Dilemma*: "Do not try to live forever. You will not succeed."[1]

FROM OEDIPUS TO TITHONUS: WHICH WAY TO DIE?

Searching for the meaning in life is a lifelong pursuit; so is the search for the best way to die. In order to understand this last issue, two figures from Greek mythology provide us with valuable insight.

Oedipus, one of the most important figures in the Theban cycle of legends, the son of King Laius, is primarily remembered today for a phrase (the Oedipus complex), referring to his unfortunate marital choice.[2] But his highly eventful life is also noteworthy for his uneventful death. In fact, the peaceful departure of Oedipus from life is something we might all aspire to. According to the Delphic Oracle, Oedipus was destined to kill his father and marry his mother. Therefore, his father wanted to dispose of him shortly after birth in order to avert catastrophe. But the baby Oedipus was found and was adopted by King Polybus and his wife, the childless, ruling couple of Corinth. Not knowing that his adoptive parents were not his true parents, Oedipus fled his new home when the Delphic Oracle revealed to Oedipus his tragic destiny.

And, in a bizarre turn of events, Oedipus ultimately killed his true father, King Laius.[3]

Before this tragic event occurred, Oedipus experienced great moments of glory. At Thebes, he solved the riddle of the sphinx and thereby freed the city from that monster. In Greek mythology, the sphinx, a monster with the body of a lion and head of a woman, was most notable for propounding riddles. Anyone who encountered the sphinx was forced to answer the riddle correctly, or die. Oedipus, on his way to Thebes, was confronted with the riddle, "What has sometimes two feet, sometimes three, sometimes four, and is weakest when it has most?" Oedipus answered promptly, "Man, for he crawls on all fours as a baby, walks on two feet as a youth, and needs a cane in old age." The sphinx, in chagrin killed itself.

As a reward for his triumph, Oedipus was made king and married the widowed queen Jocasta, his true mother. After discovering that his wife was his mother, Oedipus blinded himself, cursed his sons, and moved to Attica for a self-imposed exile with his daughter, Antigone. Jocasta, his mother–wife, committed suicide.

The rest of Oedipus's life was uneventful. Indeed, he lived a very peaceful and long life with his daughter. Furthermore, his death was uneventful and peaceful. According to Sophocles's immortal Greek drama entitled *Antigone*,

> When it was time for Oedipus to die, his daughter, Antigone, with help from her younger sister, Ismene, bathed him and dressed him in a ritual preparation for death. Oedipus declared his love for his daughters and bid them farewell. With a background of prayer to bring him relief from suffering, it was declared: "Oedipus was taken without lamentation, illness or suffering; indeed his end was wonderful if a mortal's ever was ..."

Indeed a graceful exit!

By contrast, consider the life of Tithonus, who was the son of the Trojan King Laomedon and husband of Eos (Dawn).[4] They had one son, Memnon. Eos loved Tithonus—loved him to distraction. Eos persuaded the god Zeus to bestow eternal life on her husband, but in her fervent entreaties, she forgot to request that eternal youth go with this eternal life. As a result, Tithonus lived a life of eternal senility, decrepitude, and suffering. He kept on shrinking until he looked like a dried-up insect. This miserable existence lasted an eternity.[5]

Before the advent of modern medical technology, many people had a graceful, Oedipus-like exit. Today, too many people have a Tithonus-like end—miserable existences with decrepitude, pain from senility, accident, or disease, often maintained through high-tech machines.

WHEN MIRACULOUS TECHNOLOGY PROMOTES A MISERABLE, TITHONUS-LIKE EXISTENCE

The last three decades have seen the advent of technology that brings a new lease on life for some, but the curse of a prolonged death for others. The success of cardiopulmonary resuscitation (CPR) and the invention of new machines to aid or even take over the functions of the heart and lungs not only delay the moment of death, but render obsolete the old definition of death as cessation of "vital flow"; that is, the heart and lungs stop functioning, and consequently blood, nutrients, and oxygen necessary for keeping the body alive also stop. In 1981, a new definition of death was adopted, based upon the recommendation of the Presidential Commission for Medical Ethics and Biomedical and Behavioral Research.[6] The new definition focused on the brain rather than the heart and lungs. Death now occurs only when the whole brain ceases to function. This new definition proved useful in guiding the harvesting of organs for use in transplantation, but it has obvious shortcomings.

The perspective that death occurs only when the whole brain ceases to function led to the inescapable result that individuals who manifest even rudiments of brain function are considered to be alive. Hordes of individuals have been maintained in states of permanent unconsciousness—the so-called "permanent vegetative state"—with no reasonable hope for recovery and at an enormous cost to families and to society. According to the American Neurological Association survey results on persistent vegetative state (PVS), there are 10,000–25,000 adults and 4,000–10,000 children in PVS in the USA.[7] These beings are technically alive, according to the new definition, but functionally dead, in that they cannot carry out any of the functions that constitute personhood. They can breathe and defecate, but are unable to feel, experience, appreciate, communicate, or express emotions.

The medical profession, fearful of legal repercussions, resisted attempts to withhold or withdraw treatment from these beings. Courts had to intervene on behalf of families and their loved ones in this vegetative state to limit undesired care. But, as we shall see, the legal profession has not been able to successfully arbitrate the global issue of life and death.

LEGAL RULINGS OF LIFE-AND-DEATH IMPORTANCE

In 1976, three landmark precedents occurred, each of which had a profound effect on medical intervention at the end of a person's life.

The first court landmark decision involved the sustenance by machines of a comatose Karen Ann Quinlan.[8] Ms. Quinlan was a young lady who sustained extensive and irreversible brain damage from a medication overdose. Her "life" was maintained through artificial ventilation. The New Jersey court system arbitrated her case. Ms. Quinlan's mother asked the court to disconnect her unconscious daughter from the ventilator on the basis that her quality of existence was unacceptable by any rational standard. The treating physicians and hospital objected on the basis that Ms. Quinlan was considered alive on the basis of persistent "vegetative" subconscious functions of the brain; disconnecting the patient from the machine could result in the termination of such a "life" as defined by the Harvard report and endorsed by the President's Commission. Ms. Quinlan was alive as long as her lower brain continued to function, despite her lack of higher brain consciousness. Ms. Quinlan's physician, Dr. Robert Morse, testifying in court, made a claim that was prevailing at that time: As the treating physician, he had the right and duty to continue providing assisted ventilation to his patient. His claim was that, as a physician, he was an authority of life and death matters. He could judge whether a ventilator served a worthwhile purpose, even when his judgment conflicted with that of Ms. Quinlan's parents and many others.

The court upheld the mother's request to remove the patient from the ventilator against the advice of the treating physicians, accepting the mother's judgment as a substitute for the victim's own (Substitute Judgment Standard). Karen Ann Quinlan was disconnected from the ventilator and died several years later.

The 1976 California Natural Death Act was enacted on the heels of the Karen Ann Quinlan case and clearly was inspired by it.[9] The act allowed the withholding or withdrawal of life-sustaining intrusive measures under certain circumstances of terminal illness. It is interesting to note that although the California legislation was initiated as a result of the Quinlan case, Karen Ann Quinlan would not have qualified as terminally ill according to the California legislation; that is, she did not have a terminal illness that would have resulted in her death in two weeks, with or without treatment.

Finally, during this precedent-setting year of 1976, the Massachusetts General Hospital Critical Care Committee made its recommendations regarding the management of hopelessly ill patients at the end of life. In addition, the same committee developed some guidelines for "Do Not Resuscitate" orders. These were published in the *New England Journal of Medicine*, one of the leading medical journals. The strict criteria advanced by the Massachusetts committee guided medical care near the end of life for several years thereafter (more on this later).[10]

Legal Heat Rather Than Legal Light

Since 1976, many cases have been brought to court, some of which demanded discontinuation of treatment to spare the patient the indignity of continuing a life not worth living. Others involved cases in which relatives demanded the continuation of life support when in the judgment of medical professionals, that treatment would produce no hope of recovery. Still others demanded the active termination of life by patients in intractable pain or experiencing enormous suffering due to advanced illness or extreme incapacity. Court decisions were often incomplete, conflicting, or of limited application. Many of these provided more legal heat than legal light. But these life-and-death issues have been left up to individual physicians, or individual medical institutions.

LIVING WILL TO ARBITRATE LIFE AND DEATH

Over the past years, various states have adopted "advance directives for medical care" otherwise known as "living wills." In many states, these advance directives have evolved to incorporate durable power of attorney for individuals chosen by the patient. These surrogate individuals, who are assigned durable power of attorney, are authorized to make medical decisions on behalf of the patient in the event that he or she loses the ability and competence to make such decisions, or to express them. Living wills received increasing attention when the supreme court tried the Cruzan case in 1990.[11,12]

Nancy Cruzan was a young lady from Missouri, who experienced extensive brain injury as the result of a car accident. She was sustained in a persistent vegetative state by intrusive means, including the feeding of food and the giving of water through tubes. The Cruzan family asked that their daughter not be sustained by these artificial means. The state of Missouri objected on the basis that the state has an obligation to preserve the "life" of its citizens. The Supreme Court upheld the State of Missouri's rationale that there be "clear and convincing evidence" that the family's request reflected Ms. Cruzan's personal desire. If Ms. Cruzan had had a living will that specified her desires regarding medical intervention under such specific circumstances, the outcome of the case might have been different. The much-awaited Supreme Court hearings on the Cruzan case came as a shock to many. The media rushed to interpret the court decision to mean that unless you have executed a valid living will, you should expect to be medically treated to death. Some promoted the slogan: "The living will, don't leave home without it." In fact, what the Supreme Court did was to assert that, for a Missouri citizen, existing Missouri law applied. This law was revoked shortly thereafter by legislative action from the Missouri Congress.

The Limitations of Living Wills

For many reasons, living wills are not widely used by the general public. Under many circumstances, these advance directives regarding medical intervention are not legally binding. They also contain many caveats and shortcomings. It is unlikely that, in their present form, advance directives will have a substantial impact on medical care in the United States. Of note is the fact that living wills are unpopular in other Western countries, with the exception of Denmark. As we shall see later in this book, a recently enacted living will legislation is quite popular among Danish people.

THE LEGAL AND MEDICAL PROFESSIONS FRUSTRATE THE PUBLIC

With the wide publicity of the Cruzan case and the intensification of public debate, American citizens became increasingly involved in end-of-life discussions. There is hardly any citizen who has not witnessed a loved one or known of a neighbor or co-worker who has gone through a myriad of costly, painful, almost torturous medical interventions that helped only to prolong the moment of death and extend a life void of intellect, will, and passions. More and more Americans do not wish to be forced into a miserable and expensive dependent existence, largely void of all that we associate with personhood. Recent polls show that the vast majority of Americans would prefer to be respected as a person rather than manipulated as a set of organs when their condition becomes terminal and hopeless. This respect for the person often would require the health-care professional to refrain from any "heroic" interventions, to let the person die peacefully. The public's desire for preserved dignity near the end of life has been frustrated by the legal and medical tribunals that seem unable to set guidelines that will arbitrate this vitally important issue. Legal opinions are often based on minute technicalities. Furthermore, judges react to this issue on a case-by-case basis—a process that is unlikely to provide consistent or general solutions.

TURFING THE ISSUE OF TERMINAL CARE

In a sense, the legal profession turfed the issue of medical care at the end of life to the profession with which they thought it belonged, the medical profession. The weight of legal opinion pointed to the medical profession as the party responsible for making the highly complex decisions relevant to issues of life and death and terminal illness. No physician had yet been found guilty of medical negligence for withholding or withdrawing unnecessary medical treatment, as long as the medical decision was based on a rational, deliberate, and scientifically sound approach, a fact not widely known to medical professionals.

But these life-and-death issues have been left up to individual physicians, who systematically err on the side of preserving life rather than letting people die, or to individual medical institutions. The result is that health-care professionals, like their legal colleagues, have been unable to arrive at a consensus as to the appropriateness of medical interventions when these are questionable, or when they offer marginal utility at the end of a person's life.

TERMINAL MEDICAL CARE: USEFUL OR USELESS?

I define *futile care* as care that fails to produce its desired benefits or a medical intervention that is not directed toward regaining or preserving qualities that define an individual as a person. Whether others agree with this definition or not, it is imperative that society-at-large seek consensus regarding this issue. All people—physicians, lawyers, judges, ethicists, and the average American citizen—must ponder this issue. All people, not just special classes of professionals, ultimately need to make these life-and-death decisions. Only then can systematic guidelines for limiting futile care proceed. Dealing with this issue, rather than engaging in virtuoso feats of medical technology, is the truly heroic undertaking.

Futile care is not always enacted at the behest of the medical establishment. Some recent court cases involving hopelessly ill patients revolved around families' demands for access to futile, unnecessary, and expensive high-tech intervention. In a number of these cases, the court noted that these individuals had a right to such care. Noted authorities on medical ethics are as divided in their views about futility as the legal and medical establishment. A more elaborate review of these cases will be presented later.

LIMITING FUTILE CARE: FISCALLY AND MORALLY SOUND

Futile health care at the end of life continues to exhaust valuable resources to the extent of tens, and probably close to $100 billion annually. According to Victor Fuchs, the noted Stanford economist and a respected authority in health-care economy, 1% of the total gross national product is spent on the last year of life. A system that limits futile care would provide a win/win situation.[13] It is humane, ethical, and cost-effective. The patient is spared the indignity of intrusive intensive care, the family will be relieved of having to endure the burden of watching a loved one die a prolonged, expensive, and painful death, and society will enjoy substantial savings that enable the reallocation of limited health-care resources to where they are most useful.

AN APOLOGY IN THE FORM OF A PROPOSITION

I robbed Mr. Jones of an Oedipus-like graceful exit, and I have regretted it ever since. An unwanted fate had been visited upon him and his family as the result of my "heroic" action. As recompense, I would like to help others avoid the Tithonus-like ending that Mr. Jones had the misfortune to endure. I propose that we stop letting medical high technology control our final destiny by dictating the manner in which we shall die. We cannot let judges, lawyers, politicians, ethicists, or even physicians determine what type of medical intervention we receive at the end of our lives. All laypeople should have input in this most personal of decisions.

QUALITY OF DEATH: A CONCEPT AS IMPORTANT AS QUALITY OF LIFE

As difficult as this idea may be, the time has come for all Americans to engage in the serious debate on how we can best deal with the current legal, ethical, political, and economic dilemmas surrounding life and death. The standard by which intrusive medical interventions challenge the endurance limits of each of the body's organs until the very end is neither sensible nor humane. This book is intended to spur the debate by equipping people with a knowledge base relevant to this global issue of life and death.

Finally, a new living will is proposed that will remedy the inadequacies of existing living wills, helping to ensure that all Americans achieve a graceful exit when their time comes.

Tithonus

Alfred Lord Tennyson (1809–1892)

The woods decay, the woods decay and fall,
The vapours weep their burthen to the ground;
Man comes and tills the field and lies beneath,
and After many a summer dies the swan.
Me only cruel immortality ...

I asked thee, "Give me immortality."
Then dist thou grant mine asking with a smile,
But thy strong Hours indignant worked their wills,
And beat me down and marred and wasted me,
And though they could not end me, left me maimed,...

To hear me? Let me go; take back thy gift.
Why should a man desire in any way
To vary from the kindly race of men,
Or pass beyond the goal of ordinance
Where all should pause, as is most meet for all?...

Release me, and restore me to the ground.
Thou seest all things, thou wilt see my grave;
Thou wilt renew thy beauty morn by morn,
I earth in earth forget these empty courts,
and Thee returning on thy silver wheels.

NOTES

1. Quoted from Editorial, "Who Owns Medical Technology?" *Lancet*, 345, 1995, 1126.
2. TR Cole, "Oedipus and the Meaning of Aging: Personal Reflections and Historical Perspectives." N Jecker, ed. In: *Aging and Ethics* (Totowa, NJ: Humana Press, 1991), pp. 93–111.
3. I Asimov, *Asimov's Guide to Shakespeare* (Doubleday, 1978), p. 438.
4. *The Chiron Dictionary of Greek and Roman Mythology*, trans. Elizabeth Burr (Wilmette, IL: Chiron Publications, 1994), pp. 204–295.
5. "Tithonus" by Lord A. Tennyson, O. Williams, ed. *Immortal Poems of the English Language*. (New York: Washington Square Press, 1952), pp. 381–383.
6. President's Commission for the Study of Ethical Problems in Biomedical and Behavioral Research, *Defining Death: Medical, Legal, and Ethical Issues in the Determination of Death*. (Washington, DC: U.S. Government Printing Office, 1981).
7. RB Daroff, *The American Neurological Association Survey Results on PVS*. (Presented at the 115th Annual Meeting of the American Neurological Association, October 14–17, 1990.)
8. *In re Quinlan* (New Jersey, 1976), p. 647.
9. *California Natural Death Act* (California Health & Safety Code, 1976) ch. 7187.
10. A Report of the Clinical Care Committee of the Massachusetts General Hospital, "Optimum Care for Hopelessly Ill Patients," *New England Journal of Medicine*, 7 (1976), 362–364.
11. *Cruzan v. Director* (US 261, 1990), p. 497.
12. A Meisel, "The Current State of the Right to Die." In: *The Right to Die*, 1994 supplement (New York: Wiley Law Publications, 1989), pp. 23–29.
13. VR Fuchs, *The Future of Health Policy* (Cambridge, MA: Harvard University Press, 1993), p. 165.

Chapter 2

A Whirlwind History of Technology's Impact on Life and Death

> Science without religion is lame. Religion without science is blind.
>
> —Albert Einstein (1941, in *Science, Philosophy and Religion,* Chapter 13)

Medical technology has advanced at breathtaking and heart-stopping speed in the last half of the 20th century. Health-care professionals, let alone the average citizen, have often been staggered by the pace of development, scrambling to keep up with the latest techniques. Because of this accelerated pace, we have not had the luxury to gain a perspective on this technology. Indeed, our technological advances have, in a sense, outdistanced the social and ethical context in which they should be enacted. The result has been that technology often seems to control our destinies. As we shall see, advanced medical technology forced health-care professionals to adopt a new definition of life and death, with the unintended sequela of promoting miserable, terminal existences for many.

This chapter is designed to give the reader a sense of the accelerated pace of medical technology in this century, based on my own personal experience as a physician.

When I graduated from medical school in 1955, the accelerated pace of medical advances had just begun. But even having been exposed to this nascent technology, no medical person in the mid-1950s would have imagined the shape of today's medicine. Even the most enlightened of cardiologists of the 1950s, if transported in a time capsule to the present, would be bewildered in this new world and be overtaken by its new wonders. The breathtaking pace of scientific advances in the diagnosis and treatment of disease has taken us to a totally new world, totally foreign to the practitioner of yesteryear. For me, it has been an enormously exciting, although demanding experience to be part of this total technological transformation.

It is difficult to reconstruct the medical world of yesteryear. Just imagine a yesteryear in which the greatest drama was caused by the poliomyelitis virus (i.e., polio) for which there was no vaccine. The infection paralyzed or killed hordes of individuals, young and old. Iron lungs were used to enable these victims to stay alive while they struggled for various degrees of recovery. Not anymore—thanks to polio vaccine.

In the year of my graduation, the world was barely recovering from a devastating Second World War. War has traditionally been the great incentive for technological advances. Many of these advances have, in turn, spurred medical research. The imperatives of the war accelerated several engineering and technical innovations that proved to be applicable to medical research. These included monitoring devices to track vital body functions, new techniques for imaging the human body (such as methods utilized to enhance X-ray pictures) and the use of radioisotopes and ultrasound waves in the identification of disease and in guiding treatment.

The discovery of penicillin and its use to combat infection inaugurated a new antibiotic era that enabled us to overcome previously lethal microbial infections. We are now able to control epidemics. Advances in war surgery led to improvements not only in operating techniques but also in anesthesia. Complex surgical procedures, deemed impossible a few years earlier, became commonplace. Trauma and orthopedic surgery witnessed enormous progress during the war. Much knowledge was gained in the areas of blood storage and transfusion. Limb prosthesis and rehabilitation techniques improved.

A MANIPULATION OF LIFE

All these technological advances essentially resulted in a manipulation of life.

Then surgeons accomplished the ultimate—something that was previously unthinkable. They began operating on the heart to remove foreign bodies, thus opening a whole new frontier in surgery. The heart was no longer considered "beyond surgery," as it was earlier in the century. In the mid-1950s, surgeons performed operations to close congenital defects in the heart through cooling of the body. A few years later, we learned to use machines to stop the heart by cooling it at much lower temperatures, and to restart the heartbeat with warming. These machines, designed to bypass the heart and take over the functions of the lungs, ultimately were put to greater use, enabling heroic advances in heart surgery. Now, the most complex of heart defects can be corrected or at least improved using these techniques.

Soon thereafter, organ-replacing machines were invented to take over the functions of the kidneys and lungs and, gradually, renal dialysis and assisted ventilation were perfected, finding wide application and acceptance.

Not only were organs such as the heart and kidney manipulated in this era, but also the cell—the basic unit of life—was manipulated. Indeed, no less than the secret of life in the form of chromosomes and genes was discovered. The noted biochemists Wilkins, Crick, and Watson from Cambridge University in England were awarded the Nobel Prize in 1953 for defining the chemical composition of DNA, the chemical that defines us and gives us our genetic instructions. This discovery opened up a whole new vista of genetic research. Genetic research not only allowed us to uncover the secrets of relatively rare genetic diseases, but also to engineer new treatments and antibiotics for more common disease, such as cancer, infections, and blood clots.

Many of the technological advances that have become part of the vocabulary of the common person were unheard of in the early 1950s. These advances included the advent of CT (computerized tomography) scanners, MRI (magnetic resonance imaging) devices, ultrasound imaging techniques, sophisticated nuclear imaging of the heart and brain, as well as many other diagnostic techniques. Even X-ray machines, which were considered high technology at the time of my graduation, became so advanced and the images so refined that you could hardly recognize the similarities. The use of electron microscopes and scanning microscopes, as well as new magnification and laboratory techniques, allowed the visualization of smaller and smaller subcellular structures.

CARDIOLOGY: A HEARTENING NEW MEDICAL SPECIALTY

In the 1950s, the specialty of heart disease, or cardiology, was in its infancy. Cardiologists depended on the clinical examination, chest X-ray, and electrocardiogram (EKG), the electronic monitoring of heartbeats, to diagnose disease. In American textbooks of medicine from that era, the chapters on tuberculosis, syphilis, and typhoid fever exceeded all that was written about diseases of the heart. Because high blood pressure is a symptomless disease, and because its causal connection to strokes and heart attacks was not yet known, big debate was still raging over whether to treat high blood pressure or whether high blood pressure was one of the varying characteristics of the individual person, like a large nose or large ears. When blood pressure was extremely high, leeches were applied to the patient's temples to suck out some of the patient's blood! And remember, this was the 20th century, not the 17th century. Together, patients were prohibited from eating anything other than boiled rice free of salt. Today, the treatment of high blood pressure in America is a multibillion dollar industry (according to pharmaceutical company data), involving many sophisticated monitoring devices and drugs.

Before the advent of technology and the formal codification of the medical specialty known as cardiology, cardiologists relied on bedside diagnosis. The first tools of cardiologists were their hands, eyes, ears, brain—and the stethoscope, an instrument that amplifies the sounds of the heart. These early cardiologists would glean information by looking at the dancing of the veins in the neck; they would place their hands over the chest wall to discern changes in the movement of the heart. And through use of the stethoscope, they obtained information by listening to sounds and noises produced by the heart. Generally, the more distinguished a cardiologist, the larger his stethoscope. Even today, the stethoscope is a symbol to distinguish physicians from other professionals and laypeople.

Catheters, thin tubes that are threaded through a patient's circulatory system, were the next tool that augmented the cardiologist's diagnostic ability. Forsmann went so far as to disobey his chief's prohibition and inserted a catheter in his own heart.[1] A few years later, Radner used the same technique to visualize the arteries feeding the heart.[2] In the 1950s, heart catheterization enabled physicians to diagnose and evaluate congenital abnormalities (birth defects) of the heart and rheumatic valvular heart disease—the latter caused by rheumatic fever and resulting in damage to the heart valves that control blood flow. The combination of newly found scientific information with previously discovered ways to image the heart with X-rays and monitor it with electrical recording devices (i.e., EKG), established the new specialty of cardiology. The elucidation of heart problems obtained from catheterization contributed to our better understanding of information that was obtained from the patient's history and physical examination.

Initially, surgery on certain types of valve narrowing and some simple forms of congenital heart abnormalities was done while the heart was beating. These included the opening of a narrowed mitral valve (the valve between the left atrium and ventricle) as a result of rheumatic involvement. The valve was opened with the surgeon's finger or a special knife. A congenitally persistent defect between the two atria was closed by direct suture or by placement of a patch. More involved surgery on the heart itself would have been impractical on a throbbing organ that moved 60 times per minute. But soon, machines that allowed oxygen to travel through the body without the help of a beating heart (i.e., assisted circulation of the blood and artificial ventilation) were perfected, and heart surgery for complex types of heart and vessel disease became commonplace. Thanks to the pioneer work of Forsmann and Radner, hardening of the coronary arteries has become easy to visualize and quantify using cinematographic imaging techniques. Aortocoronary bypass surgery became possible through the efforts of the Argentinean surgeon Favaloro, working at the Cleveland Clinic in 1967. Eleven years later, another maverick physician, Andreas Grunzig from Germany, introduced balloon angioplasty. A tiny balloon is threaded into the blood vessel and is carefully placed at the site of narrowing. By inflating the balloon, the narrowed segment is remodeled, relieving the blockage.

Another new technological development involved electronic means to take over the pacemaker activities of the heart. These permanent pacemakers replace the heart's own electrical system when that system has become dysfunctional. Pacemakers are now old-hat technology. The newest electrical system for the heart is an implantable defibrillator (a small device that is placed under the skin and connected to the heart chambers by wires). This enables the spontaneous return of the heart's rhythm whenever its beat becomes chaotic and hence life threatening. The small device monitors the rhythm and appropriately sends a timed, measured electric shock to bring the heart back into rhythm.

At the same time, new discoveries in antibiotics applied to the treatment of heart disease, in addition to new ways to treat high blood pressure, changed the landscape even further. In 1955, rheumatic heart disease was the number-one concern of cardiologists. Patients were cared for and rehabilitated in special wards and in some cases, a sanitorium. When I visited England in the late 1950s, I had the opportunity to visit Taplow Hospital outside London and observe firsthand the management of hundreds of children with acute rheumatic fever, in addition to the consequences of rheumatic valvular heart disease.

Rheumatic fever is now almost eradicated from the Western world, thanks to the discovery of penicillin, which treats the streptococcus bacterial infection responsible for rheumatic valvular disease. Now the number-one enemy of the heart is coronary artery disease, commonly known as "hardening of the arteries," a condition that accounts for half the deaths in the United States. Hardening or narrowing of the arteries, the blood vessels going to the heart, can cause coronary artery disease, the underlying cause of heart attacks. Just 30 years ago, one in every three patients experiencing a heart attack died of its complications.

Four decades ago, a patient with a myocardial infarction (i.e., heart attack) was treated with complete bedrest for at least six weeks. This was followed by a few months of gradually increasing activity. By the time the patient left the hospital, he or she would have become weak and depressed. Back pains, stiff joints, constant constipation, and not infrequently, hemorrhoids were inevitable consequences of this event. A heart attack meant disability for life. Contrast this with the situation today. Intensive-care units have reduced the death rate due to heart attacks to one-third what it was. New "clot-busting" drugs that dissolve blood clots to open clogged arteries and prevent adverse events, and other interventions, have reduced death further by yet another half. Most patients with heart attacks leave the hospital in a few days. If they require further interventions, such as bypass surgery, their stay may be extended by up to two weeks. Most patients return to a normal, or near-normal, active life. And besides bypass surgery, there are other possible interventions to open up narrowed arteries: angioplasty utilizing tiny balloons to open up the area of narrowing, laser beams, and metal coils, to name a few.

For those with weak hearts, there is an armament of new and effective medicines that not only relieve symptoms of shortness of breath, but also improve the ability to exercise. And, yes, these agents also prolong life.

The greatest miracle of all has been organ transplantation, including heart and heart-and-lung transplants. Pioneer heart surgeons became recognized as heroes, held in awe for their ability to control life. Some became instant celebrities on a par with movie stars and world-class athletes.

These new medical advances attracted some of the brightest young minds into the healing profession. Scientific progress was supported by substantial grants from government institutions, industries, and entrepreneurs wanting to cash in on new discoveries. No doubt, these advances had a profound effect in further accelerating a process already in progress.

THE NEW TECHNOLOGY: PROLONGING LIFE AND PROMPTING A NEW SET OF PROBLEMS

Implementation of these new technologies and drugs has resulted in a longer and better life for most people. According to the National Center of Health Statistics, Hyatsville, Maryland, the mean life span of a person has increased by more than five years since the middle of this century. Since 1968, death from heart attacks dropped by 50%, and the incidence of strokes decreased by almost 60% in all age-adjusted groups. High blood pressure complications dropped by two-thirds, and rheumatic fever and its ravages have been almost eradicated.

Increasing the life expectancy of people through these advances was not an unalloyed boon; it caused a whole new set of problems. Although fewer people die from acute disease, more patients today are dying of heart failure than in decades earlier, in spite of advances in the treatment medications, just because they are living longer (see Figure 1). The steady increase in the inci-

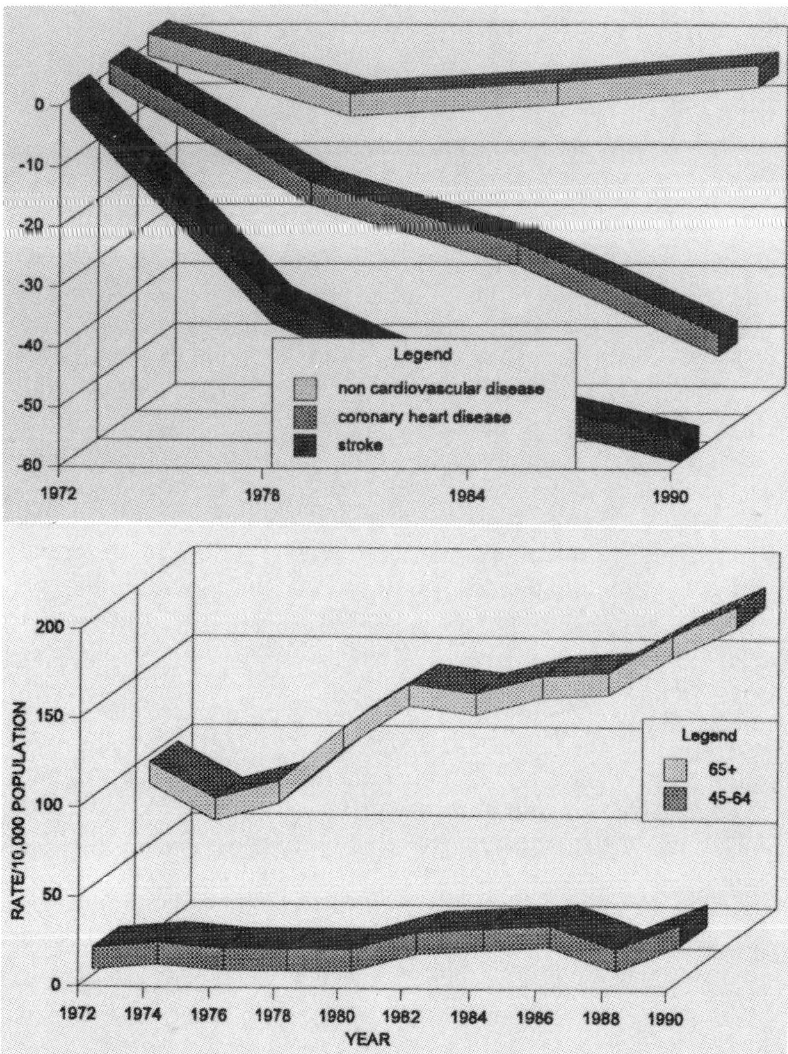

Figure 1. Percent decline in age-adjusted mortality rates since 1972 from heart disease and stroke compared to increased rates of hospitalization for heart failure (ages 45–64 and 65+, U.S. 1971–1991).

dence of heart failure has been reviewed in an article, *Prevalence and Mortality Rate of Congestive Heart Failure in the United States,"* by Dr. Douglas Schocken of the University of South Florida. This article was published in the *American Journal of College of Cardiology* in 1992.[3] As we will see later, the increase in the elderly population and in their attendant debilitating diseases will have a profound influence on the main subject of this book. The aging of the population and the growth of the postwar baby-boom generation predicts a 40% further increase in the prevalence and cost of coronary heart disease in the elderly in the next three decades, according to Dr. Weinstein and associates in an article titled "Forecasting Coronary Artery Disease Incidence, Mortality and Cost," published in 1987.[4]

Not only health-care professionals, but also the public at large fell in love with these new medical services. The populace demanded more and better services and science, with its new apostles, was able to deliver. Exaggerated promises, not unexpectedly, resulted in unrealistic expectations and sometimes unreasonable demands from consumers enamored with the miracles promised by the new technologies. Hospitals found in the new technologies ways to distinguish themselves and to further their profits. The competition for the acquisition of the highest technology—CT scanners, MRI machines, heart-cath labs, and organ transplantation programs—grew at a breathtaking pace. Insurance companies paid for the services and were able to raise the premiums of willing and sometimes eager customers. Physicians learned, perfected, believed in, and almost worshiped the new technologies. They became the masters, priests, and demigods of this new found religion. As physicians, we proclaimed ourselves the protectors of life and the enemies of death, which we sought to fight with vengeance. Death is no longer viewed as a natural end of life but as a medical failure: "The medicalization of death."[5]

THE PROFITEERS OF DEATH

In this highly individualistic, technology-driven, death-denying environment, many people profited from the new technology: the inventor and producer of the machines and devices, the drug companies, the insurance providers, hospitals, and physicians. This profit has come at great cost to society, though. Health-care costs have escalated at a rate that is many times the rate of inflation. It grew as a percentage of the general national product, from less than 6% to the present 14% in the span of three decades. The genie is out of the bottle and has become a real giant. The consumer considers that he or she is entitled to the latest in technology, whether it costs a few cents or a million dollars—as long as someone else is paying for it (the insurance company for those covered with private insurance, or the government in the case of those covered by Medicare or Medicaid). Meanwhile, escalating health-care costs became a threat to the continued prosperity of our nation and its citizens, and the struggle to slow down this overheated machine has begun on many fronts.

THE SIDE EFFECTS OF TECHNOLOGY

As with every scientific advance, progress in medical science brought with it certain unique problems. Just consider the discovery of roentgen rays (X-rays). Here is a wonder tool that enabled physicians to see through skin, fat, and muscle to study bones and visualize internal organs using radiovisible dyes and the radio-opaque element, barium. Who would have predicted that this same radiation could produce leukemia, lymphoma, and other forms of cancer? Who would have thought that it would cause suppression of the bone marrow, the part of the bone that is the blood-making factory? And no one anticipated its danger to the not-yet born, its ability to cause genetic defects in the fetus.

The greatest (although, as we will see, not necessarily the most beneficial) triumph of medical technology must be in cardiopulmonary resuscitation (CPR). Just over 30 years ago, before the classic publication of *Fundamentals of Cardiopulmonary Resuscitation*) by Drs. Jude and Elam (1965), the heart stoppage resulting in the cessation of oxygen flow meant the end of life.[6] Not anymore! Now, thanks to Dr. Bernard Lown, the noted Boston cardiologist who invented the contemporary defibrillator in 1962, when the heart stops because of a disordered electric rhythm, it can be shocked back into rhythm and the patient comes back from death to life.[7] And when the heart's electric wave ceases, the heart can be paced by an artificial generator; this is the closest medical encounter to the biblical "Pick up thy bed and walk." Similarly, when someone ceases to breathe, a machine can be used that drives breathing, and the machine settings can be adjusted to deliver the proper mixture of gases to the lungs. But maintaining blood flow through technology also had a downside.

A NEW DEFINITION OF LIFE AND DEATH

As noted earlier, as recently as 30 years ago, the cessation of heart–lung function and consequently, vital flow, was used to define death. According to this criterion, death occurred when the heart stopped or when the person ceased breathing on his or her own. Closed chest CPR was popularized in the early 1960s by a group of Johns Hopkins physicians. This landmark discovery replaced the often heroic adventures of opening the chest wall with a knife and squeezing the heart by hand to help it resume pumping. Also in the early 1960s, electric generators were improved through the new capacitor invented by Dr. Bernard Lown to deliver electric jolts to the heart to put it back in orderly rhythm. These two procedures found immediate application in the Western world.

The advent of this technology rendered obsolete the traditional definition of death. Faced with the challenge of finding a more fitting definition of death, philosophers and physicians looked for an alternative. Practically all body-organ functions can be substituted for by machines, except those of the brain. A heated debate ensued between those who advocated that death of a person has occurred with the loss of the higher brain functions of consciousness and awareness and those who insisted that death should be based on total loss of brain activity. The advent of the

Harvard criteria for defining death provided a new perspective on death, centering on cessation of whole-brain function, including the primitive vegetative functions that take place at the subconscious level.[8] Heart–lung "death" was no longer true death, but a potentially reversible condition. In 1981, the President's Commission for the Study of Ethical Problems in Medicine and Biomedical and Behavioral Research confirmed this redefinition of death: "Irreversible cessation of all functions of the entire brain, including the brain stem."[9]

Because the use of machines to take over all functions of the body, except the brain, nullified the old definition of death, and because no alternative definition had yet been formulated, this definition of death was instantly adopted in the Western world. The new definition proved to be useful in dealing with extensive head injuries and acute brain catastrophes, such as occur in previously healthy individuals involved in catastrophic motor-vehicle or motorcycle accidents, gun-shot injuries to the head, and older patients with massive stroke or brain hemorrhage. It proved particularly useful in facilitating the harvesting of viable organs from potential donors for transplantation purposes. With the President's Commission report, the new specialty of medical ethics was given a new life. It attracted a consortium of philosophers, humanists, legal scholars, and physicians to address the many confounding issues that resulted from this new definition. Many professionals provided much useful guidance, but some have drifted outside mainstream and practical thinking, engaging in arcane debates. These professionals often did not clarify issues for the layperson, they obfuscated them.

A DEFINITION OF LIFE THAT PROLONGS DEATH

As a result of recent technological advances and the use of the new definitions for life and death, many individuals have been kept alive when they would have died, according to the old definition of death as cessation of flow of the vital fluids resulting from heart and lung death. The 1960s and '70s produced tens of thousands of precariously living individuals who had sustained extensive brain injuries as a result of trauma or stroke, or who suffered cardiopulmonary arrest from which they were resuscitated, but during which they suffered irreversible brain damage (i.e., damage to the cerebral cortex and thus the "higher" brain functions). These individuals had probably irretrievably lost the content of consciousness and cognition, their memories, their ability to think and make decisions. But they had a persistently beating heart and circulating blood that carried enough oxygen to all their vital organs to prevent their bodies from dying. These individuals had been sustained on machines that breathed for them. They were fed either by intravenous fluids or through tubes inserted into their stomachs. These passive slaves of high technology required enormous efforts and costs to sustain their miserable existences. The medical community has displayed total ethical paralysis on how to handle these horrible consequences of advanced medical technology. Health-care professionals may think they have mastered this medical technology, but by ignoring or avoiding the ethical context in which this technology should be enacted, the technology has in effect mastered them.

CONSTITUTIONAL RIGHTS FOR THE UNCONSCIOUS

The new definition of death had far-reaching and problematic consequences, probably not fully realized at its inception.

According to the new definition of death, human beings who will probably never regain consciousness and higher brain function are nevertheless alive and therefore entitled to all the Constitutional rights granted to American citizens. A straightforward interpretation of the law of the land leads to the inescapable conclusion that these lives, sustained by primitive brain function, must be protected and sustained at any cost and for any length of time. Therefore, any slackness in carrying out this sacred duty would be unlawful and would expose the treating physician to conviction for manslaughter. A physician's professional code of honor and obligation further complicates this matter of ending a life that is a mere vegetative life. The Hippocratic oath obliges physicians to preserve life and not intentionally to cause death; an intervention to end life would appear to be legally, ethically, and morally wrong. All this conspires to make these vegetative beings and all of society, for that matter, slaves to high-tech machines.

A REBELLION AGAINST TECHNOLOGICAL SLAVERY

Some enlightened Americans started to express their resentment for such an existence, for becoming the salves of technology. For these people, the fear that one's final months or years might be spent in a nightmare of confusion, pain, and helplessness far exceeded the fear of death. The "Right to Die" movement was born in America in the 1960s, out of disdain for the proposition that a life void of dignity should be endured as a price of medical technological advances. The Euthanasia Society of America was established, with the overriding objective to put control of the moment of death in the hands of those who are dying. Luis Kutner, the society's founder, first proposed the idea of the "Living Will" in a meeting of the society in 1967, to serve as a manifesto for the right to die. Although their intentions are laudable, the right to die seems like a strange claim in a society in which life, liberty, and the pursuit of happiness are cornerstones of civil liberties. Death, which once was viewed as an imperative, is now claimed by some to be a "right"—a right that is to be preserved against the invasion of technology.

Counterbalancing the "right to die" movement was a new class of health-care professionals who worshiped high technology. For these people, death became an enemy to be conquered. Every human existence, except for those experiencing total brain death, was to be preserved by all means and at all costs. Many physicians viewed their primary and sacred mission to be the preservation of any vestige of life for all time. An increasing segment of the American public came to believe, justifiably, that doctors cruelly and needlessly delay the process of dying for various motives, some of which are highly suspect.

This new state of confusion, with polar-opposite viewpoints, dominates our society. This has been compounded by the dramatization of exceedingly rare cases of PVS in which there is sufficient recovery of consciousness to allow the ability to communicate, contrary to medical predictions. These cases are true medical miracles that defy logic. Sensationalization of these unique cases by the media fueled the unrealistic expectations from modern technology.

A HIGHER DEFINITION OF LIFE AND DEATH

The definition of death based on whole-brain death is not person-oriented. This definition is based on the death of an organ rather than the death of an individual, a person. Furthermore, this definition, by demanding that many people remain in a vegetative state, promotes a miserable existence for many at the end of life. The adoption of a new definition of death, based on the death of higher brain function, is one of the first critical steps toward avoiding the misery experienced by many at the end of life.

Upper-Brain Death: The Part Is More Important Than the Whole

Between the heart–lung definition of death and the newly adopted definition of whole- or total brain (including brain stem) death, there is another category of brain damage that prevents the individual from ever being able to "function as a whole," as a person. This category is termed "upper brain death" and refers to that part of the brain known as the cerebral cortex. This concept, presented by the noted ethicist Dr. Bernat in the late 1970s, and redefined by Dr. Youngner, Professors of Psychiatry and Biomedical Ethics at Case Western Reserve University School of Medicine and his associates in the early 1980s, deserves further discussion.[10]

Higher brain death occurs when there is permanent loss of consciousness and cognition, when there is irreversible loss of the ability to reason, to understand, to remember, to recognize, to have passions, or to experience feelings. Another way of looking at higher brain death is that it occurs when all that constitutes a person is dead. As noted previously, the ability of high technology to take over the functions of the heart and lungs has rendered the heart–lung or vital-flow definition of death obsolete. By the same token, the ability of high technology to substitute for many lower brain functions, such as by organ replacing machines, or by triggering spontaneous breathing, or providing support of blood pressure, and regulating temperature and the level of hormones, would appear to render the "whole brain" definition of death obsolete also.

It is the higher functions of the brain that cannot be replaced or substituted for by machines. These higher functions define the person, a distinct, living being with unique intellect, will, and passions.

Figure 2 shows a picture of the brain, brain stem, and spinal cord. A brief summary of how the brain functions follows.

The brain can be divided into two basic portions: the upper brain (or cerebral cortex), and the brain stem. The upper brain consists of two large hemispheres connected horizontally by the corpus callosum. The brain stem is positioned vertically to the hemispheres and at their base.

The brain stem can be viewed as a telephone or communication center. It is actually a coordinating center that receives billions of messages from the command stations located in the hemispheres (upper brain). The hemispheres, or cerebral cortex, contain the centers of perception, feeling, and senses, such as touch, taste, smell, sight, and hearing, as well as pain and temperature. They contain the higher center for motor coordination—how you

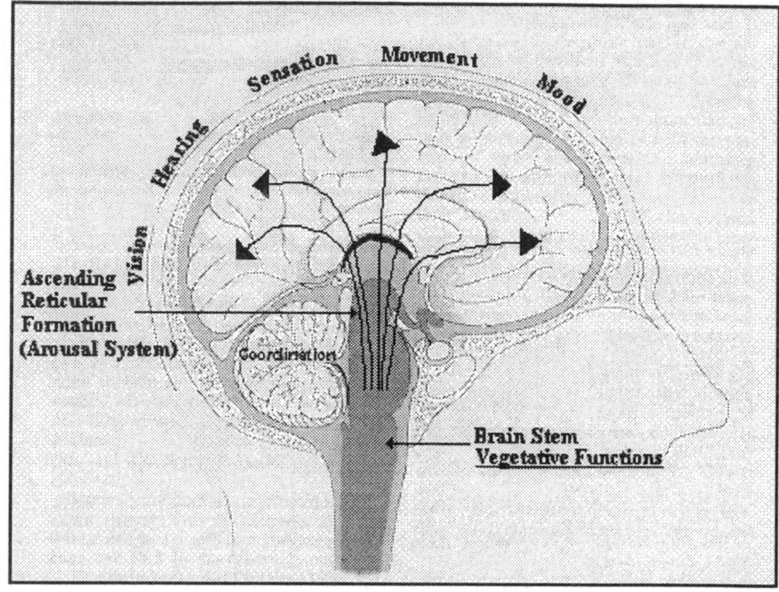

Figure 2. A simplified view of the brain: upper brain, brain stem, and spinal cord.

move your body in the world. They contain the library of memory and stored experiences. They also are responsible for our feelings and passions, our desires, our motivations, and our thinking.

The brain stem is responsible for basic functions, including the thermostats for temperature, breathing, blood pressure, and heartbeat. An ascending reticular arousal system (ARAS) rises from the brain-stem to both hemispheres and is responsible for the state of awakening. The cerebellum, located on the back side of the brain, is primarily responsible for the coordination of movement, the commands for which arise from the hemispheres. Neither the brain stem nor the cerebellum is able to interpret or initiate measured commands on its own nor to function in an orderly fashion without the decoding and command centers in the high brain, the cerebral cortex.

The Cerebral Cortex—Our Crown Jewel

The cerebral cortex is the crowning achievement of the brain. This "higher" portion of the brain, containing computer-like, specialized cells and neurons, is what distinguishes the human animal from all other animals. These neurons represent stations from which orders originate, messages are received, decoding of these messages occur, comparison of messages with past stored experiences occur, and a final reaction takes place. Genetic and cultural influences determine how and to what extent these small "computers" function, and react. The collective characteristics of these functions in turn define the *person*. The functions of the cerebral cortex are seen in Figure 3.

The neocortex, the precursor of the upper brain, developed some 200 million years ago in protohumans, our earliest ancestors.

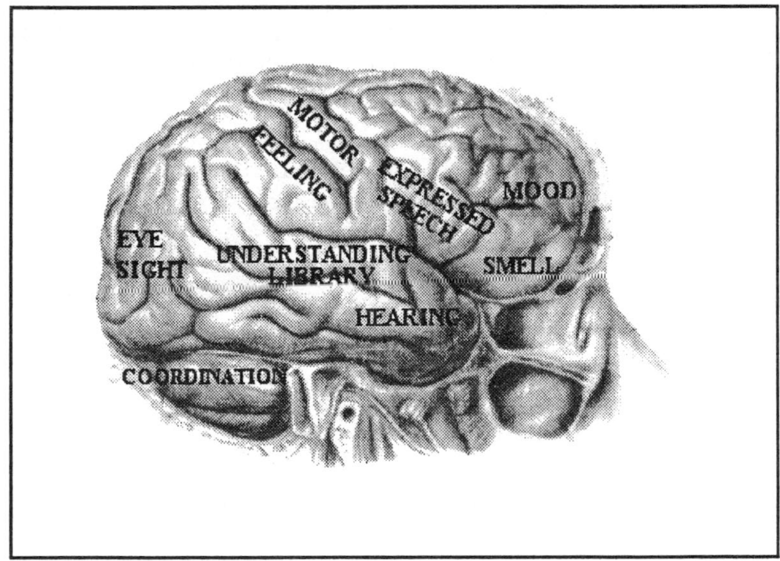

Figure 3. The upper brain: the cerebral cortex and its associated functions.

This is not a very long time relative to the four billion years since the earth was born. Our human species, *Homo sapiens*, walked on the face of the earth 50,000 years ago, and serious human civilization is less than 10,000 years old. It is the neocortex, or upper brain, that prepared man to explore, inquire, memorize, reason, invent and create, assess, adjust, and perfect. Without the neocortex, there would be no "persons" as we know them.

All cells in the body require oxygen and nutrients provided by blood pumped by the heart. But the more specialized the cell, the more fragile it is, and the more sensitive it is to any bodily changes. The neurons in the cerebral cortex are among the most specialized of cells. Consequently, they are especially sensitive to the cessation of blood, nutrients, and oxygen, and to the effects of disease. For example, a cessation of blood flow for 4 to 10 minutes may lead to extensive destruction, disruption, and death among these highly specialized cells. By contrast, the relatively less specialized brain stem cells, with their more primitive functions, are more resistant to the cessation of blood flow and may endure longer periods of interrupted blood and oxygen flow without showing serious damage.

Loss of upper-brain function is sometimes referred to as vegetative state and sometimes defined as the "inability to experience self and the environment." Complete or partial preservation of primitive and unconscious reflex brain functions remain. However, there is complete unawareness of self and the environment, accompanied by sleep–wake cycles. In addition, patients in a vegetative state show no consistent response to various stimuli, including light, sounds, touch, or pain. These patients show no language comprehension or expression. They have bowel and urinary incontinence. Unconscious reflexes, however, are preserved to variable degrees. In fact, one of the difficulties that medical professionals encounter when dealing with relatives of an individual who is in a vegetative state is how to convince the family that the patient is void of consciousness. For a relative, a patient who shows some eye movement, yawning, or jerking in response to a loud voice or touch could be easily misinterpreted as responding to a question or a gesture of love. But these are merely reactions to environmental stimuli rather than responses to another human being.[11,12]

When the loss of upper-brain function or vegetative state is the result of head trauma, recovery is unlikely after 12 months. When a vegetative state results from causes other than head injury, recovery is exceedingly rare after 3 months.

Individuals with higher brain death still demonstrate inner-brain reactions without the higher-brain sensibilities that accompany these reactions in normal people. They may react to light, but they can not see; they may respond to powerful scents, but do not appreciate the smell; they may swallow, but do not enjoy food; they respond to loud sounds, but they cannot comprehend. These people do not look forward to a meal or to a drink. Males in this state may display erections, but have no desire for sex. They may yawn, hiccup, or twitch, but these movements occur without purpose. They do not comprehend, recognize, or appreciate any person or anything in their environment. They are not capable of love, hate, rage, or happiness. They have neither memories from yesterday nor dreams of tomorrow. Yet their hearts beat, they breathe, they have warm skin, they sweat, urinate, and pass stools. They cough, yawn, display jerky movement, and appear as if they are looking at something far away.[13] There have been some recent, excellent reviews of PVS. These are quoted in the reference section.

A DEFINITION OF DEATH THAT WILL HELP CONTROL OUR DESTINIES

As mentioned in the beginning of this chapter, at times it appears as if medical technology is controlling our destinies, resulting in undignified and miserable endings for many. The adoption of a new definition of death that involves the higher brain function is one of the first critical steps in gaining control of our lives and ensuring death with dignity for all.

As difficult as it may be, we need, as a society, to adopt this definition as soon as possible. It is promising that one country, Denmark, and even one American jurisdiction in New Jersey, have already adopted this definition. Nevertheless, we still have a way to go. All other surrounding jurisdictions in New Jersey, for instance, abide by the whole-brain definition. As I mentioned, the higher brain definition standard is adopted by the Danish Council on Ethics. As we will see later in this book, the adoption of this new definition of death by Denmark, along with other innovations, such as a more useful living will document, has allowed Danish citizens to take greater control of their destiny. Of note is the fact that while health-care costs have been increasing steadily in Western nations, Denmark has experienced a drop in health-care expenditures in 1994.

NOTES

1. JM Steckelberg et al., "Werner Forsmann (1904–1979) and His Unusual Success Story," *Mayo Clinic Proceedings*, 54 (1929), 746–748.
2. S Radner, "An Attempt at Roentgenologic Visualization of Coronary Blood Vessels in Man," *Acta Radiologica*, 26 (1945), 497–502.
3. DD Shocken, MI Arrieta, and PE Leaverton, "Prevalence and Mortality Rate of Congestive Heart Failure in the United States," *Journal of American College of Cardiology*, 20 (1992), 301–306.
4. MC Weinstein, PG Coxson, LW Williams, et al., "Forecasting Coronary Artery Disease: Incidence, Mortality and Cost," *American Journal of Public Health*, 77 (1987), 1417–1426.
5. P Aries, *The Hour of Death*. (New York: Vintage Books, 1981).
6. JR Jude and JO Elam. *Fundamentals of Cardiopulmonary Resuscitation*. (Philadelphia: Davis Co., 1965).
7. B Lown, R Amarsingham, and J Newman, "New Method for Terminating Cardiac Arrhythmia: Use of a Synchronized Capacitor Discharge," *Journal of the American Medical Association*, 182 (1962), 548–555.
8. "Ad Hoc Committee of the Harvard Medical School to Examine the

Definition of Brain Death: A Definition of Irreversible Coma," *Journal of the American Medical Association*, 205 (1968), 337–340.

9. President's Commission for the Study of Ethical Problems in Medicine and Biomedical and Behavioral Research. *Defining Death: Medical, Legal, and Ethical Issues in the Determination of Death*. (Washington, DC: U.S. Government Printing Office, 1981).
10. S Youngner and ET Bartlett, "Human Death and High Technology: The Failure of the Whole-Brain Formulations," *Annals of Internal Medicine*, 99 (1983), 252–258.
11. Multi-Society Task Force on PVS, American Academy of Neurology," Medical Aspects of the Persistent Vegetative State, Part 1," *New England Journal of Medicine*, 330 (1994), 1572–1579.
12. KR Mitchell, IH Kerridge, and RJ Lovat. "Medical Futility, Treatment Withdrawal and the Persistent Vegetative State," *Journal of Medical Ethics* (1993), 71–76.
13. American Neurological Association Committee on Ethical Affairs. "Persistent Vegetative State: Report of the American Neurological Association Committee on Ethical Affairs," *Annals of Neurology*, 33 (1993), 386–390.

Chapter 3

Moral Mortality

The Ethics of Dying

> The means by which we live have outdistanced the ends for which we live. Our scientific power has outrun our spiritual power. We have guided missiles and misguided men.
>
> —MARTIN LUTHER KING (1929–1968)

It is common to think that ethical precepts are precepts to help us live. But they also provide precepts to help us die. All religions, for instance, prepare us for the moment of death. It matters not whether one is Christian, Jew, Moslem, Hindu, or Buddhist. All religions recognize and protect the sanctity of life and recognize that the ultimate human justice is to place an equal value on each human life. Christians and Jews are taught about the timing of life and death in Ecclesiastes: "To everything there is a season, and a time for every purpose under heaven: a time to be born, a time to die, a time to plant, and a time to pluck up that which is planted" (Ecclesiastes 3:1–2). The Koran advises Muslims that the dying person should dissociate himself totally from worldly affairs and anticipate the moment of meeting the Almighty:

> Mas-ala 5. At the time of one's death no such thing should be said or done which may turn his mind towards workday

> affairs because it is the time for him to present himself before Almighty Allah. Those present at that time should behave in such a manner that the mind and heart of the dying person may turn away from the world and be directed towards Allah.

Buddhists are taught that their prime concern is seeking the meaning of life, a peace and comfort that will enable them to face the suffering of illness and death:

> A man struggling for existence will naturally look for something of value. There are two ways of looking—a right way and a wrong way. If he looks in the right way, he recognizes the true nature of sickness, old age, and death, and he searches for meaning in that which transcends all human sufferings. (*Shakyamuni Buddha*, p. 8)

Religions, therefore, prepare us to accept death as natural and expected, and not as an unwelcome failure of our quest to seek immortality.

PHYSICIANS: PRIESTS AND PRIESTESSES OF THE BODY

If religious men and women are priests and priestesses of the soul, physicians could be viewed as their secular counterparts: priests and priestesses of the body and of the person. Just as religious men and women help prepare us for death, so should physicians. This type of caring for the total person, however, is often overshadowed by high-technology medicine.

When physicians take the Hippocratic oath, they pledge to protect the lives and alleviate the suffering of their patients. This commitment to protect lives, however, is often carried to extremes, driven by exaggerated promises from physicians and unrealistic expectations from patients. Enabled by the powerful tools of modern technology, physicians keep vegetative bodies alive—in a fashion.

The attitude of medical intervention *in extremis* is prevalent particularly among young physicians who are trained less in dealing with the intricate challenges of complex illnesses and more in the acquisition of information and mastering techniques. Medical intervention that is designed to sustain a vegetative existence rather than a thinking and feeling person is an example of what I term "futile care."

The inappropriateness of futile care at the end of life was recognized and well articulated by Plato, the philosopher, and Hippocrates, the father of medicine, centuries ago.

Plato chastised "the inappropriateness of persisting with treatment which leaves the surviving patient with a useless life." He went on to emphasize: "Medicine was not intended for them and they should not be treated even if they were richer than Midas."[1]

Hippocrates, in his famous oath, advises physicians to "[r]efuse to treat those who are overmastered by their diseases, realizing in such cases [that] medicine is powerless."[2] This part of the oath is rarely referred to in the day-to-day practice of contemporary medicine. Discussions about the inappropriateness of futile care have been rekindled through the realization of the limits of medicine, the inevitability of death, the horrors of intensive care or a confused life in isolation, the enormity of waste of resources at the end of life, and the mounting pressures to limit cost of medical care by the new health-care alliances.

WITHHOLDING CARE: SOMETIMES THE BEST TYPE OF CARING

As far back as 1927, in an address to the graduating class of Harvard Medical School, Dr. Francis Peabody, the Chief of Medicine at Boston City Hospital and humanist noted:

> The most common criticism made at present by older practitioners is that young graduates have been taught a great deal about the mechanism of disease, but very little about the

> practice of medicine ... or to put it more bluntly, they are too scientific and do not know how to take care of patients ...

He went on to emphasize that the best form of patient care is in caring for the patient.[3] If Dr. Peabody's words were relevant in 1927, they must be much more relevant today. Patients, families, and young physicians must realize that withholding certain forms of treatment does not mean withholding care. In fact, many times the withholding of treatment is the best form of care. It takes a real professional to advise against more intrusive treatment; it merely takes a technician to undertake one more procedure.

A basic ethical principle (*Ex Ante Pareto*) states, "If no one is worse off with a certain choice, and at least someone is better off, then that choice should prevail." Conversely, I interpret this principle to mean that if no one is better off with a certain choice and at least someone (or society) is worse off, that choice should not be granted. According to the teachings of Hippocrates, the mission of medicine as a profession is wellness for the healthy, wholeness for those who are ailing, and comfort and encouragement for the ones with incurable disease. Ethicists and health-care professionals may disagree on the definition of futility (see Appendix A), but a medical intervention undertaken with no hope of benefiting a patient is a misplaced intervention and could be considered unethical. Professional integrity and social responsibility should preclude a physician from recommending such a procedure. I would also add that it is unreasonable for patients or their families to ask for such treatment.

A MEDICAL FATE WORSE THAN DEATH

As all physicians and many laypeople can attest through personal experience, there are fates worse than death. Consider the case of a friend of mine, a 78-year-old psychiatrist, who suffered multiple strokes and lost all of his cognitive functions. He didn't know where he was, or what time of the day it was. He didn't recognize his family members. He didn't even know who he was. He couldn't swallow food, so a tube was placed in his stomach. He couldn't cough up secretions from his lungs, so he developed pneumonia. There was once a saying among physicians: "Pneumonia is the old man's friend." A few decades ago, pneumonia often allowed the elderly to depart peacefully. At the behest of the family and with concurrence of the treating physician, my friend, rather than be allowed to expire peacefully, was intubated and given intravenous antibiotics. A multitude of expensive laboratory tests guided the choice of drugs and treatment. He bled from his stomach and received pints of blood through transfusion. An endoscopy was performed to determine the cause of the bleeding; the threadlike tube with light at the end showed that he had developed a perforating stomach ulcer, requiring removal of the stomach. This major surgery was undertaken. Before the wound healed, he developed gangrene of the gallbladder that necessitated another major surgery—and more antibiotics—and more blood transfusions. Because he had been maintained on assisted ventilation for over two weeks, a tracheostomy was performed; that is, a hole was made in the trachea (the air pipe below the voice box) and oxygen was administered. His kidneys and his liver started to fail. Renal dialysis, a costly procedure that allows machines to filter toxins and other substances from the body, was initiated. The heart stopped after two months of struggle to maintain his marginal existence. Before this last event, I had a long discussion with the family and advised against resuscitation. The family agreed reluctantly. After death, his hospital bill exceeded $500,000 for treatment that, under the best of circumstances, would not have restored health, consciousness, or independence. This is a true but not unique story. It is an everyday occurrence in the practice of medicine in America. For those who do not believe it, ask to take a tour of any busy intensive-care unit in any highly specialized referral acute-care hospital. Sustaining a life in a body that is irreversibly incapacitated and without a mind is no longer a miracle of medicine but a routine in American intensive-care units. Who benefited from the prolongation of my friend's miserable existence? Society-at-large was debited over $500,000. And some wonder why insurance premiums have been going up beyond the cost-of-living adjustment.

AVOIDING MEDICAL FATES WORSE THAN DEATH

The objective of medicine is not, and must never be, to treat people to their death! This treatment exacts an enormous emotional and financial cost and cannot be construed as "caring" for the patient, caring for the person.

In a recent review of people who were in persistent vegetative states in 1993, the famed English neurologists, Drs. Kenneth R. Mitchell, Ian H. Kerridge, and J. Lovat from the University of Newcastle, England, asked the following rhetorical question in the *Journal of Medical Ethics*:

> Why do we persist in the relentless pursuit of artificial nourishment and other treatments to maintain unconscious existence? Will they be treated because of our ethical commitment to their humanity, or because of an ethical paralysis in the face of biotechnical progress?[4]

Indeed, this statement should not be construed as putting a lesser human value on a person who has lost what constituted his or her personhood. Simply, it underscores that once the ingredients of reason, passions, and desires defining a person are permanently and irretrievably lost, there is no ethical imperative to sustain such an existence.

The Council on Ethical and Judicial Affairs of the American Medical Association in 1990 endorsed this view:

> For humane reasons, with informed consent, a physician may do what is medically necessary to alleviate severe pain or cease or omit treatment to permit a terminally ill patient to die when death is imminent.... However, the physician should not intentionally cause death.[5]

Also in 1993, the American Neurological Association Committee on Ethical Affairs published a position paper that defined PVS, classified nutrition and hydration as forms of medical treatment, stated that patients or surrogates could decide to terminate treatment, and that there were no medical or ethical distinctions between withholding and withdrawing treatment.[6]

In a recent statement, the British Medical Association recommended that consent is not needed to discontinue a treatment that is deemed to have proven futile (i.e., with no reasonable hope for recovery of higher brain functions). Also, it emphasized that a family member's views about PVS should not be relevant to the decisions to cease treatment. (This particular statement may seem odd to the American reader. It is the rule in the United Kingdom and most European countries that useless care is not offered, and when asked for, it is not granted.) Nevertheless, I feel that in all circumstances, the physician has to inform the patient's family of the decision to forego or cease treatment and the reasons for it. This is required as a matter of decency and in order to maintain goodwill and promote understanding among various family members and the healing physician.[7]

It must be emphasized strongly and in no equivocal terms that whenever there is a reasonable chance for a decent recovery, it is the physician's duty to battle death aggressively. However, when there is no decent chance for recovery of the higher brain, or with multiple organ failure, death should be treated as a rational expectation rather than a remote contingency.

RELIGIOUS AUTHORITY CONCURS WITH MEDICAL AUTHORITY

All monotheistic religious institutions and other prevailing religions generally concur with these ethical positions taken by medical authorities. Almost without exception, they recommend that the physician and family should make the passing of a terminally ill patient as painless as possible. Of interest is that in 1980, the Vatican described contemporary high-technology applications at the end of life as "technologic attitude that threatens to become an abuse."

As early as 1957, in his address to the Congress of Anesthesiologists, Pope Pius XII noted that "while every reasonable effort should be made to maintain life and restore health, there comes a time when these efforts may become excessively burdensome for the patient and others." He also predicted that this issue would become a major one for the rest of the century. Recently, the Bishops of Texas and the Texas Conference of Catholic Health Facilities, in their Pastoral Statement on Artificial Nutrition and Hydration in 1990, stated: "If the means used to prolong life are disproportionately burdensome compared with the benefits to the patients, then these means need not be used. They are morally optional." These pronouncements by religious authorities give further credence to the proposition that death occurs when the upper brain irretrievably ceases to function or with failure of multiple vital organs. In this case, treatment is of no benefit to the patient. Indeed, such treatment will result in a medical fate worse than death. Of note is that the Catholic Bishop's Committee reports continue to be excessively cautious about notions of letting die and intending to bring about the death of a patient.[8]

MAY THE DEBATE ON TREATMENT FUTILITY NOT PROVE FUTILE

Unfortunately, the discussion regarding the definition of death and futility of medical care has not been settled yet. These issues are unlikely to be completely resolved until society-at-large comes to grips with the issues at hand. In the meantime, many respected authorities are still resisting the eminently rational definition of death based on death of the higher brain. Furthermore, enormous gaps exist among philosopher-ethicists in their definition of futility and in what they might consider as futile medical treatment and the scientific use of the term.

Futility derives from the Greek word *futilis*, which refers to a useless vessel, broader on the top than at the bottom. In ancient times, this *futilis* was used only in religious ceremonies but had no useful, secular function. Futile medical care could be considered a technological ceremony, of no real use in bringing a functioning person back into the world.

A CONGRESS ON FUTILE CARE: CONTROVERSY OVERWHELMS CONSENSUS

On March 24–25, 1993, a distinguished group of scholars assembled at the invitation of the Congress of Clinical Societies to discuss the question of medical futility.[9] The congress was a testimonial to the differences in how futility is understood among abstract theoretical ethicists and physicians. Proceedings of the congress were published in a 1994 issue of the *Journal of American Geriatrics Society*. In a paper entitled "Necessity, Futility, and the Good Society."[10] Dr. Callahan (Ph.D.), Director of the Hastings Center, highlighted the differences in the understanding of futility in the United States and abroad. Dr. Callahan is a highly respected leader in the ethics community. Even though he is not a physician, he described it as "unfitting to perform heart bypass surgery on octogenarians." Dr. Callahan noted that individualism in America impedes Americans' embracing shared values. He asserted our need, as one society, to establish a consensus on futility and medical necessity. Dr. Callahan has been a staunch advocate of limiting health care to the elderly who have already lived their normal life span.

Dr. Robert Veatch (Ph.D.), another authority in the philosophical approach to medical ethics, who also is not a physician, questioned whether physicians are even capable of making futility determinations.[11] In his paper "Why Physicians Cannot Determine if Care Is Futile," he contends "that the physician cannot and ought not try to determine futility." He further argues, "An appeal to justice or keeping a promise to a patient is sufficient justification to provide care deemed futile when an appeal to autonomy or beneficence is not." He invoked physicians' opinions to buttress his contention. He noted that Dr. Robert Morse, speaking for physicians in the Quinlan case, 1976, argued that keeping an unconscious patient alive on a ventilator represented proper medical care. Dr. Veatch further noted as bizarre that physicians would now contend that such treatment is futile. Unfortunately. Dr. Veatch has ignored the historical fact that physicians' and laypeople's attitudes about certain treatments have changed over the years with more knowledge about outcomes.

Dr. Howard Brody, a physician from the Center for Ethics and Humanities in the Life Sciences at Michigan State University, offered two basic ideas[12] to guide physicians:

1. Treatments are inappropriate if they cause harm disproportionate to any foreseeable benefit.
2. Doctors should not fraudulently represent the knowledge or skill of medical practice to their patients.

Dr. John Lantos, from the Department of Pediatrics and Center for Clinical Ethics, University of Chicago, argued that the debate about futility is simply a question of economics. In his essay, "Futility Assessments and the Doctor–Patient Relationship," Dr. Lantos contends that concerns about futility stem from the emergence of a prospective payment system. The cost-containment imperatives of such a system compelled physicians to discover the once forgotten Hippocratic ethic to refrain from providing useless medical treatment.[13]

Dr. Lawrence Schneiderman, Professor of Family and Preventative Medicine at the University of California, San Diego, presented a paper entitled "The Futility Debate on Effective Versus Beneficial Interventions." He offered two definitions of futility, using both quantitative and qualitative criteria.[14] According to Dr. Schneiderman, a futile intervention based on quantitative criteria is one that has not worked in the last 100 attempts (clearly not an easy standard, unless outcome research has shown that a certain treatment has a less than 1% chance to succeed). A futile intervention based on qualitative criteria is one that does not achieve its desired ends, a point agreed upon by physicians.

Dr. Youngner of Case Western Reserve University highlighted the difficulties between physicians on the one hand, and patients and families who desperately want to save or mend a life on the other. He noted how the motivations of even a well-intentioned practitioner who asks a patient to forsake a futile therapy may be suspect in the absence of a long-standing doctor–patient relationship.[15]

In his essay "Families and Futility," Dr. James Linderman Nelson of the Hastings Center presented the American Society's responsibilities in this debate. He emphasized that the question of integrity pertains to families as well as to practitioners and patients. He highlighted the importance of the roles played by families, friends, and of a meaningful doctor–patient relationship in guiding the difficult decisions about futility.

Other participants in the conference highlighted the difficulties with clinical definitions, the need for social consensus, cooperation in interdisciplinary organizations, and uniform case law.

Is it realistic to reach a consensus when leading theoretical experts in medical ethics are as far apart as Drs. Veatch and Callahan? Dr. Veatch supports the absolute right of a patient to receive a treatment deemed useless by scientific standards, and Dr. Callahan contends that society does not owe expensive care for anyone who has lived a natural life span. No doubt, the views of these experts need to be heard and pondered. However, I dare to say that the utility and futility of a medical treatment is the domain of the healing professionals. After all, ethics are not freestanding universal truths; rather, they are precepts derived from real circumstances. The definition of medical futility should be based entirely upon scientific facts, not abstract thinking. The lessons from the conference included the following:

- The question of futility of a treatment is primarily the responsibility of the medical establishment. A medical intervention must have a clear goal of restoring health or improving the patient's condition. An intervention without a therapeutic goal is improper.
- Abstract ethics are subject to enormous variation in interpretation, particularly when they pertain to complex medi-

cal issues. Ethical principles guiding medical care at the end of life are not revealed to the chosen few on the Road to Damascus. They must represent the shared values of our democratic society.

- A societal consensus should be the backbone for any policy regarding the perimeters of medical futility or marginal utility in order for the policy to succeed and meet wide acceptance.
- There is no substitute for a physician's professional integrity and a meaningful doctor–patient relationship in handling the vexing issues pertaining to an imminent death.
- It is about time to engage the public in the debate about such vital issues. To politicize an enormously complex issue such as this, reducing it to sound bites and slogans, does a great disservice to our citizens and our country.
- Medical students and the medical community at large must be better educated in how to discuss issues of life and death. They must be trained in communicating with patients and families under the dire circumstances of an imminent death.
- Guidelines for futility should be developed by a consortium of organized medicine to be presented for review by an independent, mainstream, blue-ribbon commission that does not have a political agenda. Recommendations should then be translated into common law, accompanied by the appropriate procedures to carry out the laws.

We may not be able to prevent death, but we can prepare for it and lessen the emotional and financial burden for all.

NOTES

1. Plato, In *Grube* (Hackett Publishing, 1981), pp. 76–77.
2. SJ Reiser, AJ Dyuck, and WJ Curran, *Ethics in Medicine: Historical Perspectives and Contemporary Concerns* (Cambridge, MA: MIT Press, 1977), pp. 6–7.

3. FW Peabody, "The Care of the Patient," *Journal of American Medical Association*, 88 (1927), pp. 877–881.
4. KR Mitchell, IH Kerridge, and RJ Lovat, "Medical Futility, Treatment Withdrawal and the Persistent Vegetative State," *Journal of Medical Ethics*, 19 (1993), 71–76.
5. Council on Scientific Affairs and Council on Ethical and Judicial Affairs, American Medical Association, "Persistent Vegetative State and the Decision to Withdraw or Withhold Life Support," *Journal of American Medical Association*, 263 (1990), 426–430.
6. American Neurological Association Committee on Ethical Affairs, "Persistent Vegetative State: Report of the American Neurological Association Committee on Ethical Affairs," *Annals of Neurology*, 33 (1993), 386–390.
7. Medical Ethics Committee of the British Medical Association, "Treatment of Patients in Persistent Vegetative State," September, 1992.
8. United States Bishops Committee Statement on Nutrition and Hydration, *Cambridge Quarterly of Health Care Ethics*, 2 (1993), 341.
9. JJ Fins, "Futility in Clinical Practice," *Journal of American Geriatric Society*, 42 (1994), 861–865.
10. D Callahan, *The Troubled Dream of Life: Living with Mortality* (New York: Simon and Schuster, 1993).
11. RM Veatch, "Why Physicians Cannot Determine if Care Is Futile," *Journal of American Geriatric Society*, 42 (1994), 871–874.
12. H Brody, "The Physician's Role in Determining Futility," *Journal of American Geriatric Society*, 42 (1994), 875–878.
13. JD Lantos, "Futility Assessments and the Doctor–Patient Relationship," *Journal of American Geriatric Society*, 42 (1994), 868–870.
14. LS Schneiderman, "The Futility Debate: Effective versus Beneficial Intervention," *Journal of American Geriatric Society*, 42 (1994), 883–886.
15. SJ Youngner, "Applying Futility: Saying No Is Not Enough," *Journal of American Geriatric Society*, 42 (1994), pp. 887–889.

Chapter 4

Treatment or Torture?

Medical Intervention at the End of Life

> Where is the life we have lost in living?
> Where is the wisdom we have lost in knowledge?
> Where is the knowledge we have lost in information?
> —T. S. Eliot, 1888–1965 (*The Rock*, 1934, Pt. I)

HAVE TECHNOLOGY, WILL INVADE

When it comes to the treatment of a patient with a terminal illness, the physician (with patient consent) is faced with two distinct philosophies: fighting for life at any cost (i.e., "heroically" doing everything possible), or administering optimal treatment, but treatment that is worthwhile.

The "everything possible" scenario is unfortunately too prevalent in our hospitals. Modern medical schools and many medical-specialty training programs emphasize training young doctors in the use of the latest technologies. Contemporary physicians are well trained and comfortable using modern high technology. Without question, American specialists are the best technicians in the world. One could even say that the very existence of technology motivates its use. The masters of the new art of high technology are always ready; have technology, will invade. Distressed family members, threatened by the loss of a loved one, are inclined to demand that everything possible be done. When one is distant from the battlefield, one can more easily be objective and rational. It is a different matter to personally be in the thick of it:

"He is too young to die, doctor ... please do everything you can!"

"We have been together for over 50 years and I can't imagine life without her!"

"Please don't tell me that you can't do more!"

"I know God will save him. He spoke to me in my dreams last night. Just keep doing all you can. I know he is going to make it!"

"No, it is not the time for him to go! Don't say it doctor!"

These are standard, everyday pleadings from genuinely caring family members who are unable or unwilling to let go of a loved one.

Occasionally, the physician is told something like the following: "We have been married for just a few years. I am his second wife. If I let go, his children might accuse me of not standing by him. Do everything you can!" Or, "Although all of us here have agreed that there is little more that can be done, one sister in California said not to give up and to keep fighting." Or, "This is a decision that has to be made by all family members. I have a brother in Germany that we can't reach at the present time. We have to persevere until we are able to reach him."

A young physician might be tempted to perform one or two more procedures before death becomes inevitable to assure the family, as well as him- or herself, that everything has been done. With this intervention comes the comfortable feeling that the doctor has acted in a legally defensible way.

I recall a nice 67-year-old woman whom I took care of while on call over the weekend a couple of months ago. Mrs. Brown* had been diagnosed with cancer of both breasts 12 years ago. Both

*Unless otherwise indicated, names have been fictionalized in deference to the person's right to privacy.

breasts had been removed. Her ovaries were also removed to deprive the body of the hormones necessary for the growth of the tumors. She had received radiation therapy and chemotherapy. A few years ago, she was also treated with a new antihormone medicine. Her cancer had been arrested for 10 years.

Two years prior to our encounter, tumor metastases (i.e., growth of the tumor beyond the original site) had afflicted her lungs and bones; another course of chemotherapy had limited success. She was subsequently given a megadose of chemotherapy. This final blast of chemotherapy knocked out her immune system. Her physician then ordered a bone marrow transplantation. (Bone marrow is the source of the body's immune factors.) Following these procedures, it was discovered that her heart had suffered massive damage as a result of the cumulative effects of chemotherapy. She presented to the emergency room with severe heart failure. A blood count showed that the bone marrow transplantation did not take, and the blood count had become extremely low. At this stage, one physician might say, "We have gone as far as is reasonable. Let us now make this patient's last hours of life as comfortable as possible." This physician would have explained the situation to the family in these terms: "Everything worthwhile has been done. Any more treatment, other than that which brings comfort, is meaningless." Instead, the actual treating physician presented his recommendation to an anxious and almost distraught husband: The patient should be placed on a ventilator; her heart failure can be treated aggressively. This course of action was taken. A fulminant pneumonia caused by a rare organism took hold in her body. A multitude of antibiotics were administered. The patient bled profusely from her stomach. An endoscope, a tool that enables specialists to look inside the stomach, showed a bleeding "stress ulcer." Blood transfusions were given. During the episode of massive bleeding from the stomach, the patient developed a drop in blood pressure. This was partly corrected with infusions of blood-pressure-sustaining medications, but it was then discovered that the kidneys were damaged from the drop in blood pressure and had stopped producing urine. Renal dialysis was initiated to replace her kidney function. The patient remained unconscious and on the ventilator. The patient's condition was described as "stable," at least on the chart.

A few days passed and the patient developed a high temperature. A new and vicious organism was found to have invaded the blood from the patient's colon (large intestine). An X-ray of the colon showed an infected sac, and her treating physician recommended that the colon be surgically removed. It was.

I saw the patient for the first time in this condition that weekend. I reviewed the chart and examined her. She had been on the ventilator for two weeks. This shrinking, unconscious being had 12 tubes coming out of her body. One tube was connected to the ventilator, one led to her stomach, and another tube connected a sac to her urinary bladder. Two tubes stuck out of her belly to drain the site of surgery, and one facilitated the movement of fecal matter out of her colon. Two tubes connected her to the dialysis machine, and one tube monitored the pressures within her heart. One tube enabled the continuous monitoring of blood pressure from within an artery. The rest of the tubes carried antibiotics and blood-pressure-sustaining medicines into her veins.

My examination of the patient revealed her to be unconscious, unresponsive, and unable to breathe on her own. Her blood pressure was low, and her kidneys were not making any urine. I looked at the laboratory sheet; toxins had accumulated in her blood, her bone marrow was not producing any blood cells, her liver was failing, her heart had become terminally damaged, and her lungs had become increasingly incapable of exchanging gases due to heart failure, pneumonia, and blood infection—even with help from a respirator.

I rested my head between my hands and sighed in an audible voice, "My God. We have done everything possible, haven't we? We have undertaken what is beyond the reasonable and the ridiculous, haven't we?" I asked my medical students who accompanied me: "What legal and ethical rights does an incompetent patient have?" Some answered, "The right to life, liberty, and pursuit of happiness." Others, well versed in ethical principles, cited autonomy, beneficence, nonmaleficence, and justice. I answered them: "The right to life? This depends upon your definition of life. This miserable being has suffered high-brain death for two weeks. She has been irretrievably unconscious and has lost all cognitive powers. I am told she used to be a lovely, warm, and articulate lady. I wish I had known her then. But the remains that we are dealing with here no longer fit that description."

"Well, let's agree that she has the right to liberty?" I said. "Where is your liberty when you are enslaved by 12 tubes connected to a bunch of machines? Does she have the right to privacy? This nice lady has had every part of her body exposed to the multitudes. People around her, including the attending medical professionals, converse as if she is nonexistent." (When I had approached her bed, the attending surgeon was talking to the nurse about an interesting movie that he had seen the night before. Scenes of naked patients become part of the decor in our profession, as awful as this may sound.)

"Finally, does she have the right to autonomy and to shared decision making? Whose decision? Which decision? Which autonomy?" I paused, then continued, "Beneficence means that you do what is good for the patient and nonmaleficence is to do no harm. What good are we doing by torturing someone in the process of dying. Sometimes the act of not letting one die peacefully is the greatest harm that you may inflict on a fellow human being."

Let the pundits of medical ethics come up with whatever rights they are capable of inventing in their comfortable armchairs. It is different out here. In this medical battlefield, someone who was once a dignified, intelligent, and lovely lady has been transformed into the remains of a human being. I turned to my students and continued, "There is one right that we can't take from anyone, anytime, anywhere. This is the *right to be respected.* Yes, she still has this right and will continue to have it even after she departs from this planet."

I walked out to talk to the patient's family: a loving, intelligent, and understanding group of people. I explained the situation in detail to her husband and to the other family members. I listened to them pour their hearts out. We decided to let their loved one depart in peace—no more tests, no more procedures, no more surgery, no more interventions; just medicine that brings peace and comfort. She departed a few hours later in a closed room, covered up, surrounded by her loved ones, and as respected as one can be in an intensive-care unit.

In the past, it has never been easy for me to talk about issues of death frankly and openly to a patient's loved ones. Not so since I developed cancer. I know one thing for a fact: If I ask myself whether I would have wanted to be treated like this, the answer would be a clear and unequivocal "no." One important ingredient of the medical profession is a firm commitment to the patient not to abandon him or her until the end. It is what makes medicine such a great profession, filled with joy and sorrow, exhilaration and sadness, but always compassionate, caring, and altruistic. Its moral authority derives from the fact that the patient's well-being is paramount from beginning to end.

WITHHOLDING TREATMENT MAY BE THE BEST THERAPY

The problem with the "everything possible" doctrine of medical treatment is that is masquerades as caring. It must be remembered that withholding an unnecessary procedure is not equivalent to withholding care. On the contrary, withholding a meaningless intervention is the only rational approach to care. The best medical intervention is often no intervention at all. When the patient is approaching the end of his or her normal life span, when the afflictions are incapacitating, and when the best that medicine can offer is an extension of suffering, withholding care is the best care.

In literature on medical ethics, it is customary to find the following "benefit–risk" type descriptions of treatment:

- Proportionate versus disproportionate
- Ordinary versus extraordinary

- Symmetrical versus asymmetrical
- Gain versus risk
- Benefit versus burden
- Fitting versus unfitting
- Necessary versus futile

These terms, however, are academic sounding and removed from real life. Personally, I prefer to use Dr. Weil's way of establishing whether treatment is worthwhile.[1] The questions that Dr. Weil, one of the world authorities in intensive care and Chairman of Medicine at the University of Chicago School of Medicine, uses are as follows:

- Is the treatment rational?
- Is it redeeming?
- Is it respectful?

When it is established with reasonable certainty that an individual has permanently and irreversibly lost the content of consciousness and cognition, or when further medical intervention is futile, the only rational treatment is that which brings comfort and deals with the patient respectfully.

When a baby is born without a higher brain, the only rational approach, according to the best medical advice, is to let go. Unfortunately, although most parents faced with such a misfortune elect to terminate the pregnancy rather than carry the baby to term, there are some notable exceptions. Multiple studies from neonatal intensive-care units have shown that a premature baby with less than 500 grams in weight, born of a mother who abused cocaine during pregnancy, has a meager chance for survival. If through enormous efforts it survives, it will probably lead a miserable, unhealthy, and unfulfilled life at a cost to society of over 1 million dollars. Dr. David Gary Smith, Chief of General Internal Medicine at Temple University in Philadelphia, summed up the problem in an article entitled, "Neonatal Intensive Care: How Much Is Too Much," published in the *Journal of Medical Ethics*.[2]

Rational medical therapy says that when a patient approaches the end of life because of advanced disseminated cancer that is unresponsive to all reasonable treatment, the rational approach to treatment is to make this person's remaining life as void of suffering as possible. I believe, as Dr. Weil recommends, that when a patient is admitted to the intensive-care unit with a burn that is so extensive that there is no prospect for recovery, merciful care is the appropriate care. A patient in terminal states of AIDS infection who reaches a state of unconsciousness (due to extensive destruction of brain cells) should not be kept on a ventilator.

In my view, when someone with advanced, end-stage heart disease, who is not a candidate for heart transplant, develops advanced kidney failure, he or she should not be treated with renal dialysis; this is irrational and futile. These are not simply my personal views, but facts borne out of solid medical data.

I do not condone paternalism in medical practice, by which the physician makes decisions on behalf of his patients without explaining to them why the decisions are made. By the same token, I do not condone the practice of doctors imposing their own views upon their patients about what constitutes an acceptable quality of life. Such judgments are outside the bounds of the medical profession. Any person is entitled to life, liberty, and pursuit of happiness. On the other hand, for someone who has lost "higher brain" function or who is in the end stages of an irreversible disease, the use of high-tech procedures does not represent autonomy, liberty, or pursuit of happiness and *should not be presented as a treatment option.*

Yes, a family in distress not infrequently asks the question of whether there is anything else that can be done. In the example I have given about the lady with terminal cancer, was the doctor right in presenting ultimately futile treatment options to the family members? "Yes, we can place her on a ventilator, support her blood pressure with a medicine, replace the lost blood and treat the infection ... and see what happens." With each additional complication, a physician who is so inclined could keep coming up with futile options: "We found a source of infection from the colon, and we can remove the colon. We can also place the patient on dialysis, which will take on the function of the kidneys."

I feel that the proper answer to the family should have been: "We have gone as far as is reasonable. Any intervention beyond this point will not be curative, nor will it allow her to live for any length of time. It simply will prolong the process of dying and make it unduly painful to all concerned." Oftentimes, after the treatment has failed, families have second thoughts about whether they have chartered the right course.

TRUST IN A PROFESSIONAL—THE NEXT BEST THING TO PATIENT AUTONOMY

In all my years of practice and particularly in recent years, I have rarely encountered family members who did not concur with a rational recommendation, so long as we have had a long and trusting relationship and they have been reasonably well prepared for treatment outcome. I have grown to realize that the concepts of patient autonomy and shared decision making are important. However, they are not as important as the right of the patient to be respected at all times. Also, I have come to realize that the most important ingredients in doctor–patient relationships are trust and trustworthiness.

As important as they are, the concepts of "autonomy" and "shared decision making" cannot be trusted to operate as intended in the setting of the intensive-care unit. This is particularly true with unexpected emergencies and when the patient's education and/or comprehension is limited. Data have shown that whereas some of the less sophisticated families develop unlimited trust in the physician and are prepared to relinquish all medical decisions to him or her, others leave all decisions in the hands of a specified family member. Many tend to be indecisive about the complex life-and-death issues, either from a lack of trust, poor communication between doctor and family, inability to understand all ramifications of treatment, lack of consensus, or sometimes due to outright resentment.

WILL LIMITING FUTILE CARE LEAD TO UNLIMITED ABUSE?

Some people feel that the limitation of any medical intervention—even futile intervention—will result in a spiraling descent into abuse, the so-called "slippery-slope argument."

Partisans of the slippery-slope argument maintain that society must protect the lives of its citizens under all circumstances and at any cost, since this is the basic value that binds the society together. Slippery-slope advocates feel that society must protect its most vulnerable members who may therefore be neglected or even by going to extremes, be exterminated. Ironically, these people are ignoring and often violating the right of the individual to have freedom, dignity, and respect near the end of life. It would be far better to have as an advocate a rational and compassionate physician who understands the futility of futile care.

Dr. Timothy Quill, the famed advocate of legalized euthanasia and author of *Death and Dignity.... Making Choices and Taking Charge*, has some harsh words for medical ethicists who advocate life and continued treatment regardless of its futility.[3] I quote him here to underscore a point of view with some validity: "The idealized, sanitized intentions of medical ethicists lead to bad medical practice because they neglect the reality and complexity of experience." He continues: "Current ethical and legal prohibitions reinforce self-deception, secrecy, isolation and abandonment. The humanizing of medical ethics requires greater clarity about intentions and responsibilities in the care of dying patients."

THE 50–50 PROPOSITION: MISREPRESENTING THE PROGNOSIS

In my experience, one of the most difficult situations in clinical practice is what I like to call the 50–50 proposition. In order to clarify what I mean, I will share my precise recollection of one such recent case.

Mrs. Elizabeth Hightower, a 66-year-old widow born in Scotland, lived most of her adult life in the United States. She had two bright, caring daughters and a charming granddaughter who lived close by, visiting Grandma frequently. Mrs. Hightower was a proud, bright, independent, feisty lady. She had had heart bypass surgery twice: six years ago and two years ago for the treatment of severe hardening of the coronary arteries (which provide blood to the heart muscle). In addition, she suffered two heart attacks and underwent two other procedures to open up clogged bypass veins that had been grafted into the coronary circulatory system. The second bypass surgery was extremely difficult technically according to the surgical report. Two bypass operations exhausted all utilizable leg veins that had been used for grafts. In addition, Mrs. Hightower developed severe heart failure as a result of a severely damaged heart muscle and a leaky heart valve. Although still fairly young, the burden of generalized hardening of the arteries had taken its toll. The kidneys became sluggish, her blood chemistry became difficult to stabilize, and Mrs. Hightower spent the better part of the last three months in intensive care. She was deemed not to be a candidate for heart transplantation and became desperate. "I can't go on like this!" she repeated to her relatives, nurses, and doctors. Unfortunately, I had known Mrs. Hightower only for a few weeks during her last hospitalization. We spoke about Scotland (where I had part of my training), her family, and her illness. In spite of the fact that she had executed a living will less than two years ago, denoting her resentment of a permanently dependent life, and her suffering was immense, she declined an order "not to resuscitate" when I approached her tactfully about the subject.

The family asked for a second opinion. A heart surgeon, new to town, reviewed her case with us. We had a joint conference with the family.

"The only options we have are either to do something or do nothing," he said. "If we do nothing, she will die," he continued. "If we do something, we have a 50–50 chance." He went on to say that he had already presented these options to Mrs. Hightower and that she was ready for a third open-heart surgery. The whole family welcomed this newfound hope.

I demurred: "Under the best of circumstances, Mrs. Hightower's outlook is dismal. Even if we assume that she has a 50% chance of surviving surgery, the period following the operation promises to be long, stormy, and loaded with complications. Her subsequent improvement will, at best, be extremely limited. She will never be able to lead a life of independence and, assuming the best-case scenario, she has less than a 10% chance of surviving one year."

The older daughter appeared startled. She asked the heart surgeon, "What is your experience in cases like this?"

"Well, I operated on a similar patient, Mr. Hunt, three months ago. They said he wouldn't survive, but he surprised us. He is alive."

"How is he doing now?" she asked me.

"He is still in the hospital in the skilled nursing facility. He is in severe heart failure. Each time we get ready to discharge him, he develops a new complication: pneumonia, urinary tract infection, clotting of leg veins, heart failure, and so on," I answered.

Mrs. Hightower's daughter gazed at me and asked in a tearful voice, "What do you think?" I asked to talk to Mrs. Hightower one more time.

"I know what you are going to tell me," said Mrs. Hightower. "Life is a gamble, isn't it? I am ready to have surgery and whatever happens, happens," she added.

The next morning, Mrs. Hightower underwent surgery. The operation lasted over seven hours. During surgery, a device to assist her heartbeat was inserted from the left groin; impending gangrene of the left leg developed, and another surgery to save her leg had to be performed.

After witnessing nine days of her continuing struggle in intensive care, the family decided that enough was enough, even though the surgeon wanted to persevere. A consultation with the ethics committee was obtained. Dr. Walker, Professor of Internal Medicine and noted ethicist, wrote,

We are asked to comment on this difficult case of a 67-year-old white female with severe coronary artery disease, hypertension, and peripheral vascular disease. In particular, we were called regarding refusal of tube feeding for the patient by the patient's daughter. This patient has a history of multiple heart attacks prior to 1982, when she had her first bypass surgery. In recent years, her case has become more complicated by further myocardial [heart muscle] damage, repeat bypass surgeries, angina, heart-failure problems with peripheral vascular disease. On 5-26-95, the patient underwent further bypass graft surgery, mitral valve repair with intra-aortic-balloon-pump assist device. Her postoperative course has been complicated by kidney failure, low cardiac output, and mental confusion. Prior to surgery, the patient was given a 50–50 chance of surgery improving her situation. But now, nine days after surgery, the patient's cardiac [heart] status has not improved. She remains in the intensive-care unit on multiple drips. Both cardiology and nephrology have assessed her prognosis as poor. In recent days, a DNR [Do Not Resuscitate] order has been written and a hospice consult placed. Currently, the patient is confused and unable to participate in discussions regarding her treatment. She did have the foresight to draft a detailed living will and proxy appointment while living in the state of Washington. Her proxy is her daughter, who is here at the bedside. As the patient lacks decisional capacity, all decisions regarding the patient's care should be consented to through the patient's daughter. We were consulted over the issue of the daughter refusing insertion of a feeding tube. First, it should be noted that patients have the legal and ethical right to refuse artificial nutrition and hydration. It should also be noted that the patient, in her advance directive, refused this sort of intervention in advance, conditioning it on her being decisionally incapacitated and having a terminal condition (i.e., life expectancy judged to be 12 months or less). In discussion with Dr. ..., the patient's cardiologist and attending [hospital physician], he

> states that the patient is in a terminal condition. Thus, the daughter's refusal of tube feeding goes with the patient's prior wishes. In discussion with the patient's daughter, she states that she and all her family members only want to honor their mother's wishes. She is now concerned that her mother does not wish to remain in intensive care. She states that surgery has not helped her mother's heart and that her mother is now in a situation she would have wanted to avoid. She tells me that after surgery, her mother pleaded with her to get the physicians to "stop doing things to her." The daughter is convinced that her mother would not want to continue aggressive care. She told me that she and other family members would prefer that their mother be transferred out of the unit and be given comfort measures only. By contrast, there is an entry in yesterday's nurses' notes that "the patient does not want to die." It is difficult to interpret this comment in view of the patient's disorientation and confusion. At other times, when the patient was judged to be more lucid, she indicated the opposite desire. In conclusion, we have a patient with end-stage coronary artery disease, whose heart function has not improved post cardiac surgery. She remains incapacitated in the intensive-care unit. Our assessment is that the daughter is the appropriate proxy decision maker for the patient, and that she should be consulted for all decisions. In view of the patient's poor prognosis and the attending's assessment that the patient is in a terminal condition, we agree with the daughter's decision to forego tube feeding. We do agree with the DNR status and the decision of consulting hospice. We strongly recommend that aggressive intervention be discontinued and that the patient be transferred to the floor for nonaggressive intervention and comfort care. All measures should be negotiated with the patient's daughter.

A few days passed and Mrs. Hightower became more lucid, but more weak. I asked her, "Why did you decide to go through surgery?"

"I wanted to die—and I thought I would die in surgery," she said.

Arrangements were made to transfer her by air-ambulance to be close to her daughter. On the way out I said to her daughter,

"You have done what you thought was best for her; no decision is perfect, and I would have been the happiest man if I was proven wrong."

With a choked voice, trying to overcome her tears, she asked, "What is the title of your book?"

"*A Graceful Exit,*" I said. There was a moment of silence that was worth a thousand words. (A few weeks later, I received a kind note from the family, in which they shared with me that Mrs. Hightower died at home.)

I turned to my students and said, "When the surgeon said 50–50 chance, he meant of surviving surgery; he didn't promise health, comfort and independence. A patient at the abyss of death is like a drowning person groping for straws. Exaggerated promises invite unrealistic expectations that lead to unreasonable demands, often followed by great disappointments."

Sometimes doing nothing is better than doing something when that intervention is without a defined realistic and achievable objective. Patients and their families should realize this. But often it is difficult for a layperson to assess medical options or realize that a specialist may be biased toward a particular procedure. It is not unethical for a physician to express his or her bias when making a recommendation. Therefore, for a surgeon to recommend bypass surgery to a patient is entirely ethical, provided the recommendation conforms with the surgeon's belief that such a course will most benefit this particular patient. Furthermore, doctors and medical professionals sometimes use, in their conversation, medical terms that may be difficult for nonprofessionals to understand. A recent research study at a leading university involved taping discussions between medical professionals and patients and their families regarding interventions. A few weeks later, most patients and family members had forgotten the content of the conversations and many did not recall that conversations about the specific subject matter had taken place.

When I was a patient, I experienced two surgeries for my prostate cancer: one in 1987, another in 1991. In both instances, I followed my doctor's advice. Yes, it is my right to share in the decision making. However, this right assumes that I am able to evaluate all available options and am capable of making an informed choice among them. I felt that I was not professionally qualified to accept or refuse any particular course of therapy. In each case, my choice of my doctor was based upon my trust in him. He lived up to my trust and I accepted his professional recommendation. As in the case of Mrs. Hightower and her family, I served as the trusted liaison between the medical establishment and the family. I was ultimately able to help effect a death with dignity for Mrs. Hightower.

Recently, the nation witnessed the passing of former President Richard Nixon and former First Lady Jacqueline Kennedy Onassis. When faced with the inevitability of an imminent death, each elected to depart peacefully in his or her own bed, surrounded by loved ones. No doubt, these two eminent and enlightened people provided an exemplary standard for how to face the moment of death. And, no doubt, they too had a trusted relationship with a primary physician who respected their wishes.

A NATURAL DEATH

The deaths of these two famous people reminded me of a long-term friend and patient, Mr. Otha Grimes. I treated Mr. Grimes for a heart attack in 1978. Subsequently, he returned to his oil and farm business in Kansas, Oklahoma, and Texas. He bred cattle and won prizes. A age 92, he had the energy of a 60-year-old and the passion of a 20-year-old man. At this advanced age, he developed a cough and his breathing became heavy. A chest X-ray showed cancer with a large collection of fluid outside the right lung. Small lumps were palpable at the root of his neck. A biopsy confirmed incurable cancer. I shared with Mr. Grimes details of our medical findings. He asked, "How much longer do I have to live?"

I answered, "A few months."

He asked, "Can we make it any shorter?"

I said, "I do not believe in euthanasia."

He said, "Neither do I, but my wife is crippled with advanced arthritis and has heart failure. I wish not to add to her burdens. Now that I am 92 years old, I have outlived my peers by over 10 years. It is time for me to go."

He asked to be admitted to a private hospital room, and I did as he instructed. He asked that I refrain from giving him any medicine other than painkillers, and I agreed. I held his hand. He winked at me with his right eye and smiled. I was overpowered by tears. He squeezed my hand as if to encourage me, closed his eyes, and slipped into a coma.

One may ask, "What caused Mr. Grimes to slip into a coma? How could it be possible that he would be alert and conversant one day and go into deep sleep the next?" I have no explanation except to say that the way he went proves the naturalness of death. I have seen this same phenomenon among many other older patients of Native American descent and in my old country. People who long for death withdraw from life and simply die. Mr. Grimes died two weeks later—quickly and without "lamentation or suffering." Indeed, his end was as "wonderful if a mortal's ever was." He chose an Oedipus-like death when he could have been transformed into another Tithonus.

Richard Nixon, Jacqueline Kennedy, and Otha Grimes could financially afford a couple of weeks on a ventilator somewhere in an intensive-care unit. However, they could not afford the indignity and futility that goes with it. They displayed wisdom, serenity, and courage even in the face of death.

NOTES

1. MH Weil, "Alternatives to Rationing, in Brooking's Dialogues on Public Policy." In *Rationing of Medical Care for the Critically Ill* (Washington, DC: The Brookings Institution, 1989), pp. 17–23.
2. DG Smith, "Neonatal Intensive Care: How Much Is Too Much?" *Medical Ethics*, 5 (1990), 13–14.
3. TE Quill, "Doctor, I Want to Die. Will You Help Me?" *Journal of the American Medical Association*, 270 (1993), 870–873.

Chapter 5

Do Not Resuscitate

A Man can die but once; we owe God a death.
—SHAKESPEARE (in *Henry IV*, III; 2:253)

A HISTORY OF RESUSCITATION

Since Biblical times, with Lazarus presumably rising from the dead, humans have been fascinated with the idea of resuscitation.[1] They have employed myriad methods to effect this feat. A recent article by Drs. Tucker and associates in the *Archives of Internal Medicine* in October 1994 cites attempts at resuscitation. These authors mentioned how whipping of the dead, burning of elixirs, smearing dried excreta over the victim, incantation, and the use of fireside bellows were employed to breathe "life" into the dead.[2] Boehm, the German pharmacologist from the University of Dorpat, is credited with the first reported method of closed-chest heart compressions (i.e., pushing down on the chest with both hands) in the cat to effect resuscitation. Koenig, a German surgeon, used single-handed, slow chest compressions to revive six patients after chloroform anesthesia. Another German scientist, Dr. Maass, modified this method in 1892 by applying 120 fast compressions over the breastbone, using this method to revive two patients after chloroform anesthesia. In 1914, Dr. Crile, a noted American surgeon, used chest compression to revive a patient who received ether anesthesia to enable neck surgery.[3] He described his method in a book published in 1914. In subsequent years, data from experiments in dogs showed the feasibility of chest-wall compressions to assist the pumping action of the heart. Nevertheless, doctors resorted to opening of the chest and direct hand massage on the hearts of patients who had experienced sudden death due to electrocution or similar accidents.

At Johns Hopkins University, the earliest studies in electrically shocking fibrillating hearts into regular rhythm were undertaken. (Fibrillation is a type of irregular heartbeat that can be fatal.) A young visiting scientist, Dr. Kouwenhoven[4] undertook these studies at the behest of the Edison Electric Company, whose management was concerned about potential electrocution of workers.

From experiments using dogs, Kouwenhoven developed in 1957 the first machine for reviving the heart rhythm by an electric shock applied through the intact chest wall.[5] Dr. Kouwenhoven, in association with Dr. Knickerbocker, was experimenting on a dog using new heavy electric paddles to shock the fibrillating dog heart. As these scientists pressed the pedals, they noticed that the pressure caused the dog heart to squeeze, even though it was not beating by itself. This chance observation resulted in the discovery that in humans, rhythmic compressions 60 times per minute applied to the breastbone at a force of 40 kg can revive an arrested heart.

On February 15, 1958, Dr. H. T. Bahnson, working with Drs. Kouwenhoven and Jude at Johns Hopkins, successfully resuscitated a two-year-old child with an arrested heart using the technique of closed-chest heart massage.[6] Shortly thereafter, mouth-to-mouth artificial ventilation was used in conjunction with closed-chest resuscitation. In 1962, Dr. Bernard Lown of Boston discovered that direct-current electric shocks can be used safely to regulate disordered heart rhythm in place of the less safe alternating-current method.[7] He built on earlier pioneer work of research workers, including Dr. Zoll. By the mid-1960s, CPR was ready for wide application. Initially, the success rate of CPR was 70%, but subsequent studies have never duplicated this figure. The success rate depends upon how soon after cardiopulmonary arrest CPR is initiated, the underlying state of health of the victim, the proficiency of the resuscitation team, the immediate availability of heart rhythm correcting devices, as well as the health circumstances that caused the arrest. Success rates of 20–30% are customary.

THE NEW RIGHT OF RESUSCITATION

As we have noted, the medical profession has been unable to develop rational and practical guidelines for life-and-death issues at the end of life. This hesitancy is also seen around the topic of resuscitation. With the wide acceptance of closed-chest CPR, Drs. Jude and Elam, the pioneer physicians, stated that the first principle for CPR was that "the patient must be salvageable."[8] Their initial recommendations for CPR appeared in a textbook on the subject in 1965. The criteria for who should receive CPR have undergone numerous modifications over the years, increasing its scope of application. In 1974, the American Heart Association proposed the need for documentation of do-not-resuscitate (DNR) orders in patients' records. CPR approached being mandatory therapy for every patient with cardiopulmonary arrest, whether they were really "salvageable" or not.

In 1976, the clinical care committee of Massachusetts General Hospital developed recommendations for the treatment of hopelessly ill patients and for orders not to resuscitate.[9] DNR orders meant that, in the event that the heart stops beating or the lungs cease to function, no efforts should be undertaken to revive the heart or place the patient on assisted ventilation devices. These recommendations were published in the *New England Journal of Medicine*.[10] These recommendations changed CPR from an intervention intended for use for victims with acute insult to a standard therapy for all cases of cardiac arrest, except for those that fulfilled the new, stringent criteria for DNR. The committee determined that DNR orders were appropriate *only* when the patient's disease has fulfilled all three of the following criteria:

1. The disease is "irreversible," in the sense that no known therapeutic measures can be effective in reversing the course of illness.
2. The physical status of the patient is "irreparable," in the sense that the course of illness has progressed beyond the capacity of existing knowledge and techniques to stem the process.
3. The patient's death is "imminent," in the sense that in the ordinary course of events, death will probably occur within a period not exceeding two weeks.

The committee also stipulated that the initial medical judgment regarding DNR orders be made by the physician primarily responsible for the patient, after discussion with an *ad hoc* committee consisting not only of the other physicians attending the patient, the nurses and other health-care professionals active in the care of the patient, but, also at least one other staff physician not previously involved in the patient's care.

Even with the medical staff's recommendation, the committee deemed that a DNR order would become effective only upon the informed choice of a competent patient. When the patient is incompetent, *all* appropriate family members must be in agreement with the views of the involved staff.

Unfortunately, these guidelines represent a tremendous burden on the treating physicians, especially the guidelines developed for the incompetent-patient situation. These guidelines also imply an unfortunate message:

1. It is the right course of action to resuscitate patients, anytime there is a cardiopulmonary arrest.
2. Had the patient been capable of making an independent decision, it is assumed that he or she would have desired to be resuscitated (implied consent doctrine).

Instead of considering resuscitation to be a form of treatment that is indicated in some instances and not in others, it is assumed to be the right course for all unless otherwise clearly stated. In effect, resuscitation is regarded as standard operating procedure.

In fact, under the conditions set forth in the guidelines by the Massachusetts General Hospital, even when irreversibility, irreparability, and the imminence of death have been established with reasonable certainly, a DNR order may not be the appropriate course unless the family approves unanimously.

CHALLENGING THE RIGHT OF RESUSCITATION

These guidelines were challenged in court in 1978 in the Dinnerstein case.[11] Mrs. Dinnerstein was an elderly woman with advanced impairment of her brain functions. She was not able to recognize or communicate with relatives or attending physicians. In addition, she suffered advanced heart disease due to hardening of the arteries and multiple heart attacks. She was in the hospital when family members requested that no resuscitation efforts be undertaken in the event of cessation of heartbeat. The treating physician, basing his decision upon the DNR criteria set forth by the Massachusetts General Hospital committee recommendations, could not honor the request. The court upheld the family's wishes stating, "Attempts to apply resuscitation, if successful, will do nothing to cure or relieve the illnesses which have brought the patient to the threshold of death...." And the court emphasized: "This case presents a question peculiarly within the competence of the medical profession of what measures are appropriate to ease the imminent passing of an irreversibly, terminally ill patient." The court went on to state, "This question is not one for judicial decision, but one for the attending physician, in keeping with the highest traditions of his profession." Individual physicians, having to abide by the need to obtain consent in order to withhold CPR, sometimes continued to limit what they regarded as inappropriate medical care by using low codes (in effect, sham codes).

New York State enacted legislation to put an end to this practice and required physicians to obtain patient or surrogate consent in all cases (see Hastings Center report by Morreim: "Profoundly Diminished Life: The Casualties of Coercion," 1994).[12] In 1991, the council of ethical and judicial affairs of the American Medical Association recommended the following: "When efforts to resuscitate a patient are judged by the treating physician to be futile, even if previously requested by the patient, CPR may be withheld." This recommendation took CPR into the realm of being a medical treatment decision, not just an automatic response to cardiopulmonary arrest.[13]

THE ODDS OF BEING RESUSCITATED

A recent study by Drs. Murphy, Burrows, and others, published in the *New England Journal of Medicine* in 1994, shows that relatively healthy elderly people have a 10% chance of being revived through CPR.[14] On the other hand, elderly people with long-term illnesses have a very poor chance (well below 5%) of being revived through CPR. This carefully conducted study showed that when *fully* informed about the outcome, including the chance of survival and possibility of recovery of brain function following CPR, 20% of all relatively healthy patients of various ages opted for CPR in the event of cardiopulmonary arrest, but only a very small minority of patients older than 86 years desired CPR. The overwhelming majority (95%) of well-informed, elderly patients did not wish to be revived by CPR, with its attendant risk of brain damage and consequent loss of autonomy and independence. This study was conducted at the Senior Citizen's Health Center, Presbyterian–St. Luke's Medical Center in Denver, Colorado and the Intensive-Care Research Unit at George Washington University Medical Center in Washington, DC. It contrasts sharply with the prevailing practice of resuscitating all cases of cardiac arrest under the doctrine of implied consent.

Two recent, large studies, one by Dr. Kellerman and associates from the University of Tennessee in Memphis and the other by Dr. Bonnin and associates from the City of Houston's Center of Resuscitation and Emergency Medical Services, are worth special mention and involved resuscitation of patients outside the hospital. Both have shown that as many as 25% of those who recover their heartbeat before arriving at the emergency room do well subsequently.[15,16] By contrast, patients who are taken to the hospital with no recovery of heartbeat have a less than 1% chance of leaving the hospital alive. In all instances, they experienced permanent brain damage. These studies argue strongly in favor of termination of unsuccessful cardiac resuscitation at the scene of cardiac arrest.

CONSENT VERSUS THERAPEUTIC PREROGATIVE DO-NOT-RESUSCITATE ORDERS

More recently, two forms of DNR orders are recognized: "consent DNR," when the order is given only according to certain guidelines; and "therapeutic prerogative DNR," which stipulates that DNR, like any other medical decision, has to be tailored to the patient's medical status. *Consent DNR* is defined in a document published by the Yale–New Haven Hospital in 1983:[17]

> The ultimate authority to determine the overall management objectives resides with the patient and/or the family.... If a patient is conscious and competent, he or she has the clear right to refuse any treatment (including resuscitation) even if such refusal may mean death.

With the therapeutic prerogative DNR protocols, the reason for terminating treatment is to avoid "prolongation of death." These protocols, according to Robert Baker, an outspoken critic of unrestricted CPR, recognize that there is no rationale, no medical justification, no moral justification for futile interventions, even when the patient or family disagrees. I wholeheartedly agree that "[t]he mere fact that a patient, or the patient's family wishes an intervention is not sufficient grounds for the physician to maintain or initiate it." When clinicians believe that intervention will no longer serve its medical objective of prolonging life, they should so inform the patient or the patient's surrogates and then alter or discontinue the treatment. As with any other medical intervention, CPR should be used only for those patients who have a good chance of being restored to a conscious living state in which some degree of autonomy, even if limited, can be preserved.[18]

Once more, court rulings, while generally supportive of DNR orders in cases of medical futility, occasionally rendered conflicting decisions based on narrow statutory grounds.[19] In "re Doe" (1992),[19] the Georgia Supreme Court upheld in the case of a 13-year-old girl suffering from severe brain degeneration and uncontrollable seizures with "no reasonable possibility of meaningful recovery" that physicians could not write a DNR order. The patient's parents were not married, and one of them disagreed with the DNR order. The court supported the wishes of the parent who asked for resuscitation efforts, while at the same time concurring with the attending physicians that resuscitation efforts would have been without any therapeutic purpose in this case. Researchers have shown that mothers tend to be extremely protective of their dying children, out of a deep sense of duty, love, and hope. Maternal devotion sometimes does not yield to rational thinking or pragmatic evaluation.

In various hospitals, protocols regarding DNR vary considerably. In some hospitals, the order is considered for all terminally ill patients. In others, more stringent limitation of its use is the norm. Drs. Waisel and Truog of the Children's Hospital, Harvard Medical School reviewed CPR policies from four institutions in a review published in 1995.[20] They highlighted policy differences between the following hospitals: Allegheny General Hospital, Pittsburgh, Pennsylvania; Veterans Affairs Medical Center, Seattle, Washington; Beth Israel Hospital, Boston, Massachusetts; and Johns Hopkins Hospital, Baltimore, Maryland. As the authors emphasized in their valuable study, problems regarding cardiopulmonary resuscitation policies should derive from scientific thought and public negotiation. At this time, they strongly support policies based exclusively on physiological evidence of futility. Allegheny General Hospital policy comes close to their criteria (see Appendix A).

Still, most DNR protocols in U.S. hospitals dismiss the consent process and bias the decision making toward aggressive interventions (resuscitate first and ask for consent later), often with disastrous consequences to the patient, family, and society.

To avoid these unfortunate consequences and the financial and emotional costs that they entail, universally acceptable guidelines need to be formulated. Therapeutic prerogative CPR protocols should be limited to patients who have a reasonable chance of regaining consciousness and function through resuscitation. Toward achieving these goals, Drs. Waisel and Truog of Harvard University proposed certain circumstances in which resuscitation is inappropriate. Table 1 shows a modified version of their recommendations. These criteria are reasonable guidelines and should

Table 1
Clinical Situations in Which Cardiopulmonary Resuscitation Is Unlikely to Prolong Life[a]

Advanced, progressive, ultimately lethal illness
- Bedfast metastatic cancer
- Child's untreatable Class C liver cirrhosis
- HIV[b] (AIDS) infection (patient has had $\geqslant$ 2 episodes of *Pneumocystis carinii* pneumonia)
- Dementia due to extensive brain damage requiring long-term care

Acute, near-fatal illness without evidence of improvement after admission to the intensive-care unit
- Coma (traumatic or nontraumatic) lasting > 48 hours
- Multiple organ system failure with no improvement after 3 consecutive days in the intensive-care unit
- Unsuccessful out-of-hospital cardiopulmonary resuscitation

[a]Modified from Waisel and Truog, 1995.
[b]HIV = human immunodeficiency virus. See also Murphy and Finucane, 1993.

be considered for universal adoption by the medical community. Life cannot and must not be measured by whiffs from a ventilation machine or by clicks from a heart monitor.

NOTES

1. HP Liss, "A History of Resuscitation," *Annals of Emergency Medicine*, 15 (1986), 65–72.
2. KJ Tucker, JA Savitt, A Idris, and RF Redberg, "Cardiopulmonary Resuscitation: Historical Perspectives, Physiology, and Future Directions," *Archives Internal Medicine*, 154 (1994), 2141–2150.
3. GW Crile, *Anemia and Resuscitation*. (New York: D. Appleton & Co., 1914), pp. 15–32.
4. WB Kouwenhoven and OR Langworthy, "Cardiopulmonary Resuscitation: An Account of 45 Years of Research," *Johns Hopkins Medical Journal*, 132 (1973), 186–193.
5. WB Kouwenhoven, "The Development of the Defibrillator," *Annals Internal Medicine*, 71 (1969), 449–1067.
6. B Lown, R Amarsingham, and J Newman, "New Method for Terminating Cardiac Arrhythmia: Use of Synchronized Capacitor Discharge," *Journal of the American Medical Association*, 182 (1962), 548–555.
7. JR Jude and JO Elam, *Fundamentals of Cardiopulmonary Resuscitation* (Philadelphia: FA Davis Co., 1965).
8. A Report of the Clinical Care Committee of the Massachusetts General Hospital, "Optimum Care for Hopelessly Ill Patients," *New England Journal of Medicine*, 7 (1976), 362–364.
9. MT Rabkin, G Dillerman, and NR Rice, "Orders Not to Resuscitate," *New England Journal of Medicine*, 7 (1976), 364–366.
10. *In the Matter of Shirley Dinnerstein* (MA, App., 380 NE 2d, 134, 1978).
11. EH Morreim, "Profoundly Diminished Life: The Casualties of Coercion," *Hastings Center Report* (1994), 33–42.
12. Council on Ethical and Judicial Affairs, American Medical Association. "Guidelines for the Appropriate Use of Do-Not-Resuscitate Orders," *Journal of the American Medical Association*, 265 (1991), 1868–1971.
13. DJ Murphy, D. Burrows, S Santilli, AW Kemp, S Tenner, B Kreling, and J Teno, "The Influence of Probability of Survival on Patients' Prefer-

ences Regarding Cardiopulmonary Resuscitation," *New England Journal of Medicine*, 330 (1994), 545–549.

14. AL Kellerman, BB Hackman, and G Somes, "Predicting the Outcome of Unsuccessful Prehospital Advanced Cardiac Life Support," *Journal of the American Medical Association*, 270 (1993), 1433–1436.
15. MJ Bonnin, PE Pepe, KT Kimball, and PS Clark, Jr., "Distinct Criteria for Termination of Resuscitation in the Out-of-Hospital Setting." *Journal of the American Medical Association*, 270 (1993), 1457–1462.
16. Committee of Policy for DNR Decisions, Yale–New Haven Hospital. "Report on Do-Not-Resuscitate Decisions," *Connecticut Medicine*, 47 (1983), 477–483.
17. R Baker, Beyond Do-Not-Resuscitate Orders. (Brookings Dialogues on Public Policy. Rationing of Medical Care for the Critically Ill (Washington, DC: Brookings Institution, 1989), pp. 52–63.
18. *In re Doe*, Civ. Action No D-93064 (Fulton County, GA, 1991).
19. DB Waisel and RD Truog, "The Cardiopulmonary Resuscitation-Not-Indicated Order: Futility Revisited," *Annals of Internal Medicine*, 122 (1995), 304–308.
20. Ibid.

Chapter 6

Active Euthanasia

Is There a Sour Note in the "Sweet Death"?

Commit the oldest sins the newest kind of ways.
—SHAKESPEARE (in *Henry IV*, IV; 5:124)

From the previous chapters, it must be apparent that I strongly favor the withholding or withdrawal of medication in the case of a terminally ill person once treatment has been deemed futile. I consider it a sacred duty that physicians terminate a counter-therapeutic treatment. When a physician embarks on a treatment plan, it must be with the purpose of restoring the patient to a reasonable physical health that is compatible with living. Once the treatment is found not to produce this desired result, the physician has no obligation to continue and commits no unlawful or unethical act by discontinuing it. Furthermore, it is the physician's duty to alleviate the patient's pain and suffering, even if that hastens the moment of death. In this context, the views of the patient or those of his or her relatives should not affect these purely medical decisions, as long as the physician keeps the family informed at all times. This position has been supported by many court decisions and conforms with the recommendations of the Council of Medical Ethics of the American Medical Association.[1]

Active euthanasia is a different matter. Literally translated from Latin, *euthanasia* means "sweet death," or peaceful death. Some believe, as does Dr. Gillon of Kings College, London University, that "when it is time to die, the medical profession has a series of duties and obligations to aid the patient in achieving that end as an autonomous and dignified individual. Also that physicians must be willing, on occasion, to take an active role in the process of death to stop suffering, to protect autonomy, and to replace technology by real people in dying situations."[2] Another author goes on to say, "When I am breathing my last breath, it is better to be touched by a hand than to be violated by a tube."

In the context of the debate about persistent vegetative state in the House of Lords, Lord Browne-Wilkinson[3] asked rhetorically,

> How can it be lawful to allow a patient to die slowly, though painlessly, over a period of weeks, from lack of food, but unlawful to produce his immediate death by a lethal injection, thereby saving his family from yet another ordeal to add to the tragedy that has already struck them?

Lord Browne Wilkinson's rhetorical question was presented to the Judicial Council of the House of Lords in England in the context of a hearing about whether it was lawful to discontinue feeding and hydration from Mr. Tony Bland, a young man with extensive brain damage as a result of suffocation in a soccer ball accident.

No doubt these are eloquent arguments in favor of controlled, active euthanasia. There are, however, legal, moral, ethical, and religious imperatives that must be taken into account. It is true that when it comes to animals, decent human beings make sure that their beloved pets do not suffer. "No decent human being would allow an animal to suffer without putting it out of its misery," writes Isaac Asimov. "It is only to human beings that human beings are so cruel as to allow them to live on in pain, in hopelessness, in living death, without moving a muscle to help them." And the author Robert James Waller reflects upon putting to sleep his favorite pet, Roadcat, in his book, *Old Songs in a New Cafe*:

> For some days after, I swore I would never go through that again. If it came to euthanasia, I would refuse to be present. But I have changed my mind ... you owe that much to good companions who have asked for little and who have traveled far and faithfully by your side.[4]

MURDER OR MERCIFUL DEATH?

It can be argued that euthanasia is not akin to murder. In murder, there is the intention to hurt; there is often hatefulness and cruelty. Euthanasia, on the other hand, is often justified by those who advocate it on the presumption that it is motivated by noble sentiments: love, caring, and mercy. Nevertheless, my beliefs, my upbringing, my faith, and above all, being a physician, prevent me from administering a medicine with the intention to end a life. In the Hippocratic oath, a physician swears, "I will give no deadly medicine to anyone if asked, nor suggest any such counsel." Furthermore, the Judeo–Christian teachings place human life over virtually all other considerations. This attitude is summed up in the Talmudic passage about Adam, "... to teach that if any person has caused a single soul to perish, scripture regards him as if he had caused an entire world to perish and if any human being saves a single soul, scripture regards him as if he had saved an entire world."

For these reasons, like many other mainstream thinkers (see Notes for some important references), I cannot bring myself to accept a role to deliberately, intentionally end the life of another, whatever the motive may be. I must admit, however, that many times I have administered fairly large doses of painkillers to terminally ill patients in order to alleviate their suffering. I knew that this act might have hastened their death, but that would have been incidental to relieving their pain. Also, I have strong suspicions that two of my terminally ill patients, for whom I prescribed medications to alleviate their pain, might have used the medicines to end their own lives. But I could not administer such drugs with the primary purpose of causing death. Multiple recent publications from the United States, Britain, Australia, and Canada have confirmed the fact that more than half of practicing physicians are willing to administer large doses of painkillers to alleviate patient suffering, even if that hastens the moment of death. The American Medical Association, in 1992, supported this practice in an official comminiqué from the Council of Ethical and Judicial Affairs, entitled "Decisions Near the End of Life."[5]

A DOCTOR OF DEATH

Dr. Jack Kevorkian, the "death doctor," has received much publicity as a physician who actively abets the suicide of strangers. Personally, I have great difficulty validating a physician like Dr. Kevorkian, who has taken the Hippocratic oath to protect life, yet dedicates himself to helping others die. I find it difficult to condone the conduct of a physician who specializes exclusively in the act of mercy killing and tapes the moments of his patient's death.

Kevorkian, the death impresario, has taken it upon himself to change the law prohibiting doctor-assisted suicide. He believes that this law is intrinsically immoral; therefore, he feels a greater duty to violate it. Indeed, in many instances his actions have been supported by the court, such as when Michigan Judge Cynthia Stephens supported the right to suicide of two terminally ill plaintiffs: "This court cannot envisage a more fundamental right than the right to self-determination."

The publicity surrounding Kevorkian and his suicide machines is indicative of how ill at ease physicians and society in general are with doctor-assisted suicide. At the very mention of "euthanasia," many groups, including members of the medical profession, throw up their hands in horror. Like many other attempts to reach consensus regarding end-of-life medical treatment, these issues are greeted with cries of the "slippery-slope" argument. Similar expressions of alarm occurred in the past regarding discussions about withholding interventions from patients whose deaths are imminent, withdrawing machines when treatment is hopeless, or when considering the cessation of feeding and hydration when life is near its close.

When Dr. Kevorkian, in 1990, attached one of his suicide machines to Janet Adkins, a 54-year-old woman with Alzheimer's disease, his proclaimed reason was that he was honoring her wishes. She no longer enjoyed life and feared a gradual, unrelenting decline with progressive disability. According to Kevorkian, his role was merely to facilitate Mrs. Adkins's own use of the suicide apparatus to end her own life.[6]

The suicide apparatus first delivered an intravenous infusion of saline (salt) solution. An anesthetic (thiopental) was ready to flow when Mrs. Adkins pushed the button; the potassium chloride, which caused a lethal heart rhythm disorder, automatically followed one minute later. By designing the device so that the patient could trigger the sequence, Kevorkian has been accused of aiding Mrs. Adkins in taking her own life.

Dr. Kevorkian's license to practice medicine in Michigan was revoked in November 1991. Without a license, he no longer has access to thiopental or potassium chloride and hence can no longer use his machine. Since Kevorkian has a fear of flying and dislikes driving long distances, he has limited his activities to the state of Michigan. In an attempt to stop him, John Engler, the Governor of Michigan, signed a law banning assisted suicide in December 1992. The law makes assisted suicide a felony punishable by four years in prison and a $2,000 fine. The law was to take effect on March 15, 1993. However, a sudden spate of Kevorkian-assisted deaths (seven in two months) led the legislature to introduce the measure and make it effective immediately on February 25, 1993. A special commission was appointed to further study the issue of physician-assisted suicide.

Michael Schwartz, Dr. Kevorkian's attorney, speaking for his client, challenged the constitutionality of the law. Kevorkian has commented that the legislators are making fools of themselves and expressed contempt that they would even think of perpetrating human misery by law. "It is the arbitrary codification of an edict for the sole benefit of a barbaric religious clique," said Kevorkian's attorney.[7] Dr. Kevorkian has never ceased his activities.

A new wave of criticism of Kevorkian erupted after it was revealed that Hugh Gale, a 70-year-old client of Kevorkian, might have changed his mind shortly before his death. Mr. Gale, a victim of advanced heart failure and emphysema, sought Kevorkian's assistance with suicide. Mr. Lynn Mills, an activist in Operation Rescue, while preparing for an anti-Kevorkian campaign, found in the garbage of a Kevorkian associate a form entitled "Final Action." In this form, Kevorkian described the last moments of life of his client. According to the document, Mr. Gale placed a mask on his face and initiated the flow of carbon monoxide (a toxic gas) from a machine prepared for him by Kevorkian. After 45 seconds, Mr. Gale became flushed, agitated, and short of breath. He asked that the mask be taken off. The mask was removed. Twenty minutes later, Mr. Gale indicated that he wanted to restart the process to end his life. Thirty seconds after starting the second time, "he again became flushed and agitated." His pleading to "take it off" was not honored, and he died eight minutes later. The incident, which was subsequently refuted by Mrs. Gale, Kevorkian, and his attorney, caused a firestorm of criticism from the Washington-based Christian Defense Coalition. Reverend Patrick Mahoney declared that "Gale did not die with dignity, he died an agonizing death asking that the mask be removed. This was clearly a murder taking place. Mr. Gale did not want to die." The allegations prompted many discussions about Kevorkian's activities, and he was banned from continuing his activities with patient-assisted suicide.[8]

Task forces in Canada, the United Kingdom, and many U.S. states were appointed to further study the appropriateness of physician-assisted suicide in selected instances. So far, there is a general agreement that letting a hopelessly ill patient die is both proper and humane. But there is a difference between letting one die and making one die.

The ban on doctor-assisted suicide did not stop Dr. Kevorkian from assisting more patients to take their lives. Supported by favorable public-opinion polls showing a slim majority in favor of Kevorkian and court rulings from three separate county circuit judges in Michigan, he seemed unstoppable. The Michigan Court of Appeals, in May 1994, invalidated the legislative ban on assisted suicide. The court also ruled that there is no constitutional right to suicide and that suicide assistance amounts to murder. Three weeks later, on May 30, 1994, the Michigan Supreme Court placed the appeals court ruling on hold.

In one of his many court appearances, the jury found Kevorkian "not guilty" in the case of the suicide of Thomas Hyde, a 30-year-old man totally paralyzed as result of a degenerative neurologic disorder. The man died from inhaling carbon monoxide provided by Kevorkian. The jurors heard Hyde's taped, anguished plea for a merciful death, along with Kevorkian's videotaped confession of aiding him.

The Michigan Commission on Death and Dying submitted its final report in the fall of 1994. The commission comprised 23 members with a wide spectrum of interests. Not surprisingly, three conflicting positions emerged. One, supported by 5 members, called for a total ban on assisted suicide. Another position, supported by 9 members, called for a "Death with Dignity" Act, by which assisted suicide would be legal in the case of terminal disease or irreversible suffering. The person would need to have engaged in repeated requests for assistance in dying and undergo examination by two physicians, a psychiatrist or psychologist, a social worker, and a pain-management specialist. The third position, supported by 9 members, only suggested procedural safeguards in the event of decriminalization of physician-assisted suicide.[9]

Dr. Kevorkian continues his devotion to the mission of making physician-assisted suicide legal. Continually, he receives numerous requests to end the lives of people suffering enormous mental anguish or physical pain caused by total body paralysis, disseminated cancer, or deteriorating mental function. Kevorkian's legal wrangling is relentless and is unlikely to stop as long as he is able to maintain the fight.

According to an article published in *Time*, dated May 31, 1993, out of frustration or fear of helplessness, an increasing portion of the American public views physician-assisted suicide as a reasonable "treatment." They applaud Kevorkian's acts and statements. They thereby express their defiance of the perceived inconsistency in medical practice: treating people to death while they are unable to voice their wishes and yet denying those who ask for a graceful exit the means to achieve their wishes. The first is committed under the doctrine of implied consent and the latter denied as unlawful. Other health-care professionals also champion him: "He tells us exactly where the health-care system stinks," proclaims one professional, Dr. Annas, a recognized authority in judicial and ethical issues of medicine and professor at the Boston University of Medicine and Public Health. "He is a total indictment of the way we treat dying patients.... We don't treat them well and they know it.... This mistreatment is a combination of deceit, insensitivity and neglect. ... Worse, doctors ignore patient's suffering." Many feel that Dr. Kevorkian is a refreshing antidote to those physicians who, for whatever motive, employ one last treatment intervention—even if the chances of it working are one in a million.[10]

When people are asked how they wish to die, most would say the following: "I choose to die quickly, painlessly, at home in my bed, surrounded by family and friends. I choose a graceful exist." Then ask them how they expect to die: "In the hospital, in an intensive-care unit, violated by many tubes, on machines, and in pain." The latter vision of dying is the contemporary equivalent of a Tithonus-like exit. Although the question about active euthanasia has come to the forefront in America, where more elderly die in the hospital and are likely to end up in an intensive-care unit, the problem is universal. In Canada, Sue Rodriguez was suffering from an incurable neurological degenerative disease that attacks the brain and the spinal cord. She was completely paralyzed and could not walk, breathe, or speak. She asked, in 1992, for someone to be legally allowed to help her die. The Canadian Supreme Court denied her wish by a slim majority. She died in February 1994, with the help of an anonymous doctor.[11] Of interest is the fact that the same court had granted another patient with a similar condition the right to be allowed to die by disconnecting her from the ventilator less than two years earlier. In *Nancy B. v. L'Hotel Dieu de Quebec,* the patient, a 25-year-old woman, was permanently paralyzed from nerve degeneration (Guillan-Barre syndrome).[12] Her life was dependent on the ventilator. The patient asked to be disconnected, and her family approved. In January 1992, the Supreme Court of Canada granted her request under the "Causation Rationale," (i.e., no crime would be committed by persons who complied with patient's informed consent to allow death through "nature taking its course"). Ramon San Pedro of Spain sustained a crippling neck injury in 1968. Since then, he has lived in a "locked state." He is conscious but can only move his head. In vain, he has pleaded repeatedly to the medical and legal establishments to put him out of his misery. So far, two Spanish courts have refused consent for assisted suicide.

DEATH ON DEMAND

The debate about active euthanasia (mercy killing) and physician-assisted suicide (prescribing a medication with the intent of assisting a person to take his or her own life) is by no means new. In two recent articles in the *Archives of Internal Medicine* and one in the Annals of Internal Medicine, Dr. Ezekiel Emanuel, Director of Ethics at the Dana Farber Cancer Institute in Boston, reviewed the history of euthanasia in the United States and Britain.[13,14] Dr. Emanual noted that euthanasia was an everyday encounter in the Greco–Roman empire, where "many people preferred death to endless agony." The practice of euthanasia in ancient times ran contrary to the Hippocratic oath "not to prescribe a deadly medicine even if they ask for it." It must be noted that Hippocratic teachings were followed by only a few doctors, graduates of the Aesculapius temple. Dr. Emanuel noted that the ascent of Christianity in the 12th century thereafter reinforced the Hippocratic teachings: "Life is a gift from God that has to be preserved." However, British and French philosophers of the 17th and 18th centuries attacked prohibitions against euthanasia out of defiance to the Christian religious authority. In an essay entitled "On Suicide," Hume, the legendary philosopher, wrote, "Suicide may be consistent with our duty to ourselves, no one can question, who allows that age, sickness or misfortune may render life a burden, and make it worse even than annihilation." These and similar writings seemed to have a limited resonance among the general public.

With the introduction of powerful analgesics, such as morphine, and with the discovery of anesthetics, it was suggested that these drugs might be used to "mitigate the agonies of death." The use of morphine preparations, chloroform, and ether anesthetics to relieve the pain of dying found wide use in Britain and in the United States (especially during the Civil War). Soon thereafter, advocates for a peaceful, quick "death on demand" promoted the idea that patients should have the right to end their lives. In 1870, Mr. Samuel Williams advocated the use of anesthesia to intentionally cause death.

> In all cases of hopeless and painful illness, it should be the recognized duty of the medical attendant whenever so desired by the patient, to administer chloroform or such other anesthetic so as to destroy consciousness at once, and put the sufferer to a quick and painless death.

Dr. Emanuel noted that, in 1899, Simeon Baldwin, in this presidential address to the American Social Science Association, advocated euthanasia by criticizing the "pride of many in the medical profession to prolong such lives at any cost of discomfort or pain to the sufferer."

Dr. Emanuel described how the debate about euthanasia came to the forefront of public debate early in this century, how a wealthy woman, Anna Hill, whose mother was dying from cancer, campaigned for the legislation of euthanasia in Ohio. Her campaign prompted the introduction by state Representative Hunt, of "an act concerning administration of drugs, etc. to mortally injured and diseased persons," in 1906. A heated debate erupted in the news media. The *British Medical Journal* characterized America as a

> land of hysterical legislation, in which the legislation of euthanasia is put forward every now and then by literary dilettantes or by neurotic intellectuals whose high-strung temperament cannot bear the thought of pain. The medical profession has always sternly set its face against a measure that would inevitably pave the way to the grossest abuse and would degrade them to the position of executioners.

The Ohio Hunt bill was rejected by an overwhelming margin.

Several instances of euthanasia on demand were publicized. Also, many leading newspapers carried commentaries on the subject. An editorial on this subject entitled "Dr. Norton on Euthanasia" was published in the *New York Times* in January 1906. After denying that human life is always and necessarily "sacred" and charging the physician with having carried too far his commendable desire to prolong the existence of his patients, Dr. Norton declared

> that no thinking man would hesitate to give a fatal dose of Laudanum to the victim of an accident from the torturing effects of which recovery was impossible, that no reasonable man would hesitate to hasten death in a case where a cancer has reached the stage of incessant pain and the patient wants to die, that it is plain duty to shorten, not to prolong the life of an old person whose mind has become a chaos of wild imaginings productive of constant distress not only to the sufferer, but to all who live with and attend him. (p. 8)

The article concludes eloquently with this commentary:

> ... and where would Dr. Norton get his physicians who could always tell with certainty the outcome of an accident or disease? ... It is an utter waste of time to worry about the few cases where a man with perfect wisdom would be justified in giving "the happy death" to another, since the man with perfect wisdom is yet to be invented or developed.[14]

The debate on euthanasia was revived in Britain in the 1930s by the President of the Society of Medical Officers in Britain. Dr. C. Killick Millard proposed a statute to legalize euthanasia in Britain.

THE DOWNSIDE OF EUTHANASIA

The debate about euthanasia took a new twist in Germany. In 1920, Dr. Hocke, a German professor of psychiatry, and Mr. Binding, a German lawyer, coauthored a book entitled *Permission to Destroy Life Unworthy of Life*. They argued that certain people with mental illness or physical infirmity, including deformed children, lead "unworthy lives." For these people, Hocke and Binding argued, "Death is a compassionate healing." They went on to make the point that these "unworthy lives" represent a financial drain on society while polluting the gene pool with unwanted genes. Hocke and Binding's views became part of the Nazi agenda and justified the notion of genetic cleansing, as well as that of mercy killing.

The Nazi experience, particularly the role of German physicians in genocide, biased the public debate about active euthanasia for some time.

THE REVIVAL OF HUMANE EUTHANASIA

The debate about humane euthanasia was rekindled again in 1972, when a Netherlands physician (Dr. Postma) administered a large dose of morphine to his senile, crippled, deaf mute, paralyzed mother upon her insistence that he relieve her from pain. Dr. Postma was given a sentence of one week in jail and one year probation. This incident rekindled the debate about euthanasia and brought it into the public forum in the Netherlands, eventually leading to the wide acceptance of euthanasia in Holland. In 1973, the Royal Dutch Medical Association issued a statement:

"Euthanasia should remain criminalized but the physicians should be permitted to engage in euthanasia for dying and suffering patients as a *force majeure*, when there is conflict between duties to preserve life and duties to relieve suffering." In 1987, the Dutch Parliament established the Remmelink Commission to review and advise the parliament regarding the practice of euthanasia in Holland.[15,16] The commission interviewed over 400 physicians and submitted its report in September 1991, recommending that physicians who engage in euthanasia not be prosecuted so long as they followed certain guidelines. The commission also felt that the practice of euthanasia should be brought into the open to guarantee against its abuse. In America, in 1988, the *Journal of the American Medical Association* published a case entitled "It's Over Debbie," in which an anonymous young physician claimed (perhaps falsely) to have given a young woman who was dying of disseminated cancer a large dose of morphine, then watched her die painlessly. The two recent cases of Dr. Timothy Quill in the United States and Dr. Nigel Cox of Britain[17,18] have fueled debate about the issue again on both sides of the Atlantic. (These cases will be discussed later in this chapter.)

The problem with legalization of active euthanasia stems from the difficulty of striking a balance between two opposing views, each of which has compelling reasons to be heard.

The euthanasia argument is summed up eloquently by Dr. Dan Brock, Professor of Philosophy and Biomedical Ethics at Brown University, Providence, Rhode Island:

> If self-determination is a fundamental value, then the great variability among people on this question makes it especially important that individuals control the manner, circumstances, and timing of their dying and death.

The argument follows that if physicians are allowed to withdraw life-sustaining treatment from their dying patients, why not hasten their moment of death? After all, "human life is sacred, but only to the extent that it contributes to the joy and happiness of the one possessing it, and those about him." These advocates would agree that it ought to be the privilege of every human being to cross the river Styx in the boat of his own choosing, when further human agony cannot be justified by the hope of future health and happiness.

The principal argument against euthanasia is that society has a vested interest in protecting all its members and in ensuring that all members of society have equal human worth under the law. It is one thing to have the right to commit suicide or to be left to die, but to be helped to die or made to die by a physician is a different issue. One of the central Christian beliefs is that life is a gift from God that individuals guard but do not own. It is a basic good on Earth. Furthermore, many believe that human suffering, by itself, is a wellspring of redemption and therefore has value. However, the question remains as to whether protracted human suffering inflicted by man-made machines is necessary, and at what point should it be considered excessive? Where should the boundary between death and meaningful life be drawn? This is the ultimate challenge.

Public and professional opinion polls are shifting toward support of euthanasia. A slim majority of the American public is in favor of legalized euthanasia with ample safeguards (see an article by R. A. Knox: "Americans Favor Mercy Killing," November 3, 1993).[19] A collaborative study between Harvard School of Public Health (Boston) and the *Boston Globe* regarding the public's attitude on euthanasia involved over 1,000 participants. The study showed two-thirds of the public favoring physicians being permitted to give a terminally ill patient in pain a lethal injection to aid in dying. Of the public, 20% supported assisted suicide or euthanasia for advanced, painful, irreversible disease. The recent passage in November 1994 of a law legalizing physician-assisted suicide in Oregon supports these polls. A recent survey of 2,500 readers of *Yours*, a U.K. pensioner's magazine, found that 9 out of 10 readers thought the doctors should be allowed to end the lives of terminally ill patients and wanted the law changed in Britain. More than 50% said they would help a friend, relative, or spouse to die in such circumstances. Surprisingly, religious faith, social class, and place of residence had little bearing on people's views about euthanasia in Great Britain. It is unlikely that active euthanasia will meet with as much overwhelming support in the United States. A report published in the *British Medical Journal* in February 1993 revealed that of 1,100 adults surveyed in Britain, 70% called for euthanasia to be removed from criminal law. The Canadian Parliament, which turned down euthanasia legislation four times, has appointed a commission to study the subject and gather public information.[20]

Of interest is the revealing statistic that in the Netherlands, where active euthanasia is not punishable by law, more people long for assisted suicide because of mental anguish rather than intolerable physical pain.

As shown earlier, several studies from the United States, Britain, and Australia find that roughly one-third to one-half of practicing physicians and consultants were asked by patients to hasten their moment of death, yet few of them have helped their patients die. It is clear, however, that Europeans and Australians are more accepting of the idea that some form of legislation allow euthanasia in certain circumstances. In the United States, laypeople and health-care professionals remain uneasy about the subject of euthanasia. This subject must be approached deliberately and cautiously. Supreme Court Justice Brennan's closing words in the Cruzan case are eminently relevant here: "The greatest dangers to liberty lurk in insidious encroachment by men of zeal, well-meaning but without understanding."[21]

EUTHANASIA: THE HOLLAND EXPERIENCE

Not infrequently, I have heard individuals refer to the "savage system" of legalized euthanasia in Holland. But in Holland (the only European country in which euthanasia is not prohibited) the legislation and the medical community have taken ample measures to ensure that active euthanasia is not applied arbitrarily.[22,23] Technically, euthanasia still is illegal in Holland; the original law prohibiting the ending of a life by a physician remains unrepealed. A law passed in 1993 protects from prosecution physicians who undertake euthanasia under certain conditions and requires them to report these cases for purposes of monitoring. There are strict criteria for determining who would be eligible for physician-assisted mercy killing.[23] Also, this system has ample safeguards against abuse. According to these "carefulness requirements," the patient's request for euthanasia must be made "entirely of the patient's own free will," without pressure from others. The patient must be "well informed" and capable of weighing the alternatives. Furthermore, the patient must demonstrate an enduring longing for death, rather than an impulse to die that is due to, say, a temporary depression. In addition, the patient, "must experience his or her suffering as perpetual, unbearable, and hopeless," and the physician must be able to conclude reasonably that the patient's suffering is unbearable. Finally, the physician is required to consult at least one experienced colleague who previously made a decision regarding euthanasia. In many instances, the patient is referred for psychiatric evaluation; a cooling-off period is required prior to carrying out mercy killing. In spite of that, 11% of all physicians in the Netherlands refuse to practice euthanasia. Those who do carry it out do so once or twice a year at the most, and they describe it as "a very emotional and heart-wrenching experience." In spite of the acceptance of euthanasia in the Netherlands and the fact that every physician undertaking it must file a detailed report in each instance, reported cases of euthanasia have accounted for only 2% of all deaths since the new laws were enacted. According to opinion polls in the Netherlands, quoted in the *Economist* and in *Biolaw*, 80% of the population support the right of terminally ill patients to ask for euthanasia and only 10% oppose it.[24,25]

In a recent fact-finding visit to Holland, I spoke with several physicians, many of whom have been involved in euthanasia. Also, I spoke to several laypeople. I have the impression that younger physicians are more accepting of euthanasia than older ones. All the physicians I talked to, without exception, indicated how seriously the medical establishment has approached the problem and that only a minor proportion (25–30%) of patients who ask for euthanasia end up receiving it. On the other hand, many cases of euthanasia go unreported. A recent editorial, "The Dutch Way of Dying," in the *Economist* issue of September 17, 1994, cited the reasons why admirers have hailed the Dutch experience and why critics say the safeguards are ineffective. They comment that Holland is skidding down a slippery slope toward licensed killing. The editorial cites an official report that found that in addition to 2,300 reported cases of euthanasia in Holland in 1990, a further 1,040 people had their death hastened without making a formal request for intervention. The article quotes Mr. Johan Legemaate, Legal Council of the Royal Dutch Medical Association: "We have succeeded in creating a large amount of openness and accountability." It is to be noted, however, that the current laws have been enacted by a Parliament comprised predominantly of Socialists and Christian Democrats. There is a real concern that the law may be reversed if a more conservative government assumes power in Holland. This fact seems to underlie why some physicians still do not report cases of euthanasia. They fear the repercussions of a change in government. Even though the Dutch have accepted euthanasia as an available option, there is a mounting consensus among physicians calling for more stringent self-regulation. Many influential voices prefer that patients who wish and are eligible for euthanasia be allowed to self-administer the lethal dose of barbiturate or morphine. In other words, place the final act in the hands of patients and not physicians.

WILL AMERICA EVER CONDONE PHYSICIAN-ASSISTED SUICIDE?

An ordinance that would legalize physician-assisted suicide with somewhat ample preconditions and safeguards was approved by the Oregon voters in November 1994. A similar ordinance was defeated previously in the states of Washington and California.

The study of California's Proposition 161 on physician-assisted dying is of special interest. This initiative was presented to California voters in November 1992 and was defeated by a margin of 54% to 46%.[26] A year earlier, a similar bill was defeated in Washington State by a narrower margin of 52% to 48%. The initiative would have legalized physician-assisted suicide under certain circumstances. The Attorney General of California prepared for the voters an official title and summary of the measure:

> Terminal Illness. Assistance in Dying. Initiative Statute. Permits revocable written directive authorizing a physician to terminate life in "painless, humane, and dignified manner" by mentally competent adult after terminal illness diagnosed. States procedures for witnessing and revoking directive and requesting medical assistance in dying. Precludes physicians, health professionals, and facilities from civil or criminal inability if initiative's provisions followed. Provides requesting or receiving authorized aid, not suicide. Allows physicians and health professionals to refuse to end life if religiously, morally, or ethically opposed. Prohibits existence or nonexistence of directive from affecting sale, renewal, cancellation terms, or premiums of insurance policies. Estimate by Legislative Analyst and Director of Finance of fiscal impact on state and local governments: This measure would result in some unknown savings due to decreased utilization of the state Medi-Cal program and other public programs, including county programs.

Polls taken just before the election suggested that the vote on the initiative was too close to predict. One newspaper story, appearing a few days before the election, ran the following headline: "Outcome of Death Measure May Rest on 11th-Hour Ads." A $2.8 million campaign against the proposition was proposed by the Roman Catholic Church, including the state's Catholic bishops, Catholic hospitals, and individual Catholic church members, who were urged to donate directly to the campaign. The organized support in favor of the initiative raised less than one-tenth as much money, $215,000. Both sides sought to sway voters in the final days of the campaign by airing paid advertisements. One of the opposition's 30-second television ads stated that Proposition 161 "allows physician-assisted suicide in secret, with no witnesses, no family notification, no psychological exam and no medical specialist." The ad had whispering voices in the background asserting: "No witnesses; no one will know." Other television ads focused on the possibility that physicians would err in diagnosing terminal illness. One ad stated, "If a diagnosis is wrong, someone you know may choose physician-assisted death by mistake. Death by mistake." Other spots in favor of the proposition featured patients diagnosed as terminally ill arguing that if physician-assisted dying had been available, they might have asked for a lethal injection.

A large amount of cash was raised by those who opposed the legislation. The opposition carried numerous television and radio ads, while the proponents, with a mere $55,000, were only able to run a single radio ad in the final days before the vote. The ad featured Dr. Griffith Thomas, a Los Angeles physician–attorney who had served on the joint committees on biomedical ethics of the county bar and medical associations. It aired several times daily but only on a few stations in Los Angeles and San Diego, according to the *Los Angeles Times*. California Proposition 161 was defeated.

The Oregon "right to die" legislation differs from the proposed legislation in California in some critical respects:[27]

- The patient request for euthanasia must be in writing.
- The request must be witnessed.
- A consulting physician must certify that the patient's condition is terminal.
- A fifteen-day waiting period must occur between the patient's request and obtaining the suicide prescription.

- The physician must ensure that the patient's decision is voluntary by providing information about diagnosis, prognosis, other options such as hospice care, and referral to a state licensed psychologist or psychiatrist if depression is suspected.

This issue, even in Oregon, remains controversial. Not surprisingly, various Oregon groups similar to the California coalitions against euthanasia voted to defeat the initiative. The populace of Oregon voted in favor of "physician-assisted suicide" with the forementioned safeguards by a very slim majority. Interestingly, it has been said that Oregon is the most "secular" of all American states, except for Nevada. More recently, a similar ordinance was enacted into law in Australia in spring 1995.

SECONDARY PHYSICIAN-ASSISTED DEATH VERSUS PRIMARY PHYSICIAN-ADMINISTERED DEATH

Discussions about active euthanasia first came to the attention of the medical community through isolated instances such as the incident related in "It's Over Debbie," published in the *Journal of the American Medical Association* in 1988, and more recently with the widely publicized cases involving Dr. Jack Kervorkian. Because the stories about Dr. Kevorkian and his patients are well known, I will review only the cases of Dr. Timothy Quill, published in the *New England Journal of Medicine* in 1991 and that of Dr. Nigel Cox, tried in England in 1992.

Dr. Quill, a primary-care physician and director of a hospice in Rochester, New York (now Professor at the University of Rochester) challenged the medical community in a previously mentioned article entitled, "Death with Dignity, A Case for Individualized Decision Making."[28] Quill admitted aiding a leukemia victim, Diane, to take her own life. He prescribed a dose of barbiturates sufficient to cause her to stop breathing. Prior to the suicide, all treatment options had been explored, tried, and rejected. The patient and family were counseled, and it was determined that the "limits of palliative care, from the patient's perspective and to Dr. Quill's satisfaction, had been reached."

This case resulted in a heated debate in the medical and lay communities. Quill was exonerated by a grand jury that found no grounds for prosecution. The New York Health Department, after careful review of the case, refused to sanction Dr. Quill, who since then has become an outspoken advocate for thoughtful, discriminate, physician-assisted suicide.

By contrast, Dr. Cox, a British rheumatologist, promised his patient relief of pain from her disabling, painful, acutely deforming rheumatoid arthritis.[29] Her suffering continued to be immense and unrelenting, and Dr. Cox tried every measure to alleviate the pain. He noted in the patient's chart, "She still wants out, and I don't think we can reasonably disagree." Increasingly large doses of morphine did not relieve the pain and Dr. Cox realized that, by continuing with conventional medications, he could not fulfill his pledge to alleviate her pain in her final days. Out of compassion, he injected her with two ampules of potassium chloride, which brought about her death. He recorded his act in the patient's chart. A Catholic nurse, after reading the doctor's note, reported the matter to the Solicitor General and Dr. Nigel Cox was charged with and tried for attempted murder. The prosecutor argued that giving injections with the primary intent of relieving pain and suffering is permissible, even if this resulted in hastening the foreseen death. This is referred to as the "rule of double effect." But he argued that Dr. Cox gave the injection with the *primary* intent of killing his patient in order to relieve her suffering, a clear violation of the law. The jury was instructed to ignore Dr. Cox's motive of compassion and to focus on his intent. The jury found Dr. Cox to be guilty. Deep sighs broke the dead silence of the courtroom as the judge addressed the jury at the end of the verdict: "There are times when, speaking for myself and, I strongly suspect, speaking for all of you, a criminal trial is an almost overwhelming burden." The judge imposed a sentence of 12 months but suspended it. Subsequently, Dr. Nigel Cox's conduct was reviewed by a committee of his peers and his license to practice medicine was reinstated.

Some may view Dr. Nigel Cox as a felon who crossed the line between what is legally right (to let a terminally ill patient die) and what is legally wrong (to cause the death of a terminally ill patient). Some may view him as a martyr, who must have agonized over his pledge to a trusting patient in extreme, uncontrollable pain. It must have been a heart-wrenching experience for him. I believe most will view him as a decent man and a great physician who might have broken the letter of the Hippocratic oath but who was loyal to its spirit.

PROPOSED GUIDELINES FOR ASSISTED SUICIDE

In the wake of these cases and following the defeat of California's Proposition 161, Drs. Quill, Cassell, and Meier proposed a policy for assisted suicide in the context of "care for the hopelessly ill." They suggested the following guiding principles to determine the correctness of euthanasia, in conjunction with a meaningful doctor–patient relationship:[30]

- Patient must have a condition that is incurable and associated with severe, unrelenting suffering;
- Patient must not be asking for death because of failure to get treatment that could relieve his or her suffering;
- Patient must "clearly and repeatedly" ask for assistance in dying;
- Patient's judgment must not be distorted by a problem, such as depression, that is reversible in a way that would substantially alter the situation.

These are similar to the guidelines set forth in the Dutch law of doctor-assisted suicide and conform with the newly enacted ordinance of physician-assisted suicide passed in Oregon.

A June 14, 1994 article in the *New York Times* described how AIDS patients seek solace in suicide but may risk added pain if they fail to commit it. In the article, AIDS patients relate the horrors some HIV-infected patients go through as they approach the moment of death. There are tremendous psychological stresses associated with AIDS—financial insecurity, homelessness, joblessness, and social isolation. "I will be dead, no question," one patient said. "I can't continue this way . . . It's awful. It's worse than being dead." This AIDS patient has stated that the act of stockpiling drugs necessary to effect his own suicide, "has made my every day better, much, much better. It has diminished my horror, as though I was facing an enemy on a battlefield stark naked and now I have an armor."

The argument is indeed powerful and compelling. In spite of this, as a physician, I find it hard to support the proposition of active euthanasia. But I understand and empathize with those who condone it in very limited circumstances and with ample strict safeguards.

Franklin Miller and John Fletcher, from the Departments of Internal Medicine and Center of Religious Studies at the University of Virginia, in an article entitled "The Case of Legalized Euthanasia," published in *Perspectives in Biology and Medicine*, offer a compromise position on euthanasia. I quote: "Decisions to die by euthanasia are too ethically problematic to be left to the privacy of the physician–patient relationships." Furthermore, they say,

> We oppose the position of leaving the law against euthanasia unchanged while conducting a social experiment . . . on grounds of respect for law and public accountability, we recommend legalizing voluntary euthanasia subject to prior committee review.[32]

THE LATEST RULING FROM WASHINGTON STATE

No doubt, active euthanasia will be hotly debated over the next few years in the United States. We have really just begun to address this controversial subject. The debate will be fueled by a recent ruling from a district court in the state of Washington, which in May 1994 overturned a statute prohibiting assisted suicide. The court cited explicit use of abortion as an analogous situation. The court rationalized that since abortion is a legal right and the decision to bear a child is a matter of private choice, so is the right to choose the moment and method of dying. A summary of this landmark case follows.

In this Washington State case, the plaintiffs were a coalition of three terminally ill patients, five physicians, and the Compassion in Dying Organization. The patients included a retired pediatrician with cancer that had metastasized to the bones, a 44-year-old artist dying of AIDS, and a 69-year-old retired salesman with terminal emphysema. In its deliberations, the court referred to a ruling on abortion: *Liberty Interest under Planned Parenthood v. Casey* (114 S Ct. 909, 911, 1994). I quote from the ruling:

> Personal decisions relating to marriage, procreation, contraception, family relationships, child rearing and abortion are constitutionally protected. These matters, involving the most intimate and personal choices a person may make in a lifetime, choices central to personal dignity and autonomy, are central to the liberty protected by the fourteenth amendment. At the heart of liberty is the right to define one's own concept of existence, of meaning of the universe, and of the mystery of human life. Beliefs about these matters could not define the attributes of personhood were they formed under compulsion of the state.[33]

The court went on to point out that the opinion in *Casey* involved a woman's right to choose abortion. This case did not precisely address the question of the liberty issues inherent in a terminally ill person's choice to commit suicide. However, the court found the reasoning in *Casey* highly instructive and almost prescriptive on the latter issue.

Judge Barbara Rothstein noted that, as in abortion, the court's duty is not to impose a particular moral standard. "Some of us as individuals find abortion offensive to our most basic principles of morality, but that cannot control our decision. Our obligation is to define the liberty of all, not to mandate our own moral code. The underlying constitutional issue is whether the state can resolve these philosophic questions in such a definitive way that a woman lacks all choices in the matter. ..."[34]

The judge further found the decision of the lower courts, in denying the plaintiffs the right to assisted suicide, inconsistent with *Casey*.[35] She granted the plaintiffs the right to assisted suicide, stating that a decision to end one's life is the ultimate act of self-determination. She ruled that the current law against physician-assisted suicide in the State of Washington is unconstitutional.

No doubt, this ruling will be appealed and it seems quite possible, even likely, that this or a similar case will find its way to the U.S. Supreme Court sometime in the not too distant future.

End-of-life decisions are not going to get easier for individuals and society. They constitute a spectrum, the colors blurring subtly and often confusingly into one another, thus making it difficult to discern where to draw the line. For some, the principle of autonomy entitles a dying patient to treatments deemed futile by medical standards.[36] For others withholding treatment and withdrawing useless care have different connotations.[37] Some view feeding and hydration to be different from the other forms of therapy.[38] For many, including the courts, withdrawal of treatment is ethical, whereas deliberately hastening the death of a patient is murder, while both carry the same intent and lead to the same results. And for an increasingly larger segment of society, the option to end one's life (assisted or not) underscores one's right to a dignified exit when one's terminal chapter is riddled with anguish and pain.[39]

NOTES

1. Council on Ethical and Judicial Affairs, American Medical Association, "Decisions Near the End of Life," *Journal of the American Medical Association*, 267 (1992), 2229–2233.

2. R Gillon, "Euthanasia, Withholding Life-Prolonging Treatment and Moral Differences between Killing and Letting Die," *Journal of Medical Ethics*, 14 (1988), 115–117.
3. Lord Browne-Wilkinson, Letter in *Airedale NHS Trust (Respondents) v. Bland* (Judgment, 1993), pp. 24–33.
4. RJ Waller, *Old Songs in a New Cafe*. (New York: Warner Books, 1994), p. 38.
5. Council on Ethical and Judicial Affairs, American Medical Association. "Guidelines for the Appropriate Use of Do-Not-Resuscitate Orders," *Journal of the American Medical Association*, 265 (1991), 1868–1871.
6. MS Ewer, "The Suicide Device: Does It Really Matter Who Pushes the Button?" *Internal Medicine World Report*, 5 (1990), 7.
7. Biolaw Special Section, *Assisted Suicide* (Bethesda, MD: University Publications of America, October, 1994), pp. 103–106.
8. "Kevorkian Aids in 2 More Suicides: Total Is 15," *New York Times* (February 19, 1993), p. A10.
9. *Final Report of the Michigan Commission on Death and Dying*. (Lansing, Michigan Death and Dying Commission, 1994).
10. GJ Annas, "Physician-Assisted Suicide—Michigan's Temporary Solution," *New England Journal of Medicine* 328 (1993), 1573–1576.
11. *Rodriguez v. British Columbia* (Attorney General, No. 23476, British Columbia, Superior Court, September 30, 1993).
12. *Nancy B. v. l'Hotel-Dieu W Quebec* (R.J.Q., 1992), 361 (Superior Court).
13. EJ Emanuel, "Euthanasia: Historical, Ethical, and Empiric Prospectives," *Archives Internal Medicine*, 154 (1994), 1890–1900.
14. EJ Emanuel, "The History of Euthanasia: Debates in the United States and Britain," *Annals Internal Medicine*, 121 (1994), 793–802.
15. "Euthanasia: To Cease upon the Midnight," *Economist*, 332 (1994), 21–23.
16. R Fenigsen, "The Netherlands: New Regulations Concerning Euthanasia," *Issues in Law and Medicine*, 9 (1993), 167–173.
17. TE Quill, "Death and Dignity: A Case of Individualized Decision-Making," *New England Journal of Medicine*, 324 (1991), 691–694.
18. C Dyer, "Rheumatologist Convicted of Attempted Murder," *British Medical Journal*, 325 (1992), 731.
19. RA Knox, "Poll: Americans Favor Mercy Killing," *Boston Globe* (November 3, 1991), sec. 1, p. 22.
20. M Dean, "Politics of Euthanasia in U.K.," *Lancet*, 345 (1995), 714.

21. B Lo and R Steinbrook, "Beyond the Cruzan Case: The U.S. Supreme Court and Medical Practice," *Annals Internal Medicine*, 114 (1991), 895–899.
22. *Statistics Netherlands, The End of Life in Medical Practice.* (The Hague, The Netherlands: SDU Publishers, 1992).
23. MA de Watcher, "Active Euthanasia in the Netherlands," *Journal of the American Medical Association*, 262 (1989), 3316–3319.
24. "The Dutch Way of Dying," *Economist*, 332 (1994), 23.
25. Netherlands. Biomedical Ethics in Biolaw (Bethesda, MD: University Publications of America, 1994), p. 47.
26. *California's Proposition 161 and Physician-Assisted Dying*. Biolaw (Bethesda, MD: University Publications of America, 1993), pp. 11–15.
27. Oregon's Ballot Measure, *Legal Issues in Medicine*, 331 (1994), p. 1241.
28. TE Quill, "Death with Dignity," pp. 691–694.
29. C Dyer, "Rheumatologist Convicted," p. 737.
30. TE Quill, CK Cassel, and DE Meier, "Care of the Hopelessly Ill: Proposed Clinical Criteria for Physician-Assisted Suicide," *New England Journal of Medicine*, 327 (1992), 1380–1384.
31. "Suicide: A Difficult Road for People with AIDS," *New York Times* (June 14, 1994), p. C1+.
32. FG Miller and JC Fletcher, "The Case for Legalized Euthanasia," *Perspectives in Biology and Medicine*, 36 (1993), 159–176.
33. *Compassion in Dying v. State of Washington U.S. District Court*. (Washington and Seattle, 1994), pp. C94–119R.
34. Ibid., in Biolaw (Special Section), June 1994.
35. *Casey v. Planned Parenthood*. (14F, 3rd, Circuit 848, 1994).
36. ED Pelligrino, "Ethics," *Journal of the American Medical Association*, 270 (1993), 202–203.
37. KF Langendoen, "The Clinical Management of Dying Patients Receiving Mechanical Ventilation: A Survey of Physician Practice," *Chest*, 106 (1994), 880–888.
38. Rabbi L Schostak, "Jewish Ethical Guidelines for Resuscitation and Artificial Nutrition and Hydration of the Dying Elderly," *Journal of Medical Ethics*, 20 (1994), 93–100.
39. "The Final Autonomy," *Lancet*, 346 (1995), 259.

Chapter 7

The High Price of Dying

> To contemplate human life for forty years is the same as contemplating it for ten thousand. In ten thousand, what more will you see?
>
> —MARCUS AURELIUS (in *Meditations* VII)

Most of the recent innovations in medicine have been employed to extend the life of people past middle age. Dr. D. Callahan, Director of the Hastings Institute in New York and outspoken critic of wasteful medical care at the end of life, quotes Dr. Jerome Avorn, Health Economist of the Harvard Medical School, who wrote in *Daedalus*: "With the exception of the birth control pill, most of medical technology interventions developed since the 1950s have their most widespread impact on people who are past their fifties—the further past their fifties the greater the impact."[1] These interventions afforded longer, happier lives for many of us past middle age.

The indiscriminate use of these interventions could only be construed as a terrible waste of resources. Unfortunately, the same scientific advances have also resulted in a prolonged, miserable existence for many. Over the past two decades, health-care costs have increased threefold as a percentage of the gross national product. Today, America devotes one-seventh of its gross national product to health care; most of these expenditures are spent on the older segment of the population. One of the most widely quoted statistics in medical and economic circles derives from the 1986 publication from the Center for Health Statistics. The data showed that 30% of Medicare expenditures are incurred during the last year of life. Furthermore, for the 6% of the elderly Medicare patients who die each year, 40% of medical expenditures go for care during the last month of life, and 50% of all medical costs are spent during the last two months.[2] According to one of America's leading economists, Victor Fuchs, "One of the biggest challenges facing policy makers for the rest of this century, will be how to strike an appropriate balance between care for the dying and health services for the rest of the population."[3]

SPENDING BILLIONS TO PROLONG PAIN

In the United States, we spend more health dollars per citizen than any other nation on earth, but we are not healthier, and we do not live longer than people in most civilized nations. This condition relates to the failure of our welfare system and to a higher cost of treating patients and much higher casualties of violence and drug addiction in our society compared to other nations. Other factors determining the high health-care expenditure in America include a complex system of administrative, legal and malpractice issues; high costs of defensive medicine; higher costs for medications; and other costly behavioral problems, such as smoking and alcohol abuse. All of these factors together, however, cannot account for all the excess in health-care spending.

In an essay entitled, "The Rise and Fall of the American Civilization," former Governor Richard D. Lamm of Colorado,[4] present director of the Center for Public Policy and Contemporary Issues, University of Denver, Colorado, describes our current health care:

> The health care system, for instance, became bloated and inefficient, taking more of the gross national product and

> representing more of a share of the overhead of American goods. In 1990, the U.S. spent $2,400 per capita on health care, Great Britain spent $600 per capita on health care, Singapore spent $300; and they all had approximately the same outcome. When the health care system took twelve cents out of every dollar spent in America, it was obviously adding a health care component to overhead that made American goods increasingly uncompetitive. They manufactured artificial hearts, but closed their steel mills. American products had health care costs that were fifty percent higher than those of their international competitors, yet it didn't keep its people as healthy as Europe, Canada, or Japan. By not having the internal discipline to say no to the excesses of the health care system, America added another nail to its economic coffin. (pp. 5–6)

No doubt, part of the waste relates to the excessive use of high technology, much of which is futile and enacted at the end of life. There are five times the number of intensive-care beds in America as in England or Denmark, per capita. The cost of high-tech care at the end of life, in relation to the total economy, is difficult to estimate. Experts vary enormously in their estimates. Some claim, as does Dr. Emanuel, Director of the Dana Farber Institute in Boston, that futile care accounts for as little as 3% of total health expenditures; others, including the noted Stanford University economist, Victor Fuchs, believe it to be well over 10% of health-care dollars. The fact remains that over 60% of America's elderly die in the hospital as compared to 50% in most other Western countries. Most patients who die in the hospital end up in intensive-care environments. This difference suggests a substantial, unnecessary cost. If we, as a society, do nothing more than match the European countries in encouraging more of us to die at home or in a nursing home, tens of billions of dollars can be saved. It is surprising that Emanuel and Emanuel dismiss the economic controversy over futile care as providing "the illusion of cost savings at the end of life."[5] Even by their calculation, which has been criticized by many, these authors claim that futile care accounts for $30 billion—not a trivial amount. This calculation is believed to grossly underestimate cost savings, since it does not take into account patients who may die at home rather than in a hospital and those in whom the realization of futility of intervention is recognized at the time of hospitalization and who are therefore spared intrusive high-tech interventions. But it is not the purpose of this book to argue with the methods of calculation for the cost of needless, futile care; whether the loss is 3% or 13% of total health-care expenditures is immaterial. What counts is that these $30–130 billion (and I believe the waste is close to $100 billion per year) are spent to buy suffering, pain, and a miserable, burdensome existence at the end of life. By preventing this unnecessary waste, the dying patient benefits, the patient's family benefits, and society benefits: this is a totally win–win situation.

WHY DO WE USE MEDICAL TECHNOLOGY? BECAUSE IT IS THERE

In 1973, the U.S. Congress passed legislation making renal dialysis (the use of a machine to take over the functions of the kidneys in clearing toxic chemicals from the blood) a right for all citizens who suffer failure of kidney function. Since then, the rate of use of renal dialysis exploded to three times the rate in Britain. Furthermore, 30% of all renal dialysis patients in America are over 65 years old. In Britain, renal dialysis for this older age group is undertaken only under exceptional circumstances. One may applaud the access to such care that we have in America, but the following American medical case illustrates the absurdity of such access under certain circumstances.

This case involved the treatment of a middle-aged woman who lived a reckless life. This woman was infected with a tuberculosis organism that was resistant to conventional antibiotic therapy. (Drug-resistant tuberculosis is one of the deadliest threats in America today.) In addition to high blood pressure, she was also infected with the AIDS virus and had very little immune system activity. She did not take her medications to treat either the high blood pressure or the tuberculosis, although these medications were dispensed to her free of charge. She was brought to the hospital in a high-blood-pressure crisis that resulted in acute heart failure, and she was placed on a ventilator to assist her breathing. It was discovered that the high-blood-pressure crisis (a result of her refusal to take high-blood-pressure medications) had caused her kidneys to be irreparably damaged. The patient's family requested that she be placed on permanent dialysis. The patient declared, in a defiant gesture, that she intended to have sex with others in the future and that she did not intend to take her medicines under any circumstances. In other words, she intended to distribute HIV and resistant tuberculosis infections, and consequently death, to the community. At the same time, she was entitled to receive dialysis! And receive it she did. She died two weeks later.

This and similar cases beg the vexing question (outside the scope of the practice of medicine) of whether one is entitled to all the rights and privileges of citizenship without being asked to make a return to the society. Since Plato's time, it has been recognized that in order to enjoy the rights of citizenship one must fulfill one's duties toward society and to others.

Or consider next the following case of absurd access to medical intervention. No story can approach this one told to me by my friend Dr. Philip Altus, Professor of Medicine at the University of South Florida.

SAVING A LIFE THAT WILL TAKE OTHER LIVES

The case of Bartolino Moya, age 37 years, has bequeathed us an unrelenting debate about the following ethical issue: Should doctors take into account a person's morals and character when considering eligibility for a heart transplant or a scarce medical treatment?

Mr. Moya was ostensibly a New York shopkeeper, born in the Dominican Republic. In July 1993, he was charged with six murders, one attempted murder, and six kidnappings. Police claimed his gang was also responsible for many other crimes, including several murders. Three of his followers were convicted to life without parole; others received less severe sentences.

In court, Mr. Moya pleaded that he was too sick to start the trial because of advanced heart trouble and that he was expected to die within a few months. The judge decided, on medical grounds, to forego trial and released him on his own recognizance, reasoning thus: "If this man is terminally ill and is going to be in intensive care ... it may very well be that there is no reason not to release him so that he can be with his family and have whatever comfort he can have."

Subsequently, Mr. Moya enrolled in the heart-transplant program at Temple University in Philadelphia, Pennsylvania. His lawyer stopped the police from passing on information about his past to the heart-transplant team. Philadelphia surgeons gave Mr. Moya a new heart, not knowing that he was the suspected ringleader of a brutal drug gang responsible for at least 12 murders and numerous kidnappings. Mr. Moya continued to attend the Temple University heart-transplant clinic on a regular basis for two months. He vanished at the end of July 1994, even though he was wearing a surveillance device. Without drug treatment, which cost $20,000 per year, Mr. Moya is expected to die in a few weeks.

Two months after the operation, police rearrested Moya and reinstituted charges. A New York judge released him on $250,000 bail so that he could continue to obtain treatment in Philadelphia. The judge added, "If he flees, he flees; too bad. I think we could determine (then) that it would be virtually suicide."

Physicians debated whether Mr. Moya's moral character should have ruled out the operation. However, Dr. Arthur Caplan, director of the Center of Bioethics at University of Pennsylvania, said in an interview to the news media, "I don't care if a person has been shot in the process of a holdup or if he is a child molester. Medicine has no business trying to judge the moral worth or the character of people." He added his own absurd deduction: "Very soon you'd stop treating couch potatoes or a person who had a criminal record as a child."

To many, this statement from a respected ethicist is surprising. It supports the position that reckless, unreliable, shady characters are entitled to scarce, expensive societal resources at the same time that they are wasting these resources at best, or continuing to destroy society at worst. Not surprisingly, soon after the Moya case became publicized, another convicted felon, Dewayne Murphey, was suing the government for $20 million in damages; he had developed severe heart disease and did not have long to live. The authorities in Minnesota refused to allow him to be considered for a heart transplant while serving four years imprisonment for drug trafficking.

DARING TO SPEAK THE "R" WORD: RATIONING OF HEALTH CARE

Our society has the right and duty to determine how to establish priorities in the allocation of resources that are, and will always be, scare. According to the national transplant registry last year, 6,200 people in America were on waiting lists for new hearts: 34% got them, whereas 12% died before a suitable heart could be found. It must never be forgotten that the care of heart-transplant recipients does not end with the surgical procedure; the recipient must be responsible for his or her own self-care. It requires a great deal of self-discipline and the motivation to engage in regular, rigorous follow-up for several years at a substantial cost.

We are an aging society. A recent article in *The Economist* asserts that the cost of health benefits and other social services are six times as much for a person over 65 years than for one less than 18 years old. People over 65 years constituted 11% of the population in 1980; they are expected to constitute 15% of the population in the year 2000; and they will constitute 21% of the population in the year 2040. Today, people over age 65 years consume 30% of health-care costs. By the year 2000, they are expected to consume 40%; and in the year 2040, they will consume 50% of all health-care expenditures (see Table 2).[6] Data are derived from the office of National Statistics, 1705 Equitable Building, 6235 Security Boulevard, Baltimore, Maryland 21207.

The problem of medical and monetary excesses is real and demands immediate attention; the proposed solutions, however, are problematic, because they circle around rationing, which is unacceptable to the majority of Americans. Dr. Muriel Gillick, Director of the Hebrew Rehabilitation Center for the Aged, in an article entitled "The High Costs of Dying—A Way Out," published in the October 1994 issue of *Archives of Internal Medicine*, quotes a review of 75 national opinion polls, which reveals that Americans, "want more medical care in the future, including insurance for catastrophic events, high-technology medicine, and long-term care."[7] If medical care rationing is not acceptable to us as a society, can we come up with a system of rational medical care that satisfies expectations without sacrificing quality? This will no doubt be the challenge of the decade and beyond.

Richard Lamm, Colorado's former governor, went to the extreme to publicly state that the very elderly, chronically ill members of the society have a moral duty to forego health care and accept their death. He added,

Table 2
People over Age 65 Years in America

Year	% population	% use of health-care cost
1980	11	29
1986	12	31
2000	15	40
2040	21	50

Source: Adapted from Schneider EL, and Gurainik JM, "The Aging of America: Impact on Health Care Costs," *Journal of the American Medical Association*, 263(1990), pp. 2335–2340.

> It is sad that we now have a system that allows the elderly to consume far more medical resources than we give to children. It is not only fair but desirable to have a different level of care for a 10-year-old than for someone who is 100. Should not public policy recognize that some people have far more statistical years ahead of them than others? I feel it is morally repugnant to use $100,000 or more of our kids' limited resources, as I'm on my way out the door.[8]

According to *The Economist* magazine, the aging of the population will represent an ever-increasing burden on young individuals. Whereas in 1970, 100 able-bodied workers supported seven elderly individuals in the United States, in 2050, 100 workers are expected to support 38 elderly individuals. If we, as a society, do not face up to this enormously complicated challenge, we will be faced with a formula for generation warfare (see Table 3).

The economic burden of caring for elderly people who still have higher brain function is great, but no one is protesting this economic investment. The use of futile care, however, for a 90-year-old or a 9-year-old is both economically and ethically untenable. Unfortunately, the widespread use of futile care has convinced some people, such as those in the medical cases that follow, that it is an entitlement, a right.

Table 3
Number of Elderly for Every 100 Employed Persons in the United States

Decade	Number of elderly employed workers
1970	7/100
1990	19/100
2050	38/100

Source: Adapted from *The Economist*, 1993.

Mrs. Doe, a 92-year-old gregarious woman, was my patient for over 10 years. She had been a music teacher. She wore heavy makeup, sweet perfume, red dresses, and flashy jewelry. She had a loud laugh and an eloquent vocabulary. During one of her visits to my office, Mrs. Doe instructed me to make her death as peaceful as humanely possible when her time came. Several months later, she developed a massive stroke, afflicting a key location in her brain stem, and quickly lapsed into a deep coma. In order to fulfill Mrs. Doe's prior expressed desire, I had a conference with the family. I knew these people very well and considered them friends. I explained the gravity of the situation, stating that death was imminent and inevitable. I advised that we should not place her on a ventilator machine and that it would not be necessary to treat a newly developed pneumonia. I believed that I had faithfully represented Mrs. Doe's wishes and clear instructions. I remember that day very clearly. It was a Tuesday. The family stunned me by asking that I place Mrs. Doe on assisted ventilation until the following Monday. Her daughter added, "We want her to stay alive until next week by any means and at any cost."

"Why are you asking me to do what your mother wanted to avoid?" I asked.

The daughter calmly answered, "Our children are scheduled to play in an important school football game next Saturday, which is being held out of town. My mother's death at this point would be disruptive. My children have been looking forward to the football game for weeks."

I objected to their request and politely asked that I dismiss myself from her care if they insisted, and the daughter did insist. Mrs. Doe was placed on a ventilator with full resuscitation orders and a multitude of tubes, just to keep her alive for a few days. I do not regret the fact that I could not do what the daughter asked. I have a clear conscience. Poor Mrs. Doe, and all the rest of us who had to pay close to $100,000 to delay the moment of death for a few days. A very expensive football game!

Consider next Mr. Williams, a 68-year-old man with advanced, end-stage heart failure. Mr. Williams had spent more than two of the previous three months in the hospital. For the last week, he had not been able to sleep, even in the sitting position, because of a sense of smothering. He required a large dose of oxygen on a continuous basis. He had ceased to respond to a multitude of medicines given in large doses intravenously in an effort to strengthen his heart muscle. In the past, his heart would respond to these medicines by showing an improvement in pumping blood, but not anymore. His body had withered away, and he had become very weak. His breathing was labored; he could only speak a few words at a time; his hands and feet were cold; his pulse was fast and weak; and his blood pressure had become quite low. All of these are signs of poor pumping function of the heart. An ultrasound image confirmed that the heart had become extremely weak, pumping very little blood. Furthermore, the heart valves, which keep blood in the proper heart chambers, were now allowing blood to leak backward. All of this indicated that death was imminent. Mr. Williams was too old to be considered for heart transplantation. I talked with Mr. and Mrs. Williams at great length, explaining the precarious nature of Mr. Williams's heart condition and how it was beyond the stage with which we could expect any improvement. I recommended to Mr. and Mrs. Williams that no resuscitation efforts be undertaken when the heart stopped. Also, I advised to make Mr. Williams's last days as comfortable as possible, even if that resulted in the shortening of his life, emphasizing that peace and comfort should be paramount at this stage. They agreed.

Two days later, Mrs. Williams stopped me in the hallway. "I changed my mind," she said. "I want you to do everything possible for my husband. If the heart stops, try to revive it. If you have to place him on a ventilator, please do." I asked Mrs. Williams that we visit in a private conference room. I thought that her change of heart represented a profound love for her husband and reflected the difficulty and pain associated with a "let go" decision. But I was mistaken. She declared: "Upon checking with my husband's boss, I found out that Mr. Williams's insurance will pay all expenses associated with his hospitalization. He has already met his deductible, and there will be no additional cost to him." I answered that my recommendations regarding Mr. Williams were based solely upon his medical condition. No consideration was given to whether he or someone else would pay for unnecessary care. I further explained that placing Mr. Williams on a ventilator in his present condition would be contrary to good medical judgment and that I could not be expected to carry out any treatment if I did not believe that the treatment would benefit the patient. She finally agreed to allow me to exercise my best medical judgment, but reluctantly.

THE FINANCIAL AND MORAL BANKRUPTCY OF FUTILE CARE

I am told by an economist friend that any service that is offered for free will be abused by consumers, the perception being that it does not cost anyone anything. The truth is, everyone pays for it. But perceived "freebies" are not the only factor that drives the use of futile care. There is no doubt that physician peer pressure and fear of legal repercussions also drive its use. There is also the "heroic" motivation to try a procedure, even if there is only a one in one thousand chance that it will work. In some cases, financial incentives are powerful motivating factors for physicians to utilize expensive high-tech procedures. The more procedures a physician performs, futile or not, the higher his or her income. Finally, the mere existence of these tools may motivate their use.

It has been argued that if patients who are potential candidates for futile care are provided with financial alternatives, much of the futile care at the end of life might be forfeited by them and their families. For the sake of argument, let us assume that futile care at the end of life costs the system 10% of its total health-care expenditures, which is a reasonable assumption. Also suppose that at age 20, individuals are asked to choose between two alternate health-insurance policies: one costs $2,000 per year and covers all health-care needs except for unnecessary care at the end of life, and the other policy costs $2,200 annually, with the added benefit that the policy covers useless terminal treatment in addition to other necessary health care. I wonder how many people would buy the latter policy. Would anyone in their sound mind pay an extra $200 per year, with a yearly escalation of 5%, to buy a few days or weeks of misery in an intensive-care unit or to lead an unconscious existence in isolation? Suppose we offer individuals approaching the end of life the options of being treated to death once it becomes clear that death is imminent or being awarded $100,000 for a grandson's education or a charity of their preference?

When we relinquish our "right" to futile care, we do, in effect, invest in our grandchildren. Can we relinquish that additional futile expense as a gift to generations to come? Can we, as we approach the end of life, willingly forego unnecessary burdensome treatment to take care of the health of the unborn or the education of the young? Or are we becoming, without our consent, the grabbers and usurpers of limited social goods as we exit from this world?

This is a pertinent question for our generation to ponder with open minds and caring hearts. Very few rational and reasonable people would want to be subjected to treatments that are clearly useless. This should be a relatively clear-cut issue. Other health-care issues are less so, such as when a dismal treatment outcome is less certain, although the odds are stacked against a favorable outcome. The two following cases exemplify more problematic situations.

In 1986, a 76-year-old woman successfully received a liver transplant at the Presbyterian University Hospital in Pittsburgh and made headline news. The cost of this surgery exceeded $200,000 dollars, when the prospects for a decent quality of life and length of remaining life were quite limited. The woman died a few days later.

In 1993, Siamese twins, both doomed eventually to perish, were operated upon in Pennsylvania to salvage one while the other died immediately. The one claimed to have been saved,

Angela Lakesburg, had complex anomalies of the heart that could not be corrected completely. Previously, the twins were evaluated by a specialized center in Chicago, and the possibility of surgery was rejected because of the complexity of the operation. It was felt that, given the best possible scenario, the surviving twin would have a life expectancy that did not exceed a few miserable years. In Pennsylvania, a multihour surgery was undertaken by multiple teams of surgeons. A million dollars were raised to enable the high-tech support of the surviving twin. She died on the ventilator after 10 months of surgeries and a tortuous postoperative course at a cost of over 1 million dollars.

DARING TO SPEAK THE "P" WORD: PRIORITIES IN HEALTH CARE

Dr. Norman Daniels, the noted health economist and professor at Tufts University, suggests a life-span approach to health-care allocation. Drs. Tristan Engelhart and Michael Rie, anesthesiologists at Massachusetts General Hospital, went further to suggest a formula for use by society to establish priorities of care based upon the outcome of a specific intervention and the cost involved.[10] The formula takes into account probability of cure (*P*), quality of life (*Q*) with treatment and expected length of lifespan (*L*; assuming the treatment proves successful). These are weighed against the cost of treatment (*C*). His formula is expressed

$$\frac{PQL}{C}$$

The higher the number, the more worthwhile the treatment. For example, an intervention that costs $100,000 promises to increase life span by 50 years in 80% of cases, with a good quality of life in 90%. Then

$$\frac{PQL}{C} = \frac{80 \times 90 \times 50}{100{,}000} = \frac{360}{100}$$

Contrast this to another intervention that costs $100,000, promises to increase lifespan by five years in 20% of cases and leads to a good quality of life in 10% of cases. In this case

$$\frac{PQL}{C} = \frac{20 \times 10 \times 5}{100{,}000} = \frac{1}{100}$$

According to this example, the first intervention would be much preferred to the second by a 360:1 margin. A similar formula guided the newly designed Oregon health-care model in establishing treatment priorities applicable to all citizens receiving state-supported medical treatment.

In the Oregon model, 709 paired medical conditions and treatments were evaluated. Priorities for care were given to the unborn, child care, and curable conditions. Out of 709 cases, 586 were found to be eligible for state support, and the rest were rejected because of poor outcomes in relation to cost. These cases included newborn infants with *no* upper brain (anencephaly), advanced cancer not responding to therapy, deep coma, and advanced vegetative states.[11]

Table 4 shows a classification of medical interventions based upon cost and outcome. At the top are conditions and treatments that have the highest return for invested dollars. At the bottom are conditions with increasing costs and diminishing returns.

Some would view the Oregon plan as a form of unacceptable rationing by which the worth of human life is measured in terms of dollars. Others would argue that with limited health-care resources, society has to establish reasonable priorities for care. Otherwise, we may end up spending a good portion of the nation's resources on expensive care that gives little benefit to society at large. Through implementation of scientifically sound outcome criteria in the setting of priorities, society-at-large (but not necessary a particular individual) will gain. Others would claim that although it is possible to design a system that takes priorities into account, society must, at the same time, make allowances for those members of the society who wish to receive health care that is not warranted by the priority list and can pay for it. This situation could be dealt with through private insurance policies. There

Table 4
Health-Care Costs and Outcomes

- Low cost, high gain
  - Preventive care
  - Immunization
- Moderate cost, excellent outcome
  - Common surgeries
  - Treatment of common disease in the young
  - Treatment of common infections including pneumonias
  - Treatment of high blood pressure, asthma, diabetes, and reversible medical illnesses
- Moderate cost, good outcome
  - Management of:
    - Acute heart attacks
    - Early heart failure
    - Early emphysema
    - Early cancer
    - Early liver disease
- High cost, limited outcome
  - Heart failure
  - Disseminated cancer
  - Advanced kidney disease
- Very high cost, very poor outcome
  - Premature cocaine babies
  - Extensive brain injury
  - Massive strokes
- Extremely high cost, futile care
  - Multiple end-stage organ failure (heart, lung, liver, kidney)
  - Premature infant (500 grams or less)
  - Advanced systemic uncontrollable infection
  - Over 90% total body burn

would be a basic policy that covers most conditions at a reasonable cost; you, the individual, would pay more for extra benefits. Clearly, these issues cannot be addressed on an *ad hoc* basis by practicing physicians. Rather, a consortium of professionals and laypersons (commonly referred to as *consumers*) must develop a policy that would be approved by society at large. Physicians will play pivotal roles in helping society to establish and accept the necessary priorities.

Even a prioritization of medical interventions and conditions will not render all cases clear cut. Medical care is always based upon reasonable, not absolute, certainties. The essence of the art of medicine is in weighing probabilities.

For example, the treatment of a patient in a persistent vegetative state costs approximately $100,000 per year. As discussed earlier, the patient in a PVS is unconscious but demonstrates sleep–waking patterns and some eye and facial movements. PVS can arise from brain injury, congenital malformations of the brain, or degenerative brain disease (such as in old age, advanced Alzheimer's disease, or after heart arrest). Recovery from a PVS due to trauma is very unlikely after 12 months. In vegetative states caused by other conditions, recovery is exceedingly rare after three months.

The difficult question is, knowing these limits, how many hundreds of people should be kept in a mindless vegetative existence at a cost of $100,000 per year per patient in the hope that one might show a late recovery, which is rarely significant? Clearly, this is not a decision for physicians to make, since it is beyond physicians' authority to allocate expensive resources. These decisions are for the patient's family to make, unless certain clear guidelines are formulated by society. To quote Paul Menzel, the noted health-care economist, "Whether to pay the real cost of saving a life in old age will always be an open question … but facing up to the real costs of what we are doing is not!! We must face up."[12] One of the most challenging exercises in medicine is to be able to determine early in the course of acute disease which patients are likely to survive in an intensive-care unit, thereby enabling the physicians to identify early on which patients will not benefit. An Acute Physiology–Chronic Health Evaluation method has been developed (APACHE scale) and modified further to APACHE II.[13]

During a recent visit to England, I observed how physicians are forced into establishing priorities for intensive care. With declining resources, recent hospital closures, and a limited number of intensive-care beds, doctors have to make hard choices. Dr. David Bihari of Guys Hospital has developed an even more refined computer program, The Riyadh Intensive-Care Program (RICP), to aid in establishing priorities. According to a recent evaluation of the program by Drs. Atkinson, Bihari, et al.[14] from Guys Hospital in London, published in *Lancet*, October 1994, the program is likely to produce 5% mistakes in judgment. By one standard, the program is deemed extremely valuable in guiding intensive-care admissions. On the other hand, one can easily imagine the controversy that would be created by such a computerized program were it considered for use to guide care in the U.S. intensive-care units.

TACKLING THE LAST TABOO: CALCULATING THE VALUE OF A LIFE

Before I became interested in the ethical and economic issues related to life and death, I did not know that societies undertake many decisions on the basis of the monetary value of life. For example, societies make decisions to hire policemen based upon a cost–benefit ratio. Even local communities hire lifeguards to monitor beaches in order to prevent people from drowning based upon the potential number of lives saved: The greater the hazards of drowning, the better the justification to hire lifeguards. When car companies place air bags in their vehicles, they take into account the cost of the bags in relation to the potential for lives saved. In a recent issue of the journal *Economist*, I encountered an interesting table relating how much a country is willing to pay to save a life after a car accident, expressed as the cost of a road accident (see Table 5).

I am sharing this information to emphasize the point that human societies have already calculated the life of a fellow human being under certain circumstances. In the same vein, societies

Table 5
The Value of Life: Cost of a Road-Accident Death by Country

Country	Cost (× 1000 dollars)
United States[a]	2,500
Sweden[a]	1,236
New Zealand[a]	1,150
Britain[a]	1,100
Germany[b]	928
Belgium[b]	400
France[b]	350
Holland[b]	130
Portugal[b]	20

[a]Willingness-to-pay basis.
[b]Human-capital-business.
Source: R. Wilkle and S. Beyoff, "Economic Cost of Road Accidents," National Transport Department.

have to determine how much should be spent to pursue an expensive treatment that promises less in life-saving potential, along with the maintenance of a reasonable quality of life.

No subject in medicine evokes such controversy and is riddled with such passions and biases as what constitutes an acceptable quality of life. A life worth living is a uniquely personal thing. Furthermore, equality of human worth is the basis for freedom and democracy. In the United States, we have a Constitution that not only values the right to life and liberty for all individuals, but also recognizes these individuals as the units which comprise the country ("We, the people").

As much as our diversity and individualism confer a wealth of heritage and a spirit of individualism, they also produce a heterogeneity that could border on chaos. Considering the variety of our heritages, religions, ethnic backgrounds, and other factors, it is no wonder that it has become quite difficult to formulate standards by which an acceptable quality of life, a life worth living, can be defined.

The difficulty is compounded by the fact that the definitions of life and death themselves are a matter of disagreement. At one extreme, a life limited by infirmity is intolerable to some. Cases of suicide after a major injury to a vital organ are all too well known. At the other extreme, there are those among us who define any human existence as a life that is worth preserving at any and all costs (e.g., there are those who would fight to maintain a permanently unconscious life to the bitter end). It is extremely difficult to develop widely acceptable standards for an acceptable life quality for a baby with congenital or acquired major infirmities, but a child born without a brain who will not achieve consciousness can be considered a mindless creature that will never develop into a person.

For an adult, at least to my way of thinking, the problem may not be as onerous, although it may still be complex and charged. Once a person has developed into a being with certain characteristics, the loss of these can justifiably be classified as poor quality of life.

In my numerous lectures on this subject to laypersons, I have not met anyone who would like to stay "alive" when he or she cannot recognize self and surroundings or interact meaningfully with others. In fact, I have seen hundreds of cases like that of Dr. Newberg, a Ph.D. who taught archeology at the University of Atlanta. He was an international lecturer and published extensively on the subject of comparative behavior in primitive societies. Five years ago, at age 72, he retired and moved his family to Oklahoma to be close to their only daughter, an articulate, bright, young woman who was an associate editor of the local, premier newspaper.

I saw Dr. Newberg in consultation over five years ago. He was complaining of increasing angina pectoris, chest pains due to lack of oxygen to the heart. Because chest pains came with mild exertion, he was unable to take his daily swim. At that time, my examination showed him to be a pleasant man who could follow most of our conversation, but early signs of forgetfulness had started to show. His wife and daughter had to repeat names and events in order to keep him aware of persons and things. I performed a procedure on Dr. Newberg's coronary arteries in order to prevent the chest pains, and he resumed his daily swimming. A few months later, Dr. Newberg tripped and broke his left hip. He was hospitalized. This time, he had become clearly forgetful and intermittently confused. He kept repeating the same questions over and over and talked continuously about old events in his life.

He was discharged from the hospital several weeks later and was advised to continue physical therapy at home. For over a year, the family had to struggle to take care of Dr. Newberg. One day, he left the house and was found after several hours of aimless wandering. His wife started to show signs of weariness. His daughter's marriage became strained because of her ever-diminishing attention to her husband and their only child.

One day, during a scheduled office visit, it became apparent to me that Dr. Newberg's dementia, caused by Alzheimer's disease, had progressed significantly. He had become incoherent, totally confused, and incontinent. He did not remember my name, where he was, or the purpose of his visit. He used abusive language when he talked to his wife and daughter. I talked to them frankly: "Dr. Newberg has a rapidly progressive, degenerative brain disease. He has deteriorated considerably," They nodded. "His management at home is going to be very difficult," I said. Mrs. Newberg's strained smile disappeared.

Her face became contracted and tears overcame her. "You can't imagine the nightmare I am living in at present. But what can I do?"

"We have to consider placing Dr. Newberg in a nursing home," I said. The wife and daughter broke down.

The mother almost choked in a flow of tears. "But I promised him that I would not place him in a nursing home," she said in a cracked voice, while still crying. "He is a very special man. I love him so much."

I reached out to the box of tissues and handed her some. "I

understand your pain and the predicament that you find yourselves in," I said. "I face this dilemma almost daily. Had Dr. Newberg been in his usual sound mind, would he have wanted to put you through this burden?"

"No," Mrs. Newberg said, and in a lower voice, she mumbled, "but he asked me not to place him in a nursing home."

I told them that they have to face the painful truth. "What is living with you now is not Dr. Newberg. It is a mindless, belligerent being. Dr. Newberg, as you knew him, is dead. This may sound insensitive, cold, and callous, but it is the truth. He is not suffering as much as you are, because he is unaware of what is happening to you or to him."

Dr. Newberg's stay in the nursing home was not easy on the family. His wife or daughter visited him every evening and ate dinner with him. The pain was not over, but it was bearable. Every now and then, Mrs. Newberg would express her feelings of guilt and tears would run down her cheeks. She missed the real Dr. Newberg: the intelligent, witty, articulate, charming man. She felt pity for what he had been transformed into and wished that he had died when he had the heart trouble a few years earlier.

THE FUTILE FRUITS OF FUTILE CARE

Unfortunately, the story is not over yet. In the fall, the nursing home medical staff is planning to give flu shots to all residents. Should Dr. Newberg receive a flu shot? Or would he be better off dying from a flu attack? They plan to vaccinate him with a shot against pneumonia, in order to lessen his chances of dying from lung infection. Pneumonia is one of the most merciful ways to go. As the old physician's saying goes, "Pneumonia is the old man's friend." What if he develops a heart attack? Or suppose his heart stops? Should his attendants start CPR, transfer him to an intensive care unit, and place him on a ventilator machine to breathe for him? Or should these heroic efforts be forfeited with the rationalization that Dr. Newberg as we knew him already died?

How many more people will be allowed to have a Tithonus-like stretched-out existence, for how long and at what cost? Should the Newbergs have to go bankrupt to sustain the existence of someone who was once loved, revered, and capable of giving so much love and inspiration?

Frankly, I told the Newbergs that I would not want my existence to be extended in such a situation. My life would have already outlasted its usefulness and meaning. If I reach this point, I would not want to be given flu or pneumonia vaccines, would not wish my infections treated if I developed any, would object to resuscitation if my heart stopped, and would want to have as comfortable an exit as possible—the sooner the better!

The problem is that, when faced with an enormously complex problem that relates to a loved one, we cannot, and for that matter, are not expected to think rationally. Our emotions and passions overtake us. Unfortunately, we confuse true love with demonstrated love. True love considers first and foremost the right of the loved ones to be respected.

What is the cost of sustaining Dr. Newberg's existence? It is reasonable to assume that Dr. Newberg could live 10 more years with proper nutrition, body hygiene, nursing supervision, preventative vaccination against infection, and other medical care as the need arises? The cost of nursing home care is roughly $30,000 per year, which adds up to $300,000 over 10 years. For all other medical interventions, including treatment at the end of life, add the reasonable estimate of $200,000 for the remainder of his life span. The total cost amounts to $500,000. And what do we show for it? A miserable existence for Dr. Newberg, a painful experience riddled with guilt and unjustified feeling of shame for his family, and $500,000 less in resources for society are the futile fruits of futile care.

One can apply the same calculations and determine the enormous costs involved in the partial salvage of a patient in a persistent vegetative state (several million dollars) or the cardiopulmonary resuscitation of an elderly patient (several hundred thousand dollars).

L. Churchill, the author of *Rationing Health Care in America*, notes:

> Neither should we extend our lives at the margins if by so doing we deprive nameless and faceless others a decent provision of care. And such a gesture should not appear to us as a sacrifice, but as the ordinary virtue entailed by a just, social conscience.[15]

Churchill concludes, "If the next generation is to flower and flourish, we must practice the wisdom of giving ground when our time comes."

A VIABLE SOLUTION: THE UNIVERSAL LIVING WILL

I cannot conclude this discussion without underscoring the fact that, in patients who have not lost their ability to think for themselves, quality-of-life issues are theirs to decide. Some patients have the strength and will to rise above life's travails, to embody what the poet Ben Jonson[16] describes:

> To struggle when hope is banished
> To live when life's salt is gone
> To dwell in a dream that's vanished
> To endure, and go calmly on.

These individuals are real heroes and they display the triumphs of the human spirit, serving as inspiration for us all. For others, the cross is too heavy to bear. These patients include those with intractable pains, "locked-in states" (when the patient is conscious but is totally paralyzed on both sides), and those with advanced AIDS. They need counseling, encouragement, and relief of pain. In spite of all sincere efforts, many yearn for a death like that in Samuel T. Coleridge's[17] poem:

> How well he fell asleep
> Like some proud river, widening towards the sea,
> calmly and grandly, silently and deep,
> life jointed eternity.

When a rational individual, faced with the fear of hopelessness, pain, financial insecurity, enormous psychological stress, and social isolation, makes a decision that life need not be prolonged, this person's wishes have to be granted. A fully informed, competent patient has an unquestionable right to refuse treatment as long as he or she fully understands the consequences of such a decision. No wonder that many rational and well-informed individuals find that terminal illness is a fate worse than death.

The living will, best exemplified by the Danish model or our proposed universal form, as imperfect as it is, can help ensure for each of us a death with dignity. But the living will also can benefit society by precluding the option of futile care and the enormous costs it entails.

NOTES

1. D Callahan, "Limiting Health Care for the Old." In *Aging and Ethics*, N Jecker, ed. (Totowa, NJ: Humana Press, 1991), pp. 219–226.
2. *National Center for Health Statistics: 1986 Summary*. National Hospital Discharge Survey. Advance Data from Vital and Health Statistics. (Hyatsville, MD Public Health Service, DHHS Publication No. 145 (PHS) 87-1250, 1987), pp. 1–16.
3. VR Fuchs, *The Future of Health Policy*. (Cambridge, MA: Harvard University Press, 1993).
4. RD Lamm, *The Rise and Fall of the American Civilization*. (The Center of Public Policy and Contemporary Issues, University of Denver, CO, June 1991), pp. 5–6.
5. EJ Emanuel and LL Emanuel, "The Economics of Dying: The Illusion of Cost Savings at the End of Life," *New England Journal of Medicine*, 333 (1994), 540–544.
6. ST Bruner, DR Waldo, and DR Makusick, "National Health Expenditure Projection through 2030," *Health Care Financing Review*, 14 (1992), 14–29.
7. M Gillick, "The High Cost of Dying: A Way Out," *Archives of Internal Medicine*, 154 (1994), 2134–2137.
8. RD Lamm, *America in Decline*. (The Center for Public Policy and Contemporary Issues, University of Denver, CO, 1990).

9. N Daniels, "Am I My Parents' Keeper? An Essay on Justice between the Young and Old." (New York: Oxford University Press, 1988), pp. 40–65, 88–102.
10. HT Engelhardt and MA Rie, "Intensive Units' Scarce Resources and Conflicting Principles of Justice," *Journal of the American Medical Association*, 225 (1986), 1162–1165.
11. DC Hadron, "Setting Health Care Priorities in Oregon: Cost Effectiveness Meets the Rule of Rescue," *Journal of the American Medical Association*, 265 (1991), 2218–2225.
12. PT Menzel, "Paying the Real Costs of Lifesaving," In *Aging and Ethics*, N Jecker, ed. (Totowa, NJ: Humana Press, 1991), pp. 285–305.
13. KM Rowan, J Karr, and Associates, "Intensive Care Society's APACHE II Study in Britain and Ireland II: Outcome Comparisons of Intensive Care Units after Adjustment for Case Mix by the American APACHE II Method," *British Medical Journal*, 309 (1993), 977–981.
14. S Atkins, D Bihari, M. Smithies, K Daly, R Mason, and I McCall, "Identification of Futility in Intensive Care," *Lancet*, 344 (1994), 1203–1206.
15. L Churchill, *Rationing Health Care in America*. (South Bend, IN: Notre Dame University Press, 1988).
16. B Jonson (*c. 1573–1637*), *Epigrams on My Son*.
17. ST Coleridge (1772–1834), *The Ancient Mariner* (1798).

Chapter 8

Is Medical Intervention Wasted on the Old?

> The days of our years are three-score years and ten; and if by reason of strength they be four-score years, yet is their strength labor and sorrow; for it is soon cut off and we fly away.
>
> —Psalms 90:10

IT'S NOT HOW OLD YOU ARE, BUT HOW YOU ARE OLD

In previous chapters, we have discussed the issue of increasing life expectancy and its implications for increasing demands on health care. I have not discussed, however, the factor of old age *per se* and how it factors into the global issues of health-care reform and reallocation of health-care dollars.

We are an aging population. The older segment of our society is its fastest growing segment, and we all now expect to live longer and healthier lives. We also have a passion for high technology, and our medical establishment is well prepared to fulfill that passion. As I noted previously, we no longer consider death as a part of the natural course of life but as a failure of medicine. High-tech medicine is almost expected to stave off death—a phenomenon often referred to as the "medicalization of death." Concomitant with this is the enormous appetite of Americans for consuming medications. This is especially true of older Americans. In summary, the greatest expenditures of health-care resources are for older Americans.

The need to control health-care costs remains a pressing issue. But despite the exorbitant amount of resources spent on older Americans, old age, in and by itself, should not be a factor in limiting expensive medical care when that care is expected to improve the quality of life of an individual. The age of the patient should only be a criterion for access to such rare resources as human organs for transplant purposes.

In the year A.D. 1000, the estimated average life expectancy of a human being was 30 years. At the start of this century, life expectancy increased to 50 years, and it will become 75 years by the year 2000. This substantial increase in longevity is evident worldwide but is more manifest in economically advanced countries of western Europe, the United States, and Japan. The biblical ideal life of "three score and ten," rarely achieved in the remote past, has become the average life expectancy in recent years. Furthermore, it is estimated that the human life-span would become 100–120 years if disease, accidents, and self-destructive behavior were eradicated, although this is clearly an elusive goal.

Not only are people living longer, but also most are leading happier lives. Many are able to pursue new challenges of learning, exploring, traveling, or just having a good time. You see oldsters who are healthy at golf courses, tennis courts, health clubs, spas, and dance halls. Retirement is no longer viewed as a time of decline and isolation; on the contrary, many view retirement as an opportunity to reap the benefits of many years of hard work and struggle. Unfortunately, senility and decrepitude can be postponed, but not indefinitely. With the sequelae of natural aging come decay, failure to remember or reason, loss of physical stamina, loss of appetite, and eventual physical decay leading to death.

Life-spans vary enormously among human beings. Human differences in physical stamina, intelligence, and other attributes account for the differences in the length of useful life. Dr. Karen Ritchie, a leading dementia expert who runs the Eugeria project in Southern France, recently undertook a fascinating project that she published in the *British Journal of Psychiatry* in 1995.[1] In November 1993, she examined the mental status of the world's oldest woman, J.C., then aged 118 years. J.C. was born in Arles, France in 1875. *Lancet* medical journal noted in an editorial that, at the time of J.C.'s birth, a republican constitution was being reestablished in France and the Paris Opera House had been just completed. The first bacteria were discovered a year before her birth, and the telephone and phonograph were invented a year after her birth. She was 13 years old when Vincent Van Gogh moved to Arles. She outlived her husband, her daughter, and granddaughter. She was independent until age 115 and lived alone until age 110. Apart from some compromise in hearing and eyesight, she was always healthy. She celebrated her 120th birthday in February 1995. Although the recent increase in life span is usually attributed to improved nutrition and sanitation, these factors could not totally explain J.C.'s long life. Dr. Karen Ritchie's assessment indicates that J.C. had attended school until the age of 16 and was of middle socioeconomic class. Her immediate ancestors also had long life-spans, indicating a genetic influence. She had always consumed a Mediterranean diet, shown in other studies to be associated with a lower incidence of certain diseases. Clinical examination by Dr. Ritchie showed that J.C. had a satisfactory degree of attention, expression, memory, language, and reasoning, and a normal to superior IQ. She was still alert and curious, and she seemed to have an extensive knowledge of early events in her life and of her relatives. Brain scans, however, showed generalized decay of J.C.'s brain that was not commensurate with her high level of intellectual functioning. Dr. Ritchie interpreted the findings to support the notion that people of average or above-average intelligence who remain socially active retain considerable intellect in spite of senile atrophy of the brain. It should be noted that J.C.'s life, with its absence of major degenerative diseases such as cancer, vascular disease, and dementia, does not represent normal aging. But her end stage can really be considered to be successful aging with its "terminal frailty."

But older people whose ages fall way short of 120 years derive considerable benefit from elaborate and costly medical treatment. For example, with modern treatment of heart attacks, 80 lives per 1,000 patients over 70 years old can be saved. The success rate with valve replacement in the elderly (who are susceptible to developing narrowing of certain valves that control blood flow in the heart) is 90%. In a carefully selected group of patients older than 70 years, death from surgery can be as low as 1%. Also, 95% of these patients benefit from coronary artery bypass surgery administered appropriately for treatment of hardening of the arteries. Relief of artery narrowing using balloon angioplasty carries a risk well below 1%. These interventions can provide otherwise healthy, older patients with many additional years of enjoyable life.

In light of this success in the United States, the Royal College of Physicians in London published a report in 1991 entitled "Cardiological Intervention in Older Patients." In this report, the college recommends expanding medical services similar to services available to older Americans to older British patients with heart problems.

Recently, Professor Ulrich Gleichmann of Ruhr University, Bohum, Germany, and his associates reported Germany's experience with the treatment of heart disease in the elderly. He showed that, in Germany, more than one-fifth of all bypass operations and nearly one-fourth of valve surgeries are performed on patients over 70 years old. He further emphasized the excellent results encountered when patients are selected carefully.[2]

However, the total picture is not all roses; there is a dim and problematic side to it. It is manifest in the larger number of patients who undergo useless or marginally useful interventions that contribute nothing to the quality of life. The elderly population is by no means a homogeneous group. Not all people senesce at the same pace. There are those individuals who suffer biological aging while in their forties and fifties as a result of debilitating chronic illnesses such as severe hypertension, diabetes, or kidney disease. Others endowed by nature with a healthy genetic makeup and who follow a healthful lifestyle advance gracefully into their eighties. For most, the process of aging in older years depends on whether one has been fortunate enough to escape the ravages of cancer or hardening of the arteries that strike in the fifties and sixties. Heart surgery has taught us that otherwise healthy older patients have outcomes similar to those of young patients. On the other hand, frail patients and those with diseases involving multiple organs face disastrous outcomes from major surgical interventions. The same applies to cardiopulmonary resuscitation. Among the healthy and old, 10–15% survive resuscitation and are discharged alive from the hospital. The percentage drops to half with each organ failure. The problem is where to draw the line. Is there a magical threshold or a reliable test that can help achieve the desired effects?

THE MEDICALIZATION OF DEATH

Just a few decades ago, death at all ages was not uncommon. Thanks to improved nutrition and sanitation, together with the advent of vaccination and antibiotics, the death of young children today has become an anomaly. Fifty years ago, a family with an average number of children had a 50–50 chance of experiencing the death of a child. Today, in Western societies, the loss of a child has ceased to be a normal, anticipated part of family life. We have grown accustomed to position dying in what we perceive to be its logical position, that is, at the close of a long, long life. When death occurs before life is experienced to its fullest, it is looked on as untimely. So, whereas to our ancestors' deaths were part of the experience of living, to us death has become a remote contingency.

In a recent article published in the *Journal of the American Medical Association*. Dr. Jack McCue makes this exact point: "The naturalness of dying at any age has become a foreign concept."[3]

Furthermore, he addresses a more problematic issue: Dying, which was once viewed as natural and expected, is now perceived as an unwelcome part of medical care. Dr. McCue argues that the event of death has been distorted from a natural event of great societal and cultural significance into the end point of untreatable or inadequately treated disease or injury.

Aries, in *The Hour of Our Death*, concludes that our current attitudes and beliefs, which he names "the medicalization of death," derive from social and scientific changes that cannot be considered wholly beneficial.[4] The percentage of patients dying in hospitals has increased steadily over the past few decades. Some patients are taken to the hospital while in the process of dying, simply out of fear of facing their death at home. Machines can control the time and method of death in many cases; the power of nature, with its unpredictable timetable is thus tamed and controlled. It is unlikely that this attitude about death will change in the foreseeable future. On the other hand, a similar attitude was successfully reversed in some European countries through a coordinated effort between the public, statespeople, and the medical establishment.

Some Americans have begun to courageously address this controversial issue. Richard Lamm,[5] the former Governor of Colorado and present Director of the Center of Public Policy and Contemporary Issues at the University of Denver, argues in one of his publications, *America in Decline*:

> No nation spends as disproportionately on the elderly. America spends eight times more on health care for those over 65 as on those under 65. No other industrial nation spends more than four times more.
>
> No nation spends as much on death and dying. We spend 11% of our Medicare dollars on the last 40 days of our lives—often merely to delay the inevitable.
>
> No society has as unrealistic expectations, i.e., that we can cure anything, even death, and that money should not be a consideration. (p. 18)

Lamm's comments are timely and appropriate: "We are using our limited capital to give hip replacements to people with Alzheimer's disease, to remove cataracts from people dying in hospices."

Daniel Callahan, Ph.D., Director of the Hastings Center and author of several books on care for the elderly, notes:

> The indefinite extension of life combined with an insatiable ambition to improve the health of the elderly is a recipe for monomania and bottomless spending. It fails to put health in its proper place as only one among many human goods. It fails to accept aging and death as part of the human condition.[6]

In one of his several publications on the subject, Dr. Callahan reports on his experience with a group of Swiss physicians.[7] Dr. Callahan observed that no heart surgery is undertaken in Switzerland on patients over the age of 70 years. This might have been true several years ago, but not anymore. Heart surgery is now available in Switzerland to the "healthy old," and heart transplantation is considered appropriate for some selected patients over 60 years old. It appears as if Europe is now following our lead rather than the other way around.

Dr. Callahan suggests three principles[8] to remedy what he considers to be the problem of misallocation of health-care resources:

1. Government has a duty, based on our collective social obligations, to help people live out a natural life-span, but not to help medically extend life beyond that point.
2. Government is obliged to develop under its research subsidies, and to pay for, under its entitlement programs, only the kind and degree of life-extending technology necessary for medicine to achieve and serve the aim of a natural life-span.
3. Beyond the point of a natural life-span, government should provide only the means necessary for the relief of suffering, not those of life-extending technologies.

In another proposition, Dr. Callahan asked whether our society should leave crucial life-and-death decisions in the hands of individuals or let them be decided, at least in great part, by commonly shared, cultural notions of what is and is not fitting. These cultural ideas should then be implemented in ordinary medical practice.

AGE: NOT AN ABSOLUTE CRITERION FOR HEALTH-CARE ALLOCATION

No doubt, Dr. Callahan's probing questions are cogent, valid, and timely. His notion that some expensive interventions are not fitting beyond a certain age is not groundless. However, getting an arbitrary limit for what constitutes a "normal life-span," beyond which medical interventions should be directed solely to help the patient in the process of dying, is, in my view, at best simplistic and at worst, outright dangerous.

In the first place, a normal life-span is contingent on many factors, especially genetic constitution and lifestyle. Therefore, a normal life-span could be 100 years for one person, 40 years for another, and only a few days for an unfortunate baby. Second, to establish arbitrary age-limit guidelines for the allocation of medical benefits degrades human worth and violates self-evident, unalienable human rights. It can be argued that our current system provides a health-care-allocation bias favoring the old. All those over age 65 are entitled to comprehensive care, and a large proportion of children are disenfranchised and do not have access to basic care. But to impose an injustice on a previously favored segment cannot be a fair remedy for an existing unfair one. Yes, a system that denies preventive care to the young is an outrage, and the loss of a young life from a potentially curable illness is a travesty. However, to deny a longer, productive, happy life for a 70-year-old person because he or she is close to the "normal life-span" is unrealistic and unjustifiable.

Limiting intrusive care for someone who has irretrievably lost his or her intellect, will, and passions is a different matter. This applies to all ages. Futile care is bad medicine, regardless of age.

The length of "years of benefit" from a medical intervention, however, justifies the allocation of expensive rare resources in favor of younger patients. Priority for organ transplantation should be given to younger individuals. Any policy of rationing, however, should meet stringent conditions, including that the policy and its rationale be approved by the public. Also, it should never be taken literally and without consideration of all mitigating circumstances.

WHEN MEDICAL INTERVENTION IS WASTED ON THE YOUNG—NOT OLD

To illustrate my point regarding the invalidity of using age as an absolute criterion, I would like to share with the reader the following two cases: one an elderly patient, one relatively young. These patients were cared for by the same physician. I saw both of them in my capacity as a consultant to the primary physician a few years ago.

Mrs. Campbell was a very bright 81-year-old widow, well known in the philanthropic community for sharing her time, talent, and resources for children's causes and the arts. Mrs. Campbell was admitted to the hospital because of shortness of breath and chest tightness that came on with exertion. She had become quite limited in her activities. Clinical examination showed her to be generally healthy except for a narrowing of a heart valve that controlled blood flow. An ultrasound study showed the valve to have been transformed into a piece of stone through calcium deposits. A tiny hole allowed the blood to be minimally pumped by a laboring heart. Laboratory tests showed all other body organs to be in an excellent condition.

I recommended heart surgery to replace the narrowed heart valve with an artificial one. She was reluctant, stating, "My husband died six months ago from heart failure. He had undergone two open-heart surgeries, one 12 years ago and the second 4 years ago. I would rather die a slow, natural death."

Her primary physician agreed with her decision, based primarily upon her age. "She is 81," he said, "already beyond the normal life-span."

I did not accept the decision without a further conversation with the patient in the presence of her primary physician. "You are quite healthy, except for this condition," I said. "Without heart surgery, your deterioration is expected to continue steadily, and death will occur within a few months. The chances of a surgical success are 95%, and you may be able to enjoy several years of good health." She pondered the decision and decided to receive the artificial valve. She is now living well and continuing her philanthropic activities for the good of society.

The second patient was an unfortunate 32-year-old woman. I was asked to see her during her third hospitalization in 15 months. She was a drug addict who used intravenous heroin and sniffed cocaine. She used unclean needles for the heroin injections. More than a year ago, she was hospitalized for treatment of an infection of a heart valve, the one between the right side of the heart and the blood vessel leading to the lungs. She received six weeks of intravenous antibiotics. She was advised against self-injections with dirty needles. Nine months later, she was readmitted to the hospital for a similar condition, caused in the same way. A different kind of microorganism, which usually resides in the intestine, destroyed another valve on the right side of her heart. Another six-week course of intravenous antibiotics was initiated. She was again admonished not to use dirty needles. She came to the hospital for a third time four months later with a similar condition, caused by yet another kind of microbe. This time the infection had destroyed yet another heart valve: the aortic valve on the left side of the heart. Well, patients can tolerate destruction of heart valves on the right side of the heart, but not the aortic valve. Quickly, and expectedly, she developed heart failure. Her physician asked me to evaluate her for immediate heart surgery. I hesitated to recommend surgery. If past behavior is the best indicator for future behavior, I reasoned, predictably this patient will return to the habit of using intravenous drugs. In the first place, artificial heart valves have a higher propensity to be infected than normal valves, and in the second place, she will have to take a blood thinner reliably for the rest of her life. I shared with her physician my doubts about her future behavior and compliance with the treatment.

"She is only 32," he argued vehemently. "I will convince her to be a good girl from now on." His tone was confident.

She received an artificial heart valve in the aortic area, completed a full antibiotic course, was given instructions about the use of the blood thinner, and was told never again to self-inject with dirty needles. Three weeks and $50,000 later, she was brought dead to the emergency room because of heart arrest. An autopsy showed the $10,000 valve to be infected and clotted.

In a recent study entitled "Survival after In-Hospital Cardiopulmonary Arrest of Noncritically Ill Patients," published in *Chest*, in September 1994, Dr. R. Berger and associates[9] of the University of Kentucky asked whether old age by itself was an important factor. He stated in the article,

> The rising health care costs and the ethical and economic implications of cardiopulmonary resuscitation (CPR) have generated interest in defining criteria to predict the appropriateness of CPR in specific patients. Age has been proposed as one such criterion.

The study included 255 patients who met the criteria. Of these, 52% were initially successfully resuscitated and 11% survived to discharge (28 patients). Four percent of the group (10 patients) were alive for two years. The 28 patients discharged alive resumed their previous ways of life. Age, by itself, was not a factor in determining outcome in this group of relatively healthy individuals. The authors concluded, "Whether in-hospital CPR in noncritical care areas is cost-effective is an issue that society at large must eventually decide." This study further confirms that the state of ill health is more important than old age in determining the outcome of treatment. A more recent review of 11 studies by Dr. Rogove and associates confirmed these guidelines.[10]

Ultimately, procedures for setting limits for futile, marginally effective, or inappropriate care require all of the following: treatment standards from organized medicine, a social consensus, statutory framework, case law, and ultimately, the exercise of the physicians' professional responsibility. Also, these decisions have to be subject to the patient's expressed preferences and convictions, and should never be based solely or predominantly upon the patient's age.

NOTES

1. K Ritchie, "Mental Status Examination of an Exceptional Case of Longevity," *British Journal of Psychiatry*, 166 (1995), 229–235.
2. U Gleichmann, H. Mannebach, BH Seggewi, KG Kleikamp, and R Korfer, "Treatment of Cardiovascular Disease on the Elderly in Germany," *American Journal of Geriatric Cardiology*, 4 (1995), 34–41.
3. J McCue, "The Naturalness of Dying," *Journal of the American Medical Association*, 273 (1995), 1039–1043.
4. P Aries, *The Hour of Our Death*. (New York: Vintage Books, 1981).
5. RD Lamm, *America in Decline*. (Denver, CO: Center for Public Policy and Contemporary Issues, 1990).
6. D Callahan, "Necessity, Futility and the Good Society," *Journal of the Geriatric Society*, 42 (1994), 866–867.
7. D Callahan, *Setting Limits: Medical Goals in an Aging Society*. (New York: Simon and Schuster, 1993).
8. D Callahan, "Limiting Health Care for the Old." In: *Aging and Ethics*, N Jecker, ed. (Totowa, NJ: Humana Press, 1991), pp. 225–226.
9. R Berger and M Kelly, "Survival after In-Hospital Cardiopulmonary Arrest of Non-Critically Ill Patients," *Chest*, 106 (1994), 872–879.
10. HJ Rogove, P Safar, K Sutton-Tyrrel, and JS Abramson, "Brain Resuscitation Clinical Trial and 11 Study Groups: Old Age Does Not Negate Good Cerebral Outcome after Cardiopulmonary Resuscitation; Analysis from the Brain Resuscitation Clinical Trials," *Critical Care Medicine*, 23 (1995), 18–25.

Chapter 9

How Our Dying Can Help the Living

Life, if well used, is long enough.
—Seneca De Trivitate (in *Vitae* II:49)

DISCOVERING NEW LIFE BY CONFRONTING DEATH

As strange as it may sound, my experience with cancer has been enlightening and enlivening. Others may have found cancer to be an awful thing, a curse to be dispelled, a nightmare to be fought. The occurrence of my cancer, on the other hand, has taught me who I am and who I am capable of becoming. It brought discipline into my life. It enabled me to look back, and it showed me the price I had to pay to rise to the top. Throughout my professional career, there were times when I did not care who I was stepping on, if, in the process, I could reach the stars. It did not matter if there were victims as long as I was declared victor.

Cancer has changed all this. I rediscovered my wonderful family. I wish we had had more laughs and fewer confrontations in years past, but now I cherish every minute I spend with them and with my one-year-old grandson, Max. With every passing day, I derive more joy out of life than I ever dreamed I would. I am thankful for every day, for the beautiful sunrises and sunsets, for the birds, the skies, the evening breezes, and for every little pleasure that life brings with it. I am grateful for the time I spend with my wife, Laila, who drives me to work every morning and home at the end of the day. I am grateful for every meal, every smile, every laugh, and every expression of friendship. Most of all, I am grateful for the little nameless, unremembered acts of kindness and love.

I do not have to fight cancer; I am grateful for it. Yes, two major surgeries and radiation in between brought with them considerable physical pain, but that is one price for being human, thank God. The deeper the wound, the tougher the scar.

THE COLLISION OF TECHNOLOGY AND HUMAN VALUES

In the news media, it is customary to refer to patients dying of cancer as if they have lost an arduous battle or as if they have displayed enormous courage in their fight with the disease. I am neither a fighter nor a hero for having cancer; I am merely human. The one thing that cancer has taught me is how fragile we all are. It is part of the human condition. It made me think about the finish line, and I discovered that as a society, we are doing a poor job meeting our fate. We are wasting billions of dollars just to buy a miserable end, so that more of us can have a Tithonus-like exit, a fate worse than death. It need not be this way—clearly, there must be a better way, and it is within our grasp. We have to rediscover that death is naturally inevitable. We need to prepare for it, accept it, and even welcome it.

NATURAL DEATH VERSUS TREATMENT TO DEATH

The fact that, technically, all Americans can have access to the latest in technology regardless of class, color, or race has been hailed as the living example of substantive social justice in America. On the other hand, when death is imminent, the way patients are treated varies enormously from patient to patient, and depends on the patient's education, level of understanding, and beliefs. Interestingly, some studies suggest that the better educated patients are more likely to demand less intervention at the close of life. The wishes of the family and the physician's bias also influence treatment. Even if we had all the resources to treat everybody to death, the wholesale application of high technology at the end of life would not be just. Performing invasive procedures on someone who does not have the capacity to consent or refuse can be justified only if that intervention has a reasonable chance of benefiting the patient or restoring his or her health and independence. Love for high technology and fear of lawsuits cannot stand as justification for the torture of hordes of decent people and the waste of society's valuable and limited resources. Neither we in the United States, nor anybody else in the world has unlimited resources to sustain for any length of time the squandering of resources at the end of life. Leland Kaiser, a noted contemporary philosopher warned, "The final crisis on this planet is the collision of technology and human values.... Technology has no ethics, but the people who employ the technology have to develop ethical standards for its use." What we need is a public policy, developed by ordinary laypeople with advice from lawyers, theologians, ethicists, and physicians, and enacted into law by Congress. This consortium needs to establish guidelines for the wise and rational allocation of resources at the end of life. This has been best expressed in a statement made by Lord Mustill of the Judicial Council of the House of Lords in England in the context of the Tony Bland case (the young man in a persistent vegetative state, whose treating physicians wanted to discontinue treatment) referred to earlier.

> The whole matter cries out for exploration in depth by Parliament and then for the establishment by legislation not only of a new set of ethically and intellectually consistent needs, distinct from general criminal law, but also of a sound pro-

> cedural framework within which the rules can be applied to individual cases.[1]

Is our Congress capable of debating and enacting such laws? We Americans have been accused of being too individualistic to see beyond our own self-interests. To put it bluntly, we are so self-centered that we cannot function as one society working together for the common good. Even so, it is in our best individual interests to rid ourselves of the fear of being treated to death, a course that will bankrupt our families and future generations in the process. Unfortunately, end-of-life treatment issues are so complex, so emotionally charged, and so controversial that they do not lend themselves to sound bites, slogans, or headlines. Also, they can be readily politicized to scare people off and achieve voter support. This is too immense a subject to be reduced to serve as a political tool.

THE IMPERSONAL USE OF TECHNOLOGY VERSUS THE PERSONAL TREATMENT OF THE PATIENT

The medical community has, by and large, refrained from discussing these issues with the public. We physicians owe it to our patients to share, in detail, what is meant by *coma*, *vegetative state*, and *terminal illness*; what the treatment entails and its possible cost and outcomes. We owe it to them, not as a matter of courtesy, but as a duty, if we are to be deserving of their trust. The birth of the Euthanasia Society of America and the emergence of the "death" doctor are living testimonials to our failure as a profession to carry our duty of educating the public about life-and-death issues and to fulfill their desires to exit life with dignity and respect. The breathtaking pace of science and technology has caused us to forget the "personal" treatment of the patient. "The application of the principles of science to the diagnosis and treatment of disease is only one limited aspect of medical practice. The treatment of disease may be entirely impersonal; the care of a patient must be completely personal," as we were once reminded by Dr. Francis Peabody, the noted Boston Internist in a series of lectures entitled *The Care of the Patient* in 1927.[2] There is no medical, legal, ethical, or moral justification for the use of unnecessary interventions in hopelessly ill patients. This type of intervention constitutes an impersonal use of technology—not the personal care of the patient. This serious failure of the medical community is underscored by the fact that a book describing how to end one's own life, *Final Exit*, was a best-selling book in the United States. Do reasonably informed people have to scream in our faces to interrupt our relentless high-tech pursuit to preserve an existence that, left undisturbed by high technology, would end in peace? That is not, and should not be, the mission of medicine. I can hear the poet Rainer Maria Rilke[3] screaming at us:

> Just another moment left!
> But what they are doing to me, they're always
>   taking the rope
> and cutting it!
> The other day it was so good!
> And there was already a little bit of eternity
>   in my intestines.
> They hold this spoon in to me,
> this spoon of life.
> Well I want it, and I don't
> I'd better throw up.
> I know that life is just fantastic fun,
> and the world is a foamy mug;
> but I don't really get strength from it,
> it just makes me dizzy.
> It heals others, it makes me sick.
> Grasp that some can't stand it.
> For at least a thousand years now
> I'll have to fast.

GUIDELINES TO ENSURE QUALITY OF DEATH

First and foremost, a generally acceptable definition of medical futility must be agreed upon between the medical community and the public at large. Clear and unambiguous practice guidelines regarding treatment of terminal illness should be developed for universal use by the medical community. The definition of *medical futility* cannot and must not be left to ethicists—philosophers whose abstract pronouncements have little relevance to the care of the sick, the suffering, and the dying. Our leading ethicists espouse views that can be so far off that they would never be reconciled. On one hand, Dr. Veatch, the Dean of Kennedy School of Ethics, maintains that keeping a brainless child on a ventilator is not medical futility and that doctors should not be allowed, and for that matter are incapable, to decide whether a medical treatment is futile. On the other extreme, Dr. Daniel Callahan, the Dean of the Hastings Institute, maintains that discussions of medical futility cannot be dissociated from medical necessity and that it is not fitting to consider bypass surgery for older people who have completed a normal life-span.

Guidelines in the United States are necessary to reconcile these opposing views. Such guidelines were developed in Denmark, in 1985, and in many other Western communities. This would alleviate physicians' fear of litigation. I believe that the concept of *upper-brain death* should be adopted as one definition of death, as it is in many European countries. The definition stipulates that permanent loss of consciousness and cognition constitutes death, and any further treatment will, therefore, be considered futile. This concept is strongly supported by the recent philosophical review by Lizza[4] and the critical review by Halevy and Brody.[5] Furthermore, I propose for the purposes of future deliberation that treatment of the following conditions be considered futile treatment:

1. End-stage disease afflicting two organ systems (heart–lung–liver–kidney) such as:

- End-stage heart disease + end-stage kidney disease
- End-stage heart disease + end-stage lung disease
- End-stage endocrine disorder + end-stage heart or kidney disease.

2. Patients with advanced dementia (with loss of capacity to recognize self, others, and the environment) who, in addition, have an end-stage disease of one major system (e.g., end-stage heart disease)
3. Disseminated cancer not responsive to chemotherapy or radiation therapy.
4. Advanced systemic (i.e., throughout the body), uncontrollable infection complicated with end-stage organ failure, including AIDS.
5. Advanced senility, decrepitude, total dependence associated with end-stage disease of one major system.

Under these circumstances, high-technology assistance devices, major surgical procedures, and major interventional procedures should not be applied unless they are strictly used to alleviate pain and suffering, such as in the case of amputation. Laboratory tests, antibiotics, and blood transfusions would no longer be considered viable treatment options. No resuscitative measures would be undertaken—even in the event of cardiopulmonary arrest. Terminal pneumonia would not be treated.

I realize that this list needs further examination and refinement. Input needs to be solicited from professional organizations, another conglomeration such as the Congress of Clinical Societies, and these proposals need to be debated in public forums.

THE "IMPOLITIC" ISSUE OF DEATH

Unfortunately, our political system has been incapable of tackling the difficult issues related to life and death. In one of his editorials, Arthur Caplan, Ph.D., an ethicolegal expert from Boston University, described America as a wasteful, extremely individualistic, technology-driven, death-denying society. Death was not always denied in Western civilization. According to the Greek philosopher Epicurus: "For the common man or woman, death, the most awful of evils, is really nothing, for so long as we are, death has not come, and when it has come ... we are not." But for our contemporary legislators, the mention of death is the most awful of evils and can ruin a career in politics. When Richard Lamm, the former governor of Colorado quoted earlier, ran for Congress, he brought up the issue of waste of medical resources at the end of life. He suggested that society had to take measures to prevent this waste. His statement was used by his political rivals to instill fears that Mr. Lamm was against the old, the frail, and the disabled. Mr. Lamm fell from grace and was defeated. That was a cautionary tale: Never again would any politician who holds or aspires to hold office bring up the question of curtailing the costs of treatment of terminal illness. The issue is very much subject to manipulation and misinterpretation and, therefore, misuse by political rivals. Futile medical care at the end of life has become the tar baby that officials have avoided like the plague. And whenever the issue is raised, the powerful AARP (American Association of Retired People) lobby will cry "foul" and claim discrimination against the old, the frail, the disabled, and the weak in our society. This subject, as controversial as it may be, is a ticking time bomb. It cries out for public policy brought forward by a grassroots coalition. This book is an invitation for one such effort, but do not depend on politicians to get the ball rolling. As long as there are no term limits for legislators' services, our politicians will tiptoe around the subject, hoping that it will go away. The dismally useless "Patient Self-Determination Act," enacted by Congress in 1990, was an effort to defuse the issue.[6,7] The act stipulates that patients should be informed about their rights to refuse treatment whenever they are admitted to a hospital. The right of a competent person to refuse treatment was recognized early in this century in this country, but so far, the self-determination act has had very limited effect on the practice of medicine. How can an elderly patient, or any patient, comprehend all possible scenarios that may follow a procedure or procedures that may come up during a hospital admission? What benefit can be derived from engaging in a cold, routine conversation about life-and-death issues at a time when we want the patient to harness all energies and good spirits on behalf of a planned procedure or surgery? Bringing up details about life-and-death issues at this time may even represent a cruel gesture. These difficulties are well articulated by Drs. Jeffrey S. Tobias and colleagues of the Meyerstein Institute of Clinical Oncology, Middlesex Hospital in London in an article, "Fully Informed Consent Can Be Needlessly Cruel," November 1993,[8] in the *British Medical Journal*. In all cases, it reflects poor taste. In a recent issue of the *Journal of Medical Ethics*, I encountered an interesting article entitled "Preventive Ethics."[9] The authors of this article recommend that treating physicians discuss the possibility of brain death with every pregnant woman in the event that she should be involved in a fatal accident, and the dilemma of whether to sustain the patient's heart and lung function to sustain the fetus presents itself. I find this to be an extreme example of poor taste that borders on absurdity.

It is unrealistic to think that physicians can cover every possible contingency with every patient everywhere and at all times. And if it were possible, I wonder whether it is at all decent. Where is the good old patient–doctor relationship? Physicians need to ask themselves, "Who are we? Slaves of medical etiquette or disciples of medicine?"

THE PRESENT LIVING WILL: NOT A VIABLE GUIDELINE TO ENSURE QUALITY OF DEATH

In its present form, the living will that pertains when death is imminent and unavoidable is a new testimonial to the failure of the medical community to live up to its sacred mission. Why on earth should anyone execute a document asking physicians not to continue to invade his body when the intervention is not indicated and imposes an unnecessary burden on the patient, his or her family, and society?

In their present forms, with their scope focused totally on terminal illness *in extremis*, living wills are meaningless. Responsible physicians do not need living wills to prevent ineffective treatments from being given. Treatment should cease once it is determined that the treatment is useless. Physicians should not need notarized documents with two witnesses in order to withhold or withdraw treatment when the patient's status proclaims what Christina Rossetti described in "song" in 1862:

> I shall not see the shadows,
> I shall not feel the rain,
> I shall not hear the nightingale sing on,
> as if in pain; and dreaming through the twilight
> That doth not rise nor set,
> Happy I may remember and Happy may forget.

The scope and application of living wills should change. Advance directives may be utilized as an expression of one's personal preferences and might address the treatment of potentially reversible diseases such as pneumonia. Additionally, they could direct the use of life-saving measures in the context of

> advanced weakness with total dependence, senile decay, accident, heart problems, or similar situations that have led to severe invalidity that he (or she) would become permanently incapable of taking care of himself (or herself) physically and mentally ...

The foregoing is taken verbatim from Denmark's living will.[10] These conditions do not, by themselves, represent futility and ordinarily should never be considered reason enough to unilaterally limit treatment by the physician. But for those of us who value personal dignity and independence more than an outstretched existence, this quality of life is not acceptable.

THE EXTRAVAGANT HEALTH-CARE SYSTEM IN THE UNITED STATES

No other country on earth devotes so much energy and money to take care of the critically ill as does the United States. True, we have more victims of violence and AIDS in our hospitals compared to other countries, yet this cannot justify five times as many intensive-care beds (relative to population size) compared to the Western Hemisphere country with the next highest ICU bed count. Many more ICU beds do not help us live longer or healthier than people in England. Whether we spend $50 billion or $100 billion on futile care is immaterial. These billions are spent to purchase misery, and these precious billions of dollars are taken away from our children and from future generations. As our society ages, the demand on high technology will increase unless we change our methods of applying high-tech care. We need to learn to discipline ourselves and to allocate our resources wisely. Unless that is done, our nation will face a generational war. In the near future, fewer working people will be supporting more and more of the retired, the senile, and the decrepit.

I wonder whether I would have been able to write this book were it not for the fact that I am over 60 years old and have cancer. Sooner or later, I shall join those of mankind who have passed away. We cannot but ask ourselves: Can we achieve wisdom and peace in our unrelenting combat with the aging process? Much of the progress in medical science has not produced vitality and happiness, and the fountain of youth remains as elusive as ever. Will we ever temper our unending pursuit of immortality? Will we elderly show generosity and consideration for future generations or each be fixed on his or her fate? How many societal resources are we going to exhaust as we exit from this life? Will each of us cost the system hundreds of thousands of wasted dollars as we leave?

A society in which each individual competes for limited resources without regard to others is a society that will bring itself to its knees and is headed for collapse. Members of the society, young and old, cannot behave as if they are entitled to their rights without making a return to the society at large. And, we, the older generation that has enjoyed the blessings that our nation has bestowed upon us, must lead the way.

HEALTH-CARE REFORM: LET OUR ELDERS LEAD THE WAY

Aristotle defined a civilized society as a group of individuals who enjoy being together, are useful to each other, and have as their prime aim the common good. How could we, the elderly, be part of this formula? We could begin by initiating the discussion of establishing priorities for medical care. First and foremost, we have to eliminate the wasteful high-tech brinkmanship that only distorts and prolongs the process of dying. End-of-life treatment policies will affect all members of society, but inevitably it will affect primarily the elderly segment. The acceptance of death must be part of dealing with our humanity. A peaceful death must become the natural conclusion of a meaningful life. It is an imperative for the renewal and rejuvenation of our society. If we, the older members of society, can help build the momentum necessary to tackle this difficult subject, we would be making a return to society at large, for the common good.

It must be clear that rationing of health care should never be at the sole discretion of the physician. As health-care resources become more limited, pressure will mount on physicians to unilaterally ration health care. It must be emphasized that it is society's responsibility to set health-care priorities, although physicians' organizations should have extensive input. For instance, establishing priorities for admission to intensive care, when circumstances dictate, is required from, and expected of, experienced physicians. In fact, Florida courts found a hospital liable for negligence in the case of *Von Stetina v. Florida Hospital* when the patient was denied admission to intensive care in the place of other, less deserving patients.[11]

We already have a policy of rationing in one area of medicine. Establishing nationwide priorities has worked fairly well in the case of organ transplants. The number of potential recipients far exceeds the number of potential donors; triage in this case is both legal and ethical. Despite the clear necessity for rationed care, and despite the role physicians must play in enacting this, physicians must be, and should remain, their patients' advocates at all times. This sacred relationship must be preserved in any system that society elects to adopt. In Denmark, practice guidelines regarding futility and end-of-life issues are formulated by a committee comprised of 17 individuals, predominantly laypeople, with almost equal representation from both genders. The committee is guided by public opinion polls and also consults with physicians, nurses, social workers and chaplains, as well as ethicists and law professionals. It advises the Parliament about guidelines on the definition of death, allocation of scarce resources (including life-sustaining treatment), as well as other health issues. The committee also has the duty to disseminate information and educational material. Can we agree on a commission composed in a similar way to study our collective values and make recommendations for appropriate legislative action? In this way, the judgment of a committee comprised of a number of chosen laypeople is used to satisfy the substitute judgment standard for the society as a whole.

A common criticism of doctors is that they often provide patients with fraudulent representations that lead to unfulfillable and unrealistic expectations about the efficacy of a futile treatment. Unjustified hope leads to unreasonable demands. This criticism is not groundless and, in many cases, is justified. Medical schools have to take seriously training of young physicians in how to communicate with their patients clearly, truthfully, and patiently. The moral weight of the doctor–patient relationship must be taken very seriously. Professional integrity should never be overshadowed by vague notions of professional authority.

I remind my students of the most poignant demonstration of

a doctor–patient relationship: lying on a table is a naked patient, overtaken by anxiety and anticipation, overburdened by the enigma of his illness, in the presence of a fully dressed, calm, informed, secure physician asking questions and giving instructions. In this scene, the patient should be viewed as king and the physician his devoted servant. This captures the essence of a doctor–patient relationship. Neither passion for technology nor the fear of the legal shutters should influence this sacred bond in which the patient's interests must remain paramount.

Conversations with patients and families in distress are never easy: A mix of patient ignorance or confusion about what can be achieved, as well as the inability of the physician to express himself clearly, impedes discourse between patient and physician.

Another impediment to this relationship occurs when physicians obtain their medical information about ethics from abstract philosopher–ethicists, or when they are not informed at all. How can a basic training such as abstract concepts of autonomy, beneficence, and nonmaleficence be realistically related to a dying patient? Decisions from patients and families are usually based upon their understanding of incomplete, simplified, brief, biased information from a physician. A patient about to be placed on a ventilator for the treatment of pneumonia does not have the thousands of medical articles at his disposal to read and evaluate before making his or her decision. The principle *primum non nocere* (first do no harm) could have been applicable to ancient medicine but not to high-tech interventions. Every procedure a physician performs, every survey he or she undertakes, every medicine he or she prescribes has hazards, side effects, and sometimes serious complications. I have great respect and even reverence for theoretical ethicists. I learn from their writing, although I must confess sometimes I have difficulty understanding them. However, in the world of intensive care, or when life is at stake, I have little use for theoretical ethics. It troubles me when a highly respected ethicist (e.g., Dr. Veatch) recommends that a permanently comatose 87 year old, or a brainless newborn be maintained on a ventilator in the name of justice. What about social responsibility? How could a doctor justify an expensive treatment with no hope of any benefit, such as in these two cases?

The definition of *futility* is the prime responsibility of organized medicine. Not groundlessly, physicians are asked, why is the question of futility important now? Why did doctors resist attempts to take unconscious patients off the ventilator 20 years ago and now are championing the drive? It may seem bizarre and self-serving for physicians to carry the banner of establishing priorities for medical care when they avoided similar efforts before. Frankly, because of escalating costs, physicians can no longer evade this issue. No one could have predicted the enormous escalation of health-care costs over the past two to three decades. With the wide use of CPR and artificial ventilation, medical miracles became possible. But who would have predicted that thousands of mindless victims would be left in persistent vegetative states or comas?

The breathtaking progress of medical science is quickly eliminating acute disease as the main killer. Most cases of pneumonia are cured. Acute heart attacks, which were 50% lethal to victims before intensive care, now kill less than 10% of their victims. Now patients live longer and die slower, many in isolation, confusion, anguish, and pain.

Doctors, self-proclaimed advocates of life (without having a chance to review the Hippocratic oath to discover that terminal comfort is also part of their duty), went about fighting death, preserving life, and defending any vestige of it. But physicians alone cannot establish guidelines for life-and-death issues.

LET US SUBJECT FUTILE CARE TO A PUBLIC FORUM

Yes, the economic imperatives are so great, and our country has realized that the wild application of technology in cases of futility or marginal utility must be tamed. Yes, the rapid growth of managed care is applying new, sometimes unhealthy, pressures to limit expensive care. But generational responsibility, rationality, and social conscience more than any other motives necessitate that we put an end to this madness. There are limits to what can be expected of medicine. Not all care can or will be beneficial. The vexing questions about when to withhold, when to withdraw, and whom to resuscitate are part of the clinical landscape. They have spawned a troubling debate among abstract thinkers, but ultimately the limits have to be set through public consensus, under the guidance of primary-care physicians and specialists. Unfortunately, these weighty issues have been conspicuously left out of national deliberations about health-care reform. This troubling phenomenon must be remedied as soon as possible or the consequences will be disastrous.

It is time to reform health care without sacrificing the core value of medicine. Our nation is in the process of rediscovering the values that made this country great. Let us resurrect the values that made our medicine great: (1) a strong, trusting doctor–patient relationship in which the moral authority of the physician is neither overlooked nor undervalued, and in which the doctor's devotion to his patient's best interests is never suspect; (2) scientifically superior, technologically advanced medicine that is applied judiciously, as well as skillfully.

In the context of futile medical care, we need to establish unified, proactive CPR procedures based upon our extensive current knowledge of outcomes. We should also be prepared to modify the guidelines as new technologies develop or as research clarifies some of the treatment outcomes of interventions for us.

In order for these changes to be effective, full participation from the lay community, legal authorities, theologians, ethicists, and legislators is needed. Yes, it is the physicians who have the responsibility to guide the development of these procedural guidelines, whereas it is society's responsibility through its elected institutions to finalize and empower these guidelines. It is customary for medical ethicists to promote the idea of autonomy as the basis for asking the patient to choose the way he or she wishes to be treated at the end of life. The basic premise of autonomy (according to Kant) is, however, that people participate in designing the laws that govern them. Therefore, society's role in developing these guidelines should reinforce, and not undermine, our individual autonomy in a democratic society.

ABANDONING ABSOLUTES IN MEDICAL CARE

The whole subject matter cries out for establishing standards, procedures, and protocols that take into account the standard of "reasonable probabilities" rather than absolutes in the practice of medicine. For example, the likelihood of a 1.1-pound cocaine baby surviving, even with prolonged intensive care, is less than 10% and at a cost of $1 million dollars. If this baby survives, the chances are high that it will be mentally retarded and subject to multiple medical problems. The weight of these facts directs us to use our efforts and resources to save babies of 2.2 pounds or more; these babies have an 80% chance of surviving at a cost of $50,000 each and a very good chance of becoming healthy. The same principles can be applied at the end of life and for the application of resuscitation efforts.

THE NEED TO PUT A PRICE ON HUMAN LIFE

It might be argued that such an exercise stifles medical progress and would bury our hopes and dreams of future medical progress in the green hash of cash. The argument goes on to say that human life, whatever its definition, is priceless, and that whether it costs a few cents or several millions of dollars to save a life is immaterial. The argument further claims that while the cost-effective syndrome masquerades as prudence, it will have the effect of demeaning the value of human life by placing a price tag on it. Although there are obvious truths to this argument, it must be emphasized that no country and no civilization, whatever their wealth, can afford to waste resources by trying to expand the limits of life beyond reason at both ends: babies who weigh less than 500 grams and citizens over 100 years of age. It is imperative that a society set its priorities straight.

A COMMISSION DEDICATED TO DEAL WITH END-OF-LIFE TREATMENT

The time has come for a national commission, properly selected from community leaders, to be empowered to develop goals and procedures for treatment near the end of life. Let it be named the Quinlan Commission in honor of Karen Ann Quinlan, whose mother was the first to challenge the high-tech maintenance of unconscious existence. The commission should be relatively independent and broadly representative, but should not be seen as representative of any particular special interest group. It should be appointed in a way similar to that of Justices of the Supreme Court. It must be insulated from political pressure or interference by lobbyists. It may work with small work groups that interface with medical authorities, legal scholars, ethics specialists, economists, and theologians representing dominant religions and scientists. The commission will have access to opinion polls, health statistics, and other pertinent information. The commission should develop substitute judgment standards for care of the incompetent and the terminally ill. The commission should be charged with the duty to recommend, review, and modify health-care legislation and establish priorities for medical care, including home care and hospice care. This commission will represent society's will, in addition to disseminating a uniformly designed "living will" that has practical applicability and legal power to limit treatment when death is near rather than imminent, in order to limit unnecessary and unwanted care at the end of life. In addition, the commission should establish strategies and instructional materials to disseminate information and educate the public at large. A similar commission was established in Denmark in 1988 and one in Sweden recently. This Swedish commission was able to establish the following "difficult priorities in health care":

1. That all human beings have equal worth
2. That society has a duty to protect the weakest and most vulnerable among its citizens
3. That cost-efficiency and maximum return to society for the amount of money spent on health care should prevail.

The German wife of a friend of mine has told me that a similar commission with a consensus viewpoint on health care at the end of life can never be implemented in America. She stated that Americans are too individualistic to come to a consensus on such issues. She noted that although our Constitution begins, "We the people," we Americans are so heterogeneous and so self-centered that we have lost our sense of community and of the "common good" that binds other societies together. I resent her reasoning, not only because I love America and am proud to be an American, but also because, if she is right, it will mean that we are a nation on the decline. No force is as powerful in bringing a civilization to its knees and hastening its collapse as a bunch of self-centered grabbers, cheaters, and usurpers of the public good. I do not believe we Americans are this way. I feel that the use of futile, high technology at the end of life was inevitable for a time. As it always is with Americans, fads come and go; fascination with high technology has been a fad carried to its extremes. A correction is overdue and must be forthcoming.

Although there is no religion, heritage, tradition, race, or belief that unites us in America, the fact that we are Americans is a force powerful enough to bring us together. If you do not believe me, just remember that when you travel anywhere in the world, Americans become instant friends with other Americans. Something compelling unites us—a force beyond description. Our love of country, our pride in being Americans is the glue that keeps us together and gives us the energy to dream about a better tomorrow for future generations.

More than 150 years ago, Alexis de Tocqueville, in his immortal classic, *Democracy in America*,[12] wrote:

> ... when an American asks for the cooperation of his fellow citizens, it is seldom refused; and I have often seen if offered spontaneously, and with great goodwill.... All this is not in contradiction to what I have said before on the subject of individualism. The two things are so far from combating with each other than I can see how they agree. Equality of condition, while it makes men feel their independence, shows them their own weakness; they are free, but exposed to a thousand accidents; and experience soon teaches them that although they do not habitually require the assistance of others, a time almost always comes when they cannot do without it ... (p. 185)

The time has come for the older people in our society to band together and lead the way toward a secure future. In order to achieve this, we must, among other things, stop the wasteful allocation of resources at the extremes of life. We are an aging nation, and health care needs for the elderly will grow steadily into the next century. We have a responsibility to guide our country in its quest to reallocate its expensive medical technology wisely. If we continue to add the cost of futile care at the end of life to our increasing health-care needs, the time will come when the younger generation will not be able to cope with our demands. They may in these circumstances feel compelled to abandon us.

Our generation is comprised of heroes who valiantly defended America during the Second World War and beyond. We are the owners of America's great scientific revolution, and among us are the architects of America's quest to become the unquestionable beacon of decency in a savage world.

It is our sacred duty to lead our beloved country through the political minefield, developing the necessary laws and procedures to stop the needless waste at the end of life. In the process, we will have, as individuals, preserved our dignity as we exit this planet.

SUMMARY OF PROPOSED SOLUTIONS

The following list summarizes the contributions needed from various contingents in our society to arrive at guidelines near the end of life:

1. *Duties of the medical societies*
   - Establish guidelines for medical futility or marginal utility
   - Develop guidelines for out-of-hospital CPR and in-hospital CPR
   - Develop guidelines for the withholding and withdrawal of care
   - Review the definition of brain death
2. *Duties of a laypeople blue-ribbon commission*
   - Review medical guidelines developed by the medical establishment, debate them, modify if necessary and recommend their adoption
   - Disseminate public education about health care issues
   - Propose laws for adoption of guidelines
   - Monitor the implementation of policies and procedures
3. *Duties of Congress*
   - Enact laws for the universal adoption of guidelines
   - Enact laws to establish the procedures for adoption of guidelines
   - Adopt a uniform health-care decision bill and a uniform living will
   - Establish a central registry for those who execute a will
   - Require health-care professionals to consult the registry on a regular basis
   - Ensure that the will is legally binding within reasonable limits

Albert Einstein once wrote, "Strange is our situation here upon Earth. Each of us comes for a short visit, not knowing why, yet sometimes to divine purpose.... One thing we do know, is that man is here for the sake of other men."[13]

All of us will someday face death. The way we die and the guidelines or lack of guidelines for death with dignity will either bankrupt future generations or allow us to invest in those generations to come. It is my sincere hope that this book will help all Americans make the right choice for themselves and loved ones to forego the relentless pursuit of high-tech prolongation of the process of dying.

NOTES

1. Lord Mustill, Letter in *Airedale NHS Trust* (Respondents) v. Bland (acting by his guardian ad litem) (Appellant). Judgment, February 4, 1993, pp. 33–48.
2. FW Peabody, "The Care of the Patient," *Journal of the American Medical Association*, 88 (1927), 877–881.
3. RM Rilke, *Selected Poems of Rainer Maria Rilke: A Translation from German and Commentary by Robert Bly*. (New York: Harper & Row, 1979), p. 119.
4. JP Lizza, "Persons and Death: What's Metaphysically Wrong with Our Current Statutory Definition of Death?" *Journal of Medicine and Philosophy*, 18 (1993), 351–374.
5. A Halevy and B Brody, "Brain Death: Reconciling Definitions, Criteria, and Tests," *Annals of Internal Medicine*, 19 (1993), 519–525.
6. "Efficacy of the Patient Self-Determination Act." (Death and Dying, *Biolaw*, University Publications of America, 1994), p. 171.
7. EJ Emanuel, DW Weingerb, R Gonin, LR Hummel, and LL Emmanuel, "How Well Is the Patient Self-Determination Act Working?" *American Journal of Medicine*, 95 (1993), 619–628.
8. JS Tobias and RL Soulami, "Fully Informed Consent Can Be Needlessly Cruel," *British Medical Journal*, 307 (1993), 1435–1439.
9. L Forrow, RM Arnold, and LS Parker, "Preventive Ethics: Expanding the Horizons of Clinical Ethics," *Journal of Clinical Ethics*, 4 (1993), 287–293.
10. "Public Uses Denmark's Living Will," *British Medical Journal*, 306 (1993), 413–415.

11. MA Strosberg, IO Fein, and JD Carroll, eds., *Rationing of Medical Care for the Critically Ill* (Washington, DC: Brookings Institution, Dialogs in Public Policy, 1986).
12. Alexis de Tocqueville, *Democracy in America: The Henry Reeve Text*, vol. 2. (New York: Vintage Books, 1945).
13. A Einstein, "From Living Philosophies." In *Living Philosophies*, Clifton Fadiman, ed. (New York: Doubleday, 1990), p. 3. (Original published in 1931.)

Chapter 10

The Birth of the Living Will

An Attempt to Direct Our Mortal Destiny

> Just as I select my ship as I am about to go on a voyage—so I shall choose my death when I am about to depart from life.
>
> —Lucius Annaeus Seneca, c. 4 B.C.–A.D. 65

THE LIVING WILL: AN INDICTMENT OF PHYSICIANS' ETHICAL PARALYSIS

As mentioned earlier, the accelerated development of new methods to reverse death and sustain life left the medical community totally paralyzed to handle the consequences of high technology in medicine. Doctors declared their proper position as patients' advocates without fully understanding what that position entailed. They were not prepared to consider the termination of ineffective, countertherapeutic measures, even if the patient or family requested it. This attitude, prevailing at this time, was exemplified by the testimony of Dr. Morse in the case of Ms. Karen Ann Quinlan, who at age 21 suffered a cardiopulmonary arrest in 1975 as a result of accidentally ingesting a combination of prescription medications and alcohol. After the cardiopulmonary arrest and coma, Quinlan was in a persistent vegetative state, with loss of all meaningful cognitive brain functions. Her parents sought permission from the court to let her die naturally by discontinuation of mechanical ventilation, which they thought was sustaining her hopeless condition. Dr. Morse, Ms. Quinlan's treating physician, justified that maintaining the permanently unconscious Ms. Quinlan on a ventilator was the right treatment and that he had a duty to provide it. Ms. Quinlan's parents prevailed. Karen Ann Quinlan died nine years later, without regaining consciousness. The public has attributed to physicians various motives to account for this perverse attitude: financial greed; a passion for technology that leads doctors to use invasive procedures to excess; insensitivity to the suffering they may inflict on patients; or fear of malpractice litigation, resulting in physicians' eagerness to suggest all treatments that have the slightest possibility of improving the patient's condition.

While the medical community was responding tentatively to these issues, a momentum was gaining among the general populace. This grassroots movement metamorphosed into political action. Living wills originated in the "right to die" movement in the United States. In 1967, at a meeting of the Euthanasia Society of America, Luis Kutner, founder and president of the society, first proposed the idea of the living will.[1] Soon, it became clear that the living will was really an expression of the right of self-determination rater than a manifesto for the right to die. Subsequently, the Euthanasia society of America abandoned its traditional advocacy for active euthanasia and directed its efforts more to protect the right of the terminally ill and to promote the living will. The following prototype document was the result:

> Death is as much a reality as birth, growth, maturity, and old age—it is the only certainty of life. If the time comes when I, __________, can no longer take part in decisions for my

> own future, let this statement stand as an expression of my wishes, while I am still of sound mind.
>
> If the situation should arise in which there is no reasonable expectation of my recovery from physical or mental disability, I request that I be allowed to die and not be kept alive by artificial means or "heroic measures." I do not fear death itself as much as the indignities of deterioration, dependence, and hopeless pain. I, therefore, ask that medication be mercifully administered to me to alleviate suffering, even though this may hasten the moment of death.

This pioneering will has the virtues of brevity and simplicity. Clearly, the person executing the will knew what he or she wanted. "I wish to be spared the pain, indignity, and cost of unnecessary care at the end of life." In other words, "I long for an Oedipus-like exit, a graceful exit." Most citizens have experienced the horrors of a prolonged, high-tech death of a loved one, a relative, a friend, a neighbor, or a work associate. In their minds, heroic measures equate with high-technology interventions. "Physical and mental disability" mean loss of independence and the ability to reason.

Not unexpectedly, the intent, spirit, and promise of this will was virtually lost in the feud between doctors, lawyers, theologians, ethicists, families, and society. Doctors viewed it as too ambiguous and nonspecific; lawyers noted its shortcomings regarding the issue of being legally binding; ethicists analyzed it, criticized it, and ostracized it; and families ignored it. Nevertheless, it represented a previous starting point for a society getting tired of the entrenched idea that people should be medically treated to death.

LEGISLATION VINDICATING THIS VITAL ISSUE

In 1976, the California Death Act reaffirmed the patient's right to refuse futile treatment, while exempting physicians from liability. That every human being of adult years and sound mind has a right to determine what shall be done with his own body was affirmed early in this century (see *Schloendorff v. Society of New York Hospitals*, 211 NY 128, 105 NE 93, 1914). The preamble of the California Death Act states:

> The ability of modern technology to prolong life beyond its natural limits can, in some cases, produce no more than precarious or burdensome existence while providing nothing necessary or beneficial to the patient ... thereby enabling physicians to legally withhold or withdraw treatment from an unwilling terminally ill patient ...[2]

Subsequent to the California Death Act, many other states adopted similar acts, such as "The Natural Death Act" and "Advance Directives." The guiding principles in these acts are as follows:

1. A competent patient has the right to refuse treatment. The patient is deemed competent when he or she is able to comprehend, evaluate, and choose between treatments. This underscores the patient's autonomy and the right to "shared decision making."
2. An incompetent patient has the same rights as a competent patient. The right to refuse treatment and the "right to die" are interpreted by the courts to be within the right of liberty and privacy and are included or implied in the Bill of Rights. The act contains a prescribed form of Living Will. For the Instructions to be binding, the declarant should sign the directive at least 14 days after having been diagnosed as suffering from a terminal condition: "which means an incurable condition caused by injury, disease, or illness, which regardless of the application of life-sustaining procedures would, within reasonable medical judgment, produce death, and where the application of life-sustaining procedures serves only to postpone the moment of death of the patient."

The concept of the living will, or advance directive, proposed by Mr. Kutner of the American Euthanasia Society, was popularized after the enactment of the California Natural Death Act. This legal document "directs" health-care professionals in "advance" as to the wishes of a person regarding medical intervention in the event that he or she becomes incompetent. The intention of a "living will" is to prevent unnecessary, intrusive, death postponing intervention at the end of life. Most states require that the document be executed by the patient while he or she is still competent and that it be witnessed. In many states, the "living will" is honored only for a few years, after which it has to be renewed or updated by the patient to remain in effect.

A second-generation form of the living will allows for a durable power of attorney to be granted to someone chosen by the patient. This designated person is given the authority to make medical decisions on behalf of the patient when the latter becomes incompetent or unable to make them.

A CASE OF SUBSTITUTE JUDGMENT

Short of living wills, the courts held to certain standards in order to grant or deny withdrawal of life-supporting measures for incompetent patients. These are:

- The subjective standard
- The substitute judgment standard
- The patient's best-interest standard

The subjective standard requires clear and convincing evidence that the patient would not have wanted to lead a medically sustained existence of unconsciousness or severe infirmity. An example is the *Brophy v. Massachusetts* case of 1986.[3] Mr. Brophy was a fireman who was involved in saving a victim from perishing in a burning truck and transported him to a Boston Hospital. The victim lived for approximately three months in a burn unit. The town of Easton, Massachusetts gave Brophy a medal for his heroic act. Mr. Brophy expressed his regret that the man he had rescued was leading a subhuman, miserable existence and that he would not have wanted a similar fate for himself. Brophy subsequently threw the commendation in the waste basket and explained to his wife, "I should have been five minutes later. It would have been all over for him." Brophy told his bother, "If I am ever like that, just shoot me, pull the plug." Years later, Brophy became permanently unconscious from a stroke. Before he slipped into a coma, one of Brophy's five children visited her father at Goddard Hospital. When Brophy pulled himself up to a half-sitting position in order to kiss his daughter, she scolded him for not lying still. Brophy told his daughter, "If I can't sit up to kiss one of my beautiful daughters, I may as well be six feet under." The court took Mr. Brophy's prior public statement as clear and convincing evidence that he would not have liked to have his vegetative existence sustained. He did not need to execute a living will; Mr. Brophy was allowed to die through the withholding of life-support measures.

THE NEED TO EXECUTE A WILL WHEN YOU ARE WILLING—AND ABLE

By contrast, the U.S. Supreme Court denied the removal of medical support from Nancy Cruzan, the young Missouri lady mentioned earlier, who sustained extensive, irreversible brain injuries in an accident.[4] The Missouri law required, "a clear and convincing evidence" that the patient, while competent prior to the accident, would have desired the discontinuation of medical intervention that would only maintain a permanently unconscious existence. In 1988, the Missouri Supreme Court ruled that no such evidence existed. In a 5–4 decision, the U.S. Supreme Court upheld the Missouri Court decision.[5] The decision, written by Chief Justice Rehnquist, said,

> Missouri requires that evidence of the incompetent's wishes as to the withdrawal of treatment be proved by clear and convincing evidence.[6,7] The question then is whether the U.S. Constitution forbids the establishment of this procedural requirement ... the state has "a general interest" in protecting life ... Justice Rehnquist went on to emphasize the due process clause requires the state not to repose judgment on these matters with anyone but the patient herself. Close family members may have a strong feeling—a feeling not at all ignoble or unworthy, but not entirely disinterested either—that they do not wish to witness the continuation of the life of a loved one which they regard as hopeless, meaningless and even degrading. But there is no automatic assurance that the view of close family members will necessarily be as the patient's would have been....

The lesson here is that if you are an adult who lives in a state that requires the rigorous standard of clear and convincing evidence, you had better execute a legally valid document indicating your wishes about end of life issues—or else!

IMPLICIT CONSENT TO BE TREATED TO DEATH

Until very recently, not every state had a living will statute. New York, Michigan, and Massachusetts have enacted advance directive statutes within the past two years, although some of the most progressive legal proceedings came from their courts. Of interest is that New York courts have accepted the validity of living wills in certain circumstances before the state had a legislation of its own. Alaska and Alabama do not have a health-care proxy law. In states that have living will laws, it is presumed that unless you have executed a legally valid advance directive or given unquestionable specific, oral instructions to the contrary, every attempt will be made to prolong your life, regardless of what you or your family would have wanted. The doctrine of implied consent supposes that lack of instructions to limit treatment equates to consent to being treated to death. Furthermore, New York and Missouri have both specifically denied family members the authority to refuse life-sustaining treatment for patients with extensive brain damage. Without advance directives, hospital and nursing homes feel committed to use all available technology for fear of allegations of negligence. A living will is therefore promoted by the legal profession as a way to prevent your family from having to fight with a hospital staff at a time of enormous distress. Living wills might also serve as a means to "save the family" from crushing medical costs.

THY WILL BE DONE—THROUGH A PROXY

Occasionally, the courts based their decisions about treatment near the end of life on the less stringent substitute judgment standard.[8,9] This standard stipulates that the judgment of a surrogate or an appointed proxy be taken as equivalent to the patient's own when the patient is incapable of voicing his or her own desires. Generally, the views of someone appointed by the patient to have a power of attorney in health-care decisions are binding so long as the surrogate's views are deemed rational and reasonable by a competent medical authority. In the Karen Ann Quinlan case, discussed earlier, the views of the mother were upheld by the court according to the substitute judgment standard. In this case, the more rigorous "clear and convincing evidence" standard did not apply, since it is not required by the state of New Jersey. Even in the Cruzan case, Justice Brennan presented a strongly worded dissent: "They have discarded evidence of (Nancy's) will, ignored her values, and deprived her of the right to a decision as closely approximating her own choice as humanly possible."

Justice Scalia issued a separate concurrent, "I would have preferred that we announce, clearly and promptly, that the federal courts have no business in this field ... the point at which life becomes "worthless" and the point at which the means necessary to preserve it become extraordinary or inappropriate are neither set forth in the Constitution nor known to the nine justices of his court any better than they are known to nine people picked at random from the Kansas City telephone directory."[10]

LET THE PEOPLE RULE

If that is the case, one cannot but ask the rhetorical yet extremely pertinent question: Why not submit to the judgment of the vast majority of the American people? Poll after poll has shown that all segments of the public, including members of all major religious groups, overwhelmingly support the right of the hopelessly ill to be allowed to die (refer to Brenner, Caralis, and associates, Cohen-Mansfield and associates, Dawson and D'Oronzio, and many others). Yet the courts often hand down decisions that contrast with the tenor of the times.

"PATIENT'S BEST INTEREST": A NEW STANDARD

More recently, various courts have increasingly adopted the "patient's best interest standard" to guide the management of a permanently unconscious individual. Much useful guidance can be gleaned from the case of *Bland v. Yorkshire* judgment in February 1993.[11] Mr. Tony Bland, a young man, was trapped against the stadium fence during a Liverpool soccer game. Multiple rib injuries resulted in the cessation of effective breathing. His brain was deprived of oxygen for a long enough time to cause permanent brain damage. The patient's recovery was limited, and it became obvious that Mr. Bland would continue to linger in a persistent vegetative state. Recognizing that the treatment was futile, the physicians wanted to remove existing support measures. The case was brought in front of the Judicial Council of the House of Lords in England. A thoughtful and probing discussion followed. I feel the best way to summarize the proceedings is to provide the reader with excerpts of statements made by members of the

House of Lords. The upshot of the case was that physicians were granted the right to allow Mr. Bland to die in peace, without further life-support measures. The following are excerpts and quotations from hearings of the Bland case in the House of Lords:

> To presume that the incompetent person must always be subjected to what many rational and intelligent persons may decline is to downgrade the status of the incompetent person by placing a lesser value on his intrinsic human worth. (Lord Goff of Cheiveley)
>
> The doctor cannot owe to the patient any duty to maintain his life when that life can only be sustained by intrusive medical care to which the patient will not consent. (Lord Browne-Wilkinson)
>
> If it is not in the interests of an insentient patient to continue the life-supporting care, the doctor will be acting unlawfully if he continued the treatment ... and would perform no guilty act by discontinuing. (Lord Lowry)[12]

Several relevant cases that came before the American courts were treated similarly. Even Nancy Cruzan of Missouri was allowed to die peacefully upon withdrawal of life support. Soon after the Supreme Court hearings, the state of Missouri withdrew from the Cruzan case, stating, "It has no interest in the outcome of this litigation." The Missouri law was changed by the state legislature and no longer requires the "clear and convincing evidence" standard. This was a welcome legislation that received wide support from the citizens and the media, and provided a welcome relief to the Cruzan family.

PHYSICIANS: IMMUNE FROM THE LIABILITY OF WITHHOLDING CARE

In spite of the seemingly conflicting court rulings on this issue of futile care, it must be stated that no physician has ever been indicted, let alone convicted, for withholding care deemed unnecessary by reasonable medical standards. This may seem odd when one considers the prevailing view among practicing physicians that they should overtreat patients for fear of legal repercussions.

In case of *People v. Barber,* heard by Los Angeles courts in 1983,[13] nurses complained to the state prosecutor that physicians withdrew treatment, including feeding and hydration, from a terminally ill patient and "watched him die." The court dismissed this case on the basis that there was

> no evidence in the record to show that the defendants were acting either in a malignant, selfish, or foolhardy manner to take the life of another. In this case, we do not have willful starvation as the proximate cause of the patient's death. To say that the attending physician sat back and watched a person starve to death is to ignore the state of bad health of Mr. Herbert.

In no case was the support for the physician withholding treatment as strong as in the case of *Spring v. Massachusetts Supreme Judicial Court* in 1980.[14] In this case, the court not only upheld that an incompetent person has the same right to respect, dignity, and freedom of choice as competent people, but also it took it upon itself to send a message to treating physicians: "... little need be said about criminal liability; there is precious little precedent, and what there is suggests that the doctor will be protected if he acts in a good faith judgment that is not grievously unreasonable by medical standards."

The legal scholar, Dr. Allan Meisel, Professor of Law and Medicine, University of Pittsburgh, and the author of *Right to Die* legal compendium in 1989, summed up a developing legal consensus in an article in 1992.[15] He indicated that the bulk of court opinions have been generally supportive of the general principle that determination of the futility of care is a decision to be made by the medical profession. These opinions would suggest that physicians are under no obligation to seek consent from patients or families before withholding or withdrawing care that is deemed ineffective. Also, physicians are not exposing themselves to legal liability if their decision is reasonable by conventional medical standards.

WITHHOLDING TREATMENT: WHO DECIDES

Occasionally, court decisions have not supported the autonomy of health-care professionals to make decisions regarding appropriate medical intervention. Take the case of Helga Wanglie, an 87-year-old Minnesota woman, maintained in an unconscious state by the use of a ventilator.[16] In 1989, Mrs. Wanglie was hospitalized for a hip fracture. During that hospitalization, she sustained a series of pneumonia attacks for which she had to be placed on a ventilator. She was weaned off the ventilator and transferred to nursing-home care. She suffered cardiac arrest and was resuscitated. This intervention left her in a persistent deep coma, with machine-assisted ventilation and a stomach tube for feeding. The hospital physicians deemed her case hopeless and advised the discontinuation of assisted ventilation. Her husband refused to have her disconnected from the ventilator. The court upheld his decision as a reasonable and loving act. Clearly, Mr. Wanglie could not bear to allow his wife, his lifelong companion, to die. The problem in this case appears to have been that the hospital asked to remove Mr. Wanglie as surrogate and guardian for Mrs. Wanglie on the basis of incompetence. The court found Mr. Wanglie to be competent and, therefore, his decision was upheld. Amazingly, Drs. Veatch and Mason-Spicer, from the Kennedy Institute of Ethics at Georgetown University, argued in 1993 that the treatment in this case should not be viewed as medically futile so long as it postponed the moment of death. They engaged in a lengthy philosophical argument of what constitutes "medical versus normative" futility. I am reminded of Mary Midgley, a philosopher herself, who said, "Philosophers have appeared to want to talk only to other philosophers and in a dialect other people do not understand." But in a peculiar way this dialect seemed to be convincing to the court. The court ordered the hospital to continue ventilator treatment for Mrs. Wanglie. Her heart stopped beating a few days later.

Also, in the 1987 case of *Evans v. Bellevue Hospital*, a New York court refused to order the termination of intravenous treatment for the comatose patient's AIDS-related infection, in spite of the directives in his living will. The court's reason was that "[a]lthough the underlying disease is incurable, the specific infection is treatable with drugs." This ruling caused a firestorm among the AIDS community, the press, and the medical profession.[17]

CONFLICTING CASES

Subsequently, many cases were brought to court in which family members demanded the continuation of life-support measures in spite of a determination that the treatment was deemed futile on medical grounds. The rulings, in many cases, were to continue assisted ventilation. As expected, most of these cases involved individuals who died days or weeks after the rulings, and after several hundred thousand wasted dollars. Some patients, however, lingered on for months or years, with no medical benefit in sight. The ultimate in contradiction is seen in the rulings regarding M. Saikewicz in 1977[18] and the case of Baby K in 1993.[19] In the Baby K case, the court ruled for unreasonable treatment, as we have seen previously. In the M. Saikewicz case, the court ruled against an eminently reasonable treatment.

Mr. Saikewicz was a mentally retarded, institutionalized young man from Massachusetts. He developed leukemia, a form of cancer of the blood cells that, with proper treatment, has a good chance for cure. Physicians who diagnosed Mr. Saikewicz's condition recommended that the treatment be initiated as soon as possible. Mr. Saikewicz's appointed guardian refused on the basis that the treatment was fairly intrusive, requiring injections and intravenous infusions that would have required Mr. Saikewicz to be confined to bed for several hours. Furthermore, it was argued that the treatment might have very disagreeable side effects. The physicians argued in court that Mr. Saikewicz's guardian was being unreasonable in denying the patient potentially curative treatment. The court upheld the guardian's request citing that, the "best interests of the patient would be served by not treating his leukemia. The negative factors of treatment outweighed the benefits, and it would be in Joseph Saikewicz's best interests not to undergo treatment."

By contrast, in the case of Baby K of Fairfax, Virginia, the mother refused to terminate her pregnancy, despite the prenatal diagnosis of anencephaly, or lack of a brain.[20] Babies with anencephaly uniformly die within days or weeks of birth. Baby K was born by caesarian section on October 13, 1992. Baby K would never grow up to see, hear, feel, or be aware of anything. The mother was not married to the father, who was opposed to efforts to keep the baby alive. Baby K needed to be maintained on a ventilator. The hospital decided to wait a reasonable time in the hope that the family would realize that aggressive treatment should be terminated. The medical staff informed the mother that no treatment existed for the anencephalic condition and that no therapeutic or palliative purpose was served by use of a ventilator. The mother continued to insist on ventilator treatment against the advice of many. The hospital, "... attempted to resolve this matter through our legal system."

The hospital's request to cease therapeutic intervention was supported by the American Academy of Pediatrics, the expert board on children's medicine. In spite of this, the court ruled in favor of the mother, citing:

> The use of a mechanical ventilator to assist breathing is not "futile" or "inhumane" in relieving the acute symptoms of respiratory difficulty.... To hold otherwise would allow hospitals to deny emergency treatment to numerous classes of patients, such as accident victims or those who have cancer or AIDS, on the grounds that they eventually will die anyway from those diseases and that emergency care for them would, therefore, be "futile."

Then the judge referred to Baby K's anencephaly as a handicap or disability. He further affirmed that the mother's decision would have been scrutinized only if the family had sought to terminate or withhold medical treatment for a minor or incompetent adult. In this case, the mother's strong Christian conviction was that all life has value and should be protected. She also believed that God, rather than human beings, should determine the moment of death. As of the time of writing this manuscript, Baby K, now in her third year, is still maintained on the ventilator.

As usual, medical ethicists weighed in on both sides of the issue. Dr. Grodin's view on this intervention, with which I agree, is as follows: "Sustaining the life of an anencephalic baby is the ultimate inappropriate use of health care resources." On the other hand, Dr. Robert Veatch, the dean of the Kennedy Institute of Ethics in Washington, D.C., who testified on behalf of Baby K, while conceding that an anencephalic baby should be regarded as brain dead, raised the following philosophical question: "Whether there is value in preserving a vegetative life is not a technical question to be left to *experts*. It is a matter of personal philosophy, religion, and judgment." The court ruling was based upon the *expert* testimony of Dr. Veatch.

These unusual and bewildering decisions could have been averted had we, as a society, accepted the concept that death occurs in the event of higher brain death with irretrievable loss of consciousness and cognition, or, in the case of irreversibly unconscious individuals.

"A CONSCIENCE OF SCIENCE" THAT TRANSCENDS CASE-BY-CASE RULINGS

This lack of general agreement in court decisions reflects the legal practice of dealing with issues on a case-by-case basis. Court cases differentiate what is legally right from what is legally wrong based upon specific circumstances and not upon criteria and definitions accepted by the society at large. Society cannot, however, hold the legal establishment responsible for the lack of guidelines. To some extent, the medical establishment should be held responsible for these conflicting, incomplete, and often puzzling legal decisions. The medical community has failed to educate society and pioneer the adoption of general principles and standards. Yes, these are very complex issues that cannot possibly be reduced to headlines, sound bites, or slogans. Yes, we live in society with an ever-present fear of being misunderstood, misinterpreted, or misquoted. Yes, incomplete information, distorted information, or misinformation is rampant. Although these fears are not groundless, they cannot justify the dangerous dissociation of the medical establishment from the society-at-large. To quote John Galbraith, the noted Harvard economist, author and Professor Emeritus, "Although there is no religion of science, there should be a conscience of science, a scientific code regarding the uses to which inventions are put, in order to warn politicians and the public of their terrible consequences." We, as a medical community, must not continue to adopt and implement new and more powerful tools of technology without conscious regard to the consequences of our actions. We can no longer afford to have our medical technology outrun the ethical context in which it should be practiced.

We should heed the experience of many European countries, including the Netherlands and Denmark.[21,22] In these two countries, there are ethics councils comprised mainly of people from the mainstream public, whose overriding charge is to guide public policy and community debates in health-care issues. In these two countries, upper-brain death (or absence of an upper brain) is accepted as death, as it is in many other European countries. In these societies, withholding or withdrawing treatment is to be expected and goes unchallenged once higher brain functions have been irretrievably lost. This change of attitude has occurred even in Germany, where citizens have been ridden by guilt for the atrocities committed by their countrymen during World War II, and presumably have been reluctant to precipitously define guidelines for allowing death. Consequently, they had strict laws against discontinuation of life-support measures. On September 13, 1994, Germany's constitutional court ruled that doctors could withdraw treatment from terminally ill patients and thereby hasten their death, as long as this was the patient's wish.

Can rational, systematic, well-thought-out policies be enacted in the United States? Or have we become as the cynics like to describe America: a wasteful, extremely individualistic, heterogeneous, medication-loving, procedure-avid, technology-driven, death-denying country? Is it possible that we, in America, can achieve public consensus on issues of life and death without sloganizing or politicizing the matter? Can we agree on a set of standards that guide our care during the sunset of our lives without fear of the heavy hand of the law or interference by men of zeal, well-meaning but with poor understanding? Hopefully, this book will offer guidelines for achieving a consensus on life-and-death matters.

NOTES

1. L Kutner, "Due Process of Euthanasia: The Living Will, a Proposal" *Indiana Law Journal* (1969), 44.
2. *California Natural Death Act, 1976 Preamble.* (California Health & Safety Code. CH 7187).
3. *Brophy v. New England Sinai Hospital, Inc.* (497 NE 2nd 626, MA, 1986).
4. G Annas, "Nancy Cruzan and the Right to Die," *New England Journal of Medicine*, 323 (1990), 670–673.
5. *Cruzan v. Director* (497 US 261, 1990).
6. A Miesel, "A Retrospective on Cruzan," *Law, Medicine and Health Care*, 20 (1992), 340.
7. A Miesel, *Cruzan v. Director. The Right to Die* (New York: Wiley Law Publications, 1989, in 1994 supplement).
8. J Cohen-Mansfield, JA Droge, and N Billig, "The Utilization of the Durable Power of Attorney for Health Care among Hospitalized Elderly Patients," *Journal of the American Geriatric Society*, 39 (1991), 1174–1178.

9. J Cohen-Mansfield, BA Rabinovich, S Lispon, A Fein, B Gerber, S Weisman, and LG Pawlson, "The Decision to Execute a Durable Power of Attorney for Health Care and Preferences Regarding the Utilization of Life-Sustaining Treatments in Nursing Home Residents," *Archives of Internal Medicine*, 151 (1991), 289–294.
10. A Miesel, *Cruzan v. Director*, p. 25.
11. *Airedale NHS Trust v. Bland*, Judgment, February 4, 1993. 2 WLR 316, 343, per Burler-Sloso LJ.
12. Lord Lowry, letter in *Airedale NHS Trust (Respondents) v. Bland* (Acting by his guardian *ad litem*) (Appellate) Judgment, February 4, 1993, pp. 33–48.
13. *Barber v. Superior Court of State of California* (Cal Rptr, 1983).
14. *In re Spring 380 Mass.* 629 405 NE 2nd 115, 119 (1980).
15. A Miesel, "The Legal Consensus about Forgoing Life-Sustaining Treatment: Its Status and Its Prospects," *Kennedy Institute of Ethics Journal*, 2 (1992), 309–312.
16. *In re Wanglie No. PX-91-283* (4th District Court, Hennepin Count, Minnesota, 1991).
17. A Miesel, *In Evans v. Bellevue Hospital. The Right to Die* (New York: Wiley Law Publications, 1989).
18. Supreme Judicial Court of Massachusetts in: *Superintendent of Belchertown State School v. Saikewicz* (370 NE 2d, 1977), p. 428.
19. "Hospital Appeals Decision on Treating Anencephalic Baby," *Hospital Ethics*, 9 (1993), 6–7.
20. *In the Matter of Baby K*, No CIV A. 93-104-1 (Ed VA: 7, July, 1993).
21. *Netherlands*. Biomedical Ethics in Biolaw (Bethesda, MD: University Publications of America, 1994), p. 47.
22. *Denmark*. Biomedical Ethics in Biolaw (Bethesda, MD: University Publications of America, 1993), pp. 43–44.

Chapter 11

Does the "Living Will" Deserve to Live?

It's not that I am afraid to die, I just don't want to be there when it happens.
—WOODY ALLEN [Allen Stewart Konigsberg]
(in *He Is Still Alive: Death*, 1975)

In over 30 years of medical practice, I have taken care of tens of thousands of people. I have talked with many about life-and-death issues. I have lectured about advance medical directives and have held many public forums about this subject matter.

In many instances during my medical practice, I entered a note in the patient's charts indicating his or her preferences when life is coming to a close and when death is near or imminent. In other instances, patients have brought me signed and notarized documents, instructing me as to what I should and should not do. In most cases, I included the documents in the patient's chart but also had a private talk with the patient about the subject matter. I often discovered that what the patient really meant was not clearly expressed in the signed, notarized document. Without exception, a patient who hands you a living will wants to tell you: "When the end is near and inevitable, make me comfortable, make this final event as short, painless, and peaceful as possible. Most importantly, I want to be assured that I will not become a burden on the ones I love, and I want to be remembered as a person worthy of respect."

In this country, we all cherish our autonomy. I am no exception. I want to take part in treatment decisions at all times, including near the end of life. True, my wife knows exactly how I feel about life-and-death issues, as do my children and my treating physicians. Nevertheless, I wanted to leave my wishes expressed clearly in writing. To me, this is a most serious business. I have cancer. Even though it is now in remission, I am afraid I might end up dying a horrible death.

I spent hours drafting what I thought was a document that reflected my feelings and covered in detail the possible medical contingencies. After all, I am a physician, and I have unlimited access to medical literature.

In preparation for writing this document, I learned all there was to be learned about my affliction, cancer of the prostate. But I also realized that I, as a 62-year-old male, could have a heart attack; consequently, this last contingency was covered also. It is possible that I might be involved in an accident, have a stroke, or develop another cancer. I covered it all. I developed what I thought was a model, water-tight, multipage advance directive. I took it to my lawyer to have it witnessed and notarized.

My lawyer's secretary greeted me with a beautiful smile and asked that I leave the document for review. She advised me that Mr. Smith (not his real name) would deliver the notarized document to my office on his way home. Sure enough, the next day, my friend, Mr. Smith, delivered a document, but not the one I authorized.[1] What an insult, I thought!

I read the form delivered to me and recognized that it was the standard Oklahoma Advanced Directive. It reads:

I, ________________, being of sound mind and eighteen (18) years of age or older, wilfully and voluntarily make known my desire, by my instructions to others through my living will, or by my appointment of a health-care proxy, or both, that my life shall not be artificially prolonged under the circumstances set forth below. I thus do hereby declare:

I. Living Will

a. If my attending physician and another physician determine that I am no longer able to make decisions regarding my medical treatment, I direct my attending physician and other health-care providers pursuant to the Oklahoma Rights of the Terminally Ill or Persistently Unconscious Act, to withhold or withdraw treatment from me under the circumstances I have indicated below by my signature. I understand that I will be given treatment that is necessary for my comfort or to alleviate my pain.

b. If I have a terminal condition:

(1) I direct that life-sustaining treatment shall be withheld or withdrawn if such treatment would only prolong my process of dying, and if my attending physician and another physician determine that I have an incurable and irreversible condition that even with the administration of life-sustaining treatment will cause my death within six (6) months

Signature ______________________

(2) I understand that the subject of the artificial administration of nutrition and hydration (food and water) that will only prolong the process of dying from an incurable and irreversible condition is of particular importance. I understand that if I do not sign this paragraph, artificially administered nutrition and hydration will be administered to me. I further understand that if I sign this paragraph, I am authorizing the withholding or withdrawal

of artificially administered nutrition (food) and hydration (water).

Signature ______________________

(3) I direct that (add other medical directives, if any)

____

____

Signature ______________________

c. If I am persistently unconscious:

(1) I direct that life-sustaining treatment be withheld or withdrawn if such treatment will only serve to maintain me in an irreversible condition, as determined by my attending physician and another physician, in which thought and awareness of self and environment are absent.

Signature ______________________

(2) I understand that the subject of the artificial administration of nutrition and hydration (food and water) for individuals who have become persistently unconscious is of particular importance. I understand that if I do not sign this paragraph, artificially administered nutrition and hydration will be administered to me. I further understand that if I sign this paragraph, I am authorizing the withholding or withdrawal of artificially administered nutrition (food) and hydration (water).

Signature ______________________

(3) I direct that (add other medical directives, if any)

____

____

II. My Appointment of My Health Care Proxy

a. If my attending physician and another physician determine that I am no longer able to make decisions regarding my medical treatment I direct my attending physician and other health-care providers, pursuant to the Oklahoma Rights of the Terminally Ill or Persistently Unconscious Act to follow the instructions of ________________, whom I appoint as my health care proxy. If my health care proxy is unable to or unwilling to serve, I appoint ________________ as my alternative health care proxy with the same authority. My health care proxy is authorized to make whatever medical treatment decisions I could make if I were able, except that decision regarding life-sustaining treatment can be made by my health care proxy or alternate health care proxy only as I indicate in the following sections.

(1) I understand that the subject of the artificial administration of nutrition and hydration (food and water) is of particular importance. I understand that if I do not sign this paragraph, artificially administered nutrition (food) or hydration (water) will be administered to me. I further understand that if I sign this paragraph, I am authorizing the withholding or withdrawal of artificially administered nutrition and hydration.

Signature ________________________

(2) I authorize my health care proxy to (add other medical directives, if any)

____

____

b. If I am persistently unconscious:

(1) I authorize my health care proxy to direct that life-sustaining treatment be withheld or withdrawn if such

treatment will only serve to maintain me in an irreversible condition, as determined by my attending physician and another physician, in which thought and awareness of self and environment are absent.

Signature ______________________________

(2) I understand that the subject of the artificial administration of nutrition and hydration (food and water) is of particular importance. I understand that if I do not sign this paragraph, artificially administered nutrition (food) and hydration (water) will be administered to me. I further understand that if I sign this paragraph, I am authorizing the withholding and withdrawal of artificially administered nutrition and hydration.

Signature ______________________________

(3) I authorize my health care proxy to (add other medical directives, if any)

____

____

III. Conflicting Provision

I understand that if I have completed both a living will and have appointed a health care proxy, and if there is a conflict between my health care proxy's decision and my living will, my living will shall take precedence unless I indicate otherwise.

____

____

Signature ______________________________

IV. Other Provisions

a. I understand that if I have been diagnosed as pregnant and that diagnosis is known to my attending physician this advance directive shall have no force or effect during my pregnancy.
b. In the absence of my ability to give directions regarding the use of life-sustaining procedures, it is my intention that this advance directive shall be honored by my family and physicians as the final expression of my legal right to refuse medical or surgical treatment including, but not limited to, administration of my life-sustaining procedures, and I accept the consequences of such refusal.
c. This advance directive shall be in effect until it is revoked.
d. I understand that I may revoke this advance directive at any time.
e. I understand and agree that if I have any prior directives, and if I sign this advance directive, my prior directives are revoked.
f. I understand the full importance of this advance directive and I am emotionally and mentally competent to make this advance directive.

Signed this day of ______________________, 19__________

City ________ County ________ State ________ Residence ________

Date of Birth ____________ Social Security Number ____________

This advance directive was signed in my presence:

______________________________ ______________________________

Signature of Witness *Address*

I became livid. How dare Mr. Smith do that to me! And to add insult to injury, enclosed was a bill from Mr. Smith for $200 for his efforts in coming up with this will written in legal jargon with over

10 signature entries. He had totally ignored my original request for him to notarize my own, original living will, the one that I had painstakingly composed. I called Mr. Smith and conveyed my dissatisfaction, disappointment, and dismay while I struggled hard to repress my anger. He said, "Your will is not valid in Oklahoma. It is not binding. It will not stand up in court." He added that the one he sent me is the one he has been using for other clients. It is the standard, new and revised Oklahoma Advance Directive. I suggested to him, politely, that we execute another, somewhat better generic form of a living will. I chose a standard will that I have used for some patients. This will is adapted from an earlier one suggested by Sissela Bok, the noted medical ethicist, in 1976 and published in the *New England Journal of Medicine*.[2] It reads:

> I, *L. Basta*, want to participate in my own medical care as long as I am able. But I recognize that an accident or illness may some day make me unable to do so. Should this come to be the case, this document is intended to direct those who make choices on my behalf. I have prepared it while still legally competent and of sound mind. If these instructions create a conflict with the desires of my relatives, or with hospital policies or with the principles of those providing my care, I ask that my instructions prevail. I wish to live a full and long life, but not at all costs. If my death is near and cannot be avoided, or if I have lost the ability to interact with others and have no reasonable chance of regaining this ability, such as in severe dementia or extensive stroke, or if my suffering is intense and irreversible, such as with disseminated carcinoma or advanced decrepitude, I do not want to have my life prolonged. I would then ask not to be subjected to surgery or resuscitation. Nor would I then wish to have life support from mechanical ventilators, intensive-care services, or other life-prolonging procedures, including the administration of antibiotics, blood products, and/or artificial feeding and hydration. I would wish, rather, to have care that brings peace and comfort, even if it hastens the moment of death, and which

facilitates my interaction with others to the extent that is possible, and which brings peace. In order to carry out these instructions and to interpret them, I authorize *Laila Basta* to accept, plan, and refuse treatment on my behalf in cooperation with attending physicians and health personnel. This person knows how I value the experience of living, and how I would weigh incompetence, dependence, pain, suffering, and dying. Should it be impossible to reach this person, I authorize *Victor or Steve Basta* to make such choices for me. I have discussed my desires concerning terminal care with them, and I trust their judgment on my behalf.

Date: ________________ Signed: ______________________

Witnessed by: ______________________________

and by: ___________________________________

I gave my lawyer, for reference, another form suggested in 1989 by Drs. Ezekiel and Linda Emanuel, Directors of the program in ethics and professors at the Kennedy School of Government, Harvard University, realizing that this form appears quite complex. It covers four different scenarios of terminal illness, coma, persistent vegetative state, and advanced dementia (such as Alzheimer's disease). There are 12 different entries that go with each choice. Although this form has been well formulated, my patients—including the better educated among them—found it quite confusing and/or were intimidated by it.[3]

THE LIMITATIONS OF EXISTING LIVING WILLS

There are multiple and major problems with currently used forms of advance directives. These problems are elaborated on in many studies referred to in the Notes at the end of this chapter. First, there is the problem of ambiguous language. When wills talk about disability, what do they mean—loss of a limb, a small stroke, dimmed eye sight, failing hearing? What is meant by mental disability? Is this simple depression, forgetfulness, or total dependence? What specifically is meant by artificial means and does the document proscribe all artificial intervention? An artificial pacemaker for an otherwise healthy heart might give an individual 10 or more additional happy years; an artificial joint may significantly improve a miserable existence and enable mobility and travel. What is meant by heroic measures? An otherwise healthy person afflicted with severe pneumonia may have to be assisted by a ventilator for a few days to effect a cure; this is an eminently reasonable form of heroic action. Assisted ventilation may also be a lifesaver in a curable episode of asthma, laryngitis, or reversible muscle paralysis. What does it mean when people talk about hopeless pain? With medicines available at our disposal today, there should rarely be such a thing. The vague description of disability (physical or mental) has rendered the living will legally unbinding, ethically problematic, and medically too ambiguous to be effective.

Another problem is the limited use a "living will" has in directing medical intervention. Standard forms of "living wills" have been transformed from "personal testaments" into "legal documents" drafted by lawyers written in legal jargon to be binding in courts. A common person would not be able to decipher the language and is often intimidated by the wordiness of the document. They are supposedly designed to direct physicians to withhold or withdraw care when the patient is *in extremis*. Because of this transformed design, they have little place, if any, in directing the treatment of patients, either because they do not anticipate all medical contingencies or they apply only when the treatment has proven futile and death is imminent, with or without intervention.

WHEN DISREGARDING A LIVING WILL IS ETHICAL

To further illustrate some of the difficulties with living wills, let me cite the following cases.

I recall a 63-year-old woman with no children of her own who was admitted to the hospital for treatment for a type of irregular heartbeat that is ordinarily neither fatal nor crippling. The patient arrived with her nephew, a handsome and articulate young man. She emphasized, "First of all, I want you to know that I do not want to be kept alive by artificial or heroic means. I am ready to go when my time comes. Also, I brought my nephew, who is a lawyer, to make sure that you honor my wishes." She handed me a notarized piece of paper—a generic "living will."

I assured her that she was quite healthy except for this new irregular heart rhythm. I did not see any reason for her to talk about death at present. Her condition at the time was not serious, but I did fully understand her wishes, which would be honored at the appropriate time. We started the patient on a medicine that regulates heart rhythm. The medicine is a derivative of quinine and is called quinidine.

Just to prepare the reader for what is coming, I will point out that a very small percentage (less than 5% or 1 in 20) of patients placed on this medicine develop a much more serious heart rhythm disturbance, called *torsades de pointes,* which can be lethal and must be treated as an emergency. Sometimes electric shocks, or *cardioversion,* must be delivered to the heart to jolt it back to normalcy. No doubt, many people would consider electric cardioversion to be an heroic measure; all would consider it a form of resuscitation. Sure enough, at 3:00 A.M., the nurse called me to declare that Mrs. Jones had developed three episodes of *torsades de pointes.* She lost consciousness during two of them and required electroconversion (electric shock resuscitation). We continued our efforts to control this life-threatening heart irregularity, knowing full well that we had disobeyed, to the letter, the patient's living will that we had pledged to honor. Would it have been more appropriate to allow this lady to die of complications caused by our treatment when such a complication could have been overcome and reversed?

Mrs. Jones recovered. She is still active, and as far as I can tell, is able to enjoy life much more than ever before. On her most recent six-month visit to my office, she reiterated how happy she was to be alive and well.

Consider next the case of Mr. Hall, who gave me a copy of his "advance directive." This document clearly indicated that, when the moment came, he did not want to be kept alive by artificial means. Subsequently, Mr. Hall passed out while mowing the lawn. His son started CPR and the ambulance brought him to the emergency room. When I saw him, he was pale and lethargic but not comatose. He could respond to questions in a feeble voice with slow, shaky, short phrases. He was clammy and sweat beads covered his face. His heart was beating very slowly, less than 30 beats per minute (the normal is about 70 beats per minute), which barely sustained him. A thorough evaluation revealed that he had no other major health problem. The EKG showed that the electric pathways of his heart were decayed, but the heart muscle was still intact. The heart is like a car motor and needs the equivalent of a battery, spark plugs, and electric wiring to initiate the heartbeats. Also, the heart needs its gas pipes, the coronary arteries, to bring gas to the motor, the heart muscle. One can have an intact motor but bad wiring, or in other situations, bad gas pipes, which are referred to as hardening of the arteries. I explained the problem to Mrs. Hall, Mr. Hall, Jr., and to the rest of the family; all agreed on Mr. Hall's behalf to place a permanent pacemaker in his heart. Twelve years have passed and Mr. Hall is still alive and active, thanks to "artificial means"—an artificial pacemaker placed in his heart.

Finally, consider Mr. Wood, who is a lay leader in our church. Mr. Wood is alive today because of two separate bypass operations—the first performed in 1985 and the second in 1991. Mr. Wood's brother was not as fortunate. He suffered a heart attack that resulted in massive upper-brain damage. He slipped into a deep coma and was maintained on a ventilator in the intensive-care unit until he died a few weeks later.

After this sad experience, my friend, Mr. Wood, asked me to let him go in peace if his heart stopped. That was three years ago. A year later, Mr. Wood started to experience smothering chest pains with the least amount of exertion. The pains became more frequent, lasted longer, and started to wake him from his sleep. I suggested that we repeat the coronary *angiograms* (pictures of his blood vessels) in order to study his heart arteries and the bypass grafts. In a bypass operation, one blood vessel, such as a leg vein that is not blocked, is used to "bypass" a coronary (heart) artery that is blocked. The angiogram showed that one of the bypass grafts had developed severe narrowing. I recommend that we open it up with a procedure called *balloon angioplasty,* in which a balloon inflates the blocked artery. A tiny balloon was advanced into the narrowed bypass vessel and positioned carefully in the middle of the narrowing. We inflated the balloon to open up the narrowed spot. Angioplasty causes a temporary interruption of blood flow and oxygen to the heart. The heart did not like the temporary cessation of blood flow, and it began beating irregularly, a condition known as *ventricular fibrillation.* The fact that the heart fibrillated (began beating in a disorganized fashion) is a common occurrence during a procedure such as the one we were performing. As a cardiologist, I may panic when I see somebody bleed from his nose, but not when I see a heart fibrillate. This is my territory.

In this situation, proper medical intervention involves deflating the balloon and shocking the heart. The use of electric-shock resuscitation will bring the patient back to life. Had we followed Mr. Wood's instructions, as set forth in his advance directive, electric shock would not have been used, and Mr. Wood would have been dead. Of course, I shocked the heart.

All these real-life instances serve as cautionary tales: Living wills should *never* be implemented blindly; neither should they be disregarded completely. Theoretically, a poorly worded living will could result in withholding useful therapy about which the patient has not been fully informed. I do not know of any such cases and have never heard of any. This hazard may become real, I fear, with the mounting pressures to limit medical treatment costs in a management-care environment. Should that ever happen, it will be a real tragedy!

ABIDING BY THE SPIRIT—RATHER THAN THE LETTER—OF THE LIVING WILL

A competent patient has the right to refuse treatment, but such refusal has to be predicated upon that patient having full information about all possible scenarios relevant to his or her condition. The patient should also be able to comprehend and evaluate these scenarios and the therapeutic options. Given these strict provisions, there will still arise scenarios that are deemed remote at the time. Not infrequently, physicians are faced with complications that would have been only remotely possible and even inconceivable in the course of treatment.

Advance directives, as well intentioned as they might be, do not allow for all possible contingencies, as stated previously. Therefore, living wills should not be taken literally and should never be implemented blindly unless the patient is terminally ill or permanently unconscious. In most of these latter cases, treatment should be deemed futile whether or not a living will exists. This position is supported by many scholars, among whom is Dr. Wicclair, the noted author of *Ethics and the Elderly*.[4]

THE LIMITATION OF LIMITED ACCESS

Another problem with living wills is the limited access that emergency health-care professionals have to them. I cannot recount how many times an emergency call results in an ambulance dispatch. Emergency medical technicians encounter a person who has recently died (i.e., has experienced cessation of heartbeat and breathing). CPR is initiated at the scene, and the patient is transported to the emergency room. Although the patient is found to be unconscious, further resuscitative measures revive the heart. Later, family members show up to tell me that Mr. X had a living will. It's too late. You cannot reverse the course of events until you are satisfied that the resuscitation treatment (which was started without the patient's consent in the first place) has proven futile.

POWERS OF ATTORNEY: BE SURE TO EMPOWER THE RIGHT PERSON

We noted earlier that a durable power of attorney allows a designated person to make medical and legal decisions on behalf of an incompetent person. Again, this legal measure is far from perfect. The requests of the designated person must be evaluated carefully by the treating physician.

Even if the patient gives a durable power of attorney to a close relative, directions from this surrogate should be followed only if they are deemed legally sound, morally just, and ethically right.

I experienced the imperfections of the durable power of attorney while treating a 76-year-old woman, Mrs. Fields, who was admitted to the hospital because of a transient ischemic brain attack, a ministroke. For a brief while, she lost eyesight in her left eye and developed some weakness of her right hand. She recovered. Upon examination, the stethoscope revealed noises heard over the big blood vessels on both sides of the neck, suggesting severe narrowing of these vessels carrying blood to the brain. This was further confirmed by an ultrasound imaging device. The amount of blood reaching the upper brain was barely keeping up with the needs of the brain. This is a condition that can be corrected with surgery that cleans up the artery; this procedure carries a low risk for the patient. Mrs. Fields refused medical intervention in spite of repeated pleas to consider surgery in order to prevent an imminent stroke. She asked to be discharged from the hospital and continued to smoke two to three packs of cigarettes daily. A week later, she developed paralysis on the right side of her body and lost her ability to speak. Because of difficulty in swallowing, a small tube was placed in her stomach to feed her. Throughout her illness, she never lost consciousness. She recognized her family and knew who I was. She watched sunsets in the evenings and woke up in the morning at regular hours. She expected her meals to be served on time and became angry at her attendant when they were late.

Mrs. Fields was a wealthy woman, a recognized socialite in

the community. She looked and acted like a lady. She had the reputation of being very stubborn. A few weeks after she had the stroke, her daughter asked to see me in my office. "Why are you allowing my mother to be kept alive by artificial means? Don't you know that my mother would never have wanted to live like this? Unable to communicate ... dependent ... helpless ... pathetic?" I tried to calm the daughter down, but she kept pounding on my desk and the decibels of her voice became higher and higher as she continued to express dissatisfaction with my care. I waited until she finished and asked her to sit down. Then I spoke, "As far as I am concerned, your mother is alive. She is able to appreciate people and things. Her consciousness is substantially intact and her ability to reason appears to be preserved to some extent. She has passions that she shares and desires that she expects to be fulfilled, and she appears to derive pleasure from being alive. You may not consider this to be an acceptable quality of life, but that is your view, and it might have been your mother's view prior to this stroke. But who am I and who are you to judge whether a life is worth living? It would have been different if your mother had lost her personhood completely and her existence depended upon the function of her brain stem. But as long as she has some attributes that constitute personhood—consciousness, awareness, and feelings to share—she has all the rights that you and I cherish. We owe that to our shared humanity. If you do not agree with me, ask me to cease to be your mother's physician." She stood up and left. I have not heard from her since then.

WHEN THE LIVING WILL DOES NOT GO FAR ENOUGH

Consider another case that illustrates yet another limitation of existing living wills. Mrs. Morgan was an 86-year-old woman brought from the nursing home for my consultation. The attendant noted that Mrs. Morgan, a widow with no children, was passing blood with her stools. While competent, she executed a standard, state-approved advance directive. The directive pertained to terminal illness, imminent death, coma, and persistent vegetative state. She had been placed in the nursing home by her niece, who could not cope with her aunt's severely deteriorated mental status. Recently, she was confused all the time. She could not tell the time, day, or year. She did not remember her late husband's name, and her vocabulary became limited to a few words that she uttered incoherently. Still, she could feel pain, cold, heat, and hunger. Her condition did not conform to the provisions of the signed living will that proscribed medical intervention. In order to find the cause of bleeding, the physician attending to Mrs. Morgan performed a procedure and subsequently discovered a tumor that, upon further examination, proved to be a cancer. It took the attending physician two days to locate Mrs. Morgan's niece, who lived in another state; she was too busy to leave work for a few days but wanted everything that was medically necessary to be done.

Since Mrs. Morgan was anemic, she required blood transfusions. Major surgery was used to remove her cancerous colon. During surgery, a metastatic nodule, another form of spreading cancer, was noted to have lodged in her liver. Surgery was followed by a cascade of complications. Mrs. Morgan became delirious, belligerent, and combative, requiring constant sedation. Restraints were placed on both wrists to prevent movement. She developed acute pneumonia, because she was unable to clear her lungs with a productive cough. She was placed on a ventilator. She required several antibiotics that caused her sluggish kidneys to deteriorate further. Because she was bedridden for several days, a clot formed in a major vein in her right leg. The clot became loose and traveled to the blood vessel supplying her lungs. A special filter was placed in the big vein in her belly to prevent further clots from migrating toward the heart. The kidneys continued to deteriorate. Her heart showed signs of failure, and she died after over three weeks of enormous suffering.

One cannot help but ask why a person who is only able to experience pain or no pain should be subjected to all of this torture? For what purpose? Would it not have been more humane to let her bleed from her colon and die peacefully in her sleep? Was her niece acting in the patient's best interest?

EMPOWERING THE POWERLESS

Human frailty in the person empowered to carry out someone's living will can also foil the intent of this document as it stands today. Consider the case of Mr. Harrison (fictitious name): "They wouldn't let him die!" his daughter, Mrs. Mary Bynum, tearfully told me, in a broken voice, the first time I met her. I reached out to a box of tissue, picked up a handful, and handed them to her. She wiped away her tears and pointed to a picture on the wall. "My poor dad, the doctor's wouldn't let him die!" she said. I looked at the picture. There was a handsome, tall man with an overpowering figure. She went on to tell me about her 86-year-old father.

I learned that Mr. Harrison was a dignified, proud man. He enjoyed golf, fishing, and hunting, which he had engaged in regularly until two years ago. His beloved wife died after a long, debilitating battle with cancer; they had been married for 62 years. He became reclusive and was overtaken by grief. His prolonged bereavement culminated in a stroke that left his right side paralyzed. He was unable to express himself verbally or through writing, a huge blow to his dignity. Mr. Harrison was moved to his daughter's house. The loving daughter attended to his needs with devotion. But all the fun in life was over for Mr. Harrison. He cried with the least provocation and, at times, without any apparent reason.

At one time, his daughter recalled that he pointed to a toy gun and put his left index finger to his head, as if to say: "I wish you would help me put an end to this prolonged unhappiness." He could not reciprocate gestures of love and caring and his life, according to his daughter, became void of fun, love, or dignity.

Mr. Harrison had executed a notarized living will and

granted his daughter power of attorney for health-care decisions. Twice that year, Mr. Harrison was admitted to the hospital for treatment of pneumonia. Pneumonia is a treatable condition and, in Mr. Harrison's case, his condition was neither hopeless, nor terminal. During the previous hospital admission, Mr. Harrison had to be placed on a ventilator for three days, but this time his pneumonia was treated early enough. Mr. Harrison had spent 10 days in the hospital and it was time to bring him back home. I asked the daughter whether she was certain that her father would not have preferred to die of pneumonia. Promptly she answered "yes." She sighed and continued: "But he never asked me before he had the stroke to allow him to die of pneumonia if he became totally dependent. This much I know: If that were me in his place, I wouldn't have chosen to go on like this. I love him." I held her shoulder as a gesture of encouragement. To this day, I cannot forget her words: "A life void of fun, true love, and dignity is a fate worse than death." Nevertheless, when a tough but humane medical decision needed to be made, the daughter was incapable of doing so; she lacked the ability to make the tough decision.

These cases are illustrative of ordinary events and not the extraordinary; they represent everyday encounters in the life of a busy practitioner.

Patients execute living wills with the intention to spare themselves and their loved ones indignity, pain, and expense at the end of life. But "living wills," in their present form, fall short of producing the desired benefits and do not avert the horrible consequences that they were designed to prevent in the first place. The medical profession's prevailing attitude is to interpret the living will with great caution. The ever-present fear of litigation from erroneously second guessing the patient's intentions causes an overcautious and often guarded interpretation of the living will. Also, whenever family members wish to override the document in favor of medical interventions, physicians have tended to go along with more, albeit marginally beneficial, medial care.

Consider the last two cases discussed. Did the niece of Mrs. Morgan and the daughter of Mr. Harrison not act properly? In the case of Mrs. Morgan, it can be argued that the niece did not have much interaction with her aunt, was too disengaged to properly evaluate her aunt's situation, and took the safest course available: My aunt has cancer; let's have the cancer removed. In the case of Mr. Harrison, the daughter knew that her father would not have wished to linger in his state of dependence. She loved him but could not find the courage within herself to ask the attending physician to forego treatment of pneumonia.

LIVING WILLS—NO SUBSTITUTE FOR NATIONAL GUIDELINES ON LIFE AND DEATH

Durable powers of attorneys and living wills, as they stand now, remind us of our failure as a medial profession in the face of technological advances, and they provide an indictment of our society and its legal system for not providing clean and consistent guidelines for treatment that is deemed appropriate at the end of life. It is morally outrageous for citizens to have to go to the trouble of executing a document that has the semblance of legal power in order to tell the treating physicians: "I have seen others who had horrible deaths as a result of unrelenting pursuit of high-tech interventions. Please spare me the agony." It need not be this way. It is sad that decent people are denied a decent way to exit life in peace. And the saddest indictment of all is the indisputable fact that the medical establishment, guided by esoteric, ethical pronouncements or fearful of legal consequences, has consistently failed to respond to the incessant pleas of rational citizens. I was horrified to hear the secretary of my friend, the chief of cardiac surgery, describe her worst nightmare to me: "My daughter has leukemia. All attempts to cure her, including a bone-marrow transplant have failed." Then with tears in her eyes and a choked voice, she continued, "I know that her death is near and in a few months, she will be no more. She is at home engaging in her favorite hobbies. But my greatest fear is that someday, if she is found dead or unconscious, the ambulance will be called and she will be revived. My nightmare is that she will be placed on a ventilator and enslaved by machines for weeks on end before she is pronounced dead." She went on to say, "I have put signs all over the house that indicate that I do not want such a horrible end for my daughter," and as tears flow down her cheeks, she continued, "I love her so much!"

How amazing is our present state of medicine? Are we incapable of taming our high-tech instruments so that they serve our human needs? Have we rendered ourselves passive slaves to a monster that we have created? In a recent conference on the care of patients with heart disease, I asked 200 nurses attending the conference as to their personal preferences regarding terminal care. Of these, 98% did not want to be resuscitated if the chance of subsequent recovery and independence is less than 5%, and none wished to be subjected to CPR when the chance for a favorable outcome is less than 1%. Nevertheless, the present standard for CPR is to resuscitate everyone with a cardiac arrest anywhere in or out of hospital, often without regard for their wishes.

The weakness of contemporary living wills should be obvious by now. In the first place, they are designed to assert one's autonomy in making decisions for health care. In the second place, they are intended to preserve one's dignity at the end of life, spare one unnecessary intrusive interventions, and in many instances, relieve loved ones of the burden of excessive cost for futile care. They fail on both counts.

The concept of patient autonomy overrides all other considerations from an ethicist's point of view. But is this really practical? It is true that a competent patient has the right to refuse treatment. But what percentage of competent people refuse rational treatment aimed at redeeming their health and well-being? What percentage of patients faced with complex health problems are able to evaluate various medical scenarios and choose their treatment from that menu? With few exceptions, there is one best option, and almost always patients elect that option, particularly when they have a trusting relationship with their doctor. The best means to preserve a meaningful autonomy for the patient is to foster that sacred doctor–patient relationship. This relationship, however, is threatened by extinction in our businesslike environment, with its HMOs and other managed-care alliances.

In the situation in which the patient is unconscious or becomes incompetent, the best way to treat him or her is to apply the "best-interest standard." However, the perspective that allows proxy decision making is deeply flawed, according to Professor John Hardwig, Professor of the program in Medical Ethics, College of Medicine, East Tennessee State University in Johnson City.[5] Surrogates are often guided by their own feelings rather than by the desire of the patient they represent. Their decisions are often tainted by feelings of guilt, fear of reproach, or desire for self-gain. Even genuine love can adversely affect a decision if the proxy is unable to let go.

Perhaps no one team has studied living wills more than Drs. Ezekiel J. Emanuel and Linda L. Emanuel of the Kennedy School of Government, Harvard University. Since its inception, they promoted the idea of the advance directive, proposed forms with various medical scenarios (which my older patients found to be confusing), and studied the effects of living wills on the practice of medicine. In two recent publications, one entitled "Advance Directives: What Have We Learned So Far," appearing in the 1993 issue of the *Journal of Clinical Ethics*,[6] and the other entitled "Advance Directives: Do They Work?", appearing in the 1995 issue of the *Journal of American College of Cardiology*,[7] they reviewed the influence of living wills on patient care. In the first place, only 25% of Americans have living wills and less than one-third of these have a provision for a durable power of attorney. Most revealing of all is that living wills achieve their intended results only when patients, families and their physicians have an open discussion about life-and-death issues that cover specific scenarios and detailed courses of action. And, I venture to say, the lucky ones among us who have such a relationship with their physicians and loved ones do not need to execute a living will. As mentioned previously, both former President Richard Nixon and former First Lady Jacqueline Kennedy Onassis recently had dignified, Oedipus-like exits from life in comfortable beds, surrounded by loved ones. Numerous articles were written about how peaceful their deaths were, and many writers ascribed it to the fact that each of these individuals had executed a living will. No distortion can be further from the truth; their Oedipus-like exits had little to do with living wills and everything to do with the fact that they each knew exactly how they wanted to be treated at the end of life. Both shared their views clearly and unequivocally with their families and physicians. They died on their own terms.

The Emanuels of Harvard University have proposed a default living will to be designed by a committee for those who do not have an existing living will at the time of death. Wouldn't it be simpler if we, as a society, developed well-thought-out practice guidelines in harmony with our shared values and had these guidelines apply to all of us? Wouldn't that spare us the agony of unnecessary, defensive medicine, prompted by fear of litigation and the confusion inflicted upon health-care professionals by professional ethicists and compounded by inconsistent court rulings?

No testimonial for my thesis can lend stronger support than a recent study, the SUPPORT study, published in 1995 in the *Annals of Internal Medicine*,[8] and a previous paper derived from the same study (Teno and associates) published in 1994 in the *Journal of Clinical Ethics*.[9] This study evaluated whether advance directives (or the Patient Self-Determination Act) affect resuscitation decisions and the use of resources for seriously ill patients. The study involved over 3,000 patients treated in 10 leading medical centers, including Harvard, Johns Hopkins, Duke, UCLA, and Case Western Reserve Universities. Researchers found no significant association between the existence of advance directives and decisions about resuscitation. Furthermore, the researchers concluded that advance directives (in their present form) were irrelevant to medical decision making near the end of life.

Using a society's judgment as the substitute judgment should bring assurance to the patient and treating physician. Substitute judgment does not violate the principle of autonomy. After all, according to Kant, the principle of autonomy is fulfilled when people are subject to laws they have helped author. The best-interest standard does not violate individual autonomy; the application of intrusive, nonconsentual medical treatment under the presumption of implied consent does.

SHOULD LIVING WILLS LIVE?

Do advance directives and living wills, in a different form, have a place in patient care? In spite of many shortcomings, some of which have been discussed, I believe advance directives have a place in helping physicians and surrogates make the more difficult choices in patient care—choices that must be made when treatment is of questionable, or only transient benefit, and at a stage when death is not imminent.

In America, advance directives apply to the management of patients *in extremis*. In that case, rational medical judgment, with or without a living will, should dictate the substitution of intrusive, interventional, contratherapeutic care by soothing, comforting care.

In Denmark, on the other hand, living wills are directed primarily toward withholding treatment of potentially curable and reversible conditions in the presence of advanced decrepitude, senile decay, accident, heart problems, or similar situations that have led to such severe states of invalidism that the patient has become permanently incapable of self-care. Under such circumstances, pneumonia would not be treated, internal hemorrhage would not be stopped, and blood transfusion would not be given. It is obvious, therefore, that this is a totally different application of a "living will" by comparison to its conventional role and intended application in the United States. Furthermore, there is one approved "living will" form used in Denmark. It is a simple form, available to all citizens, and does not require an attorney to get it executed. In the United States, not all states have statutes that result in the recognition of advance directives, and not all of those who have statutes have surrogate power-of-attorney statutes. Furthermore, some of these advance directives treat feeding and hydration differently than others forms of treatment. Some states require that only extremely complex living will forms that are appropriately notarized, be legally binding. What a complicated and inconsistent process!

If I would design a personal living will it would have looked very much like the standard living will used in Denmark today. A document such as this, and a personal and trusting relationship with a physician are the best safeguards for ensuring a death with dignity.

NOTES

1. *Oklahoma Living Will* (Oklahoma Natural Death Act, 1992).
2. S Bok, "Personal Directions for Care at the End of Life," *New England Journal of Medicine*, 7 (1976), 367–368.
3. LL Emanuel, EJ Emanuel, JD Stoeckler, LR Hummel, and MJ Barry, "Advance Directives: Stability of Patients' Treatment Choices," *Archives of Internal Medicine*, 154 (1994), 209–217.
4. MR Wicclair, *Ethics and the Elderly*. (New York: Oxford University Press, 1993).
5. J Hardwig, "The Problem of Proxies with Interests of Their Own: Toward a Better Theory of Proxy Decisions," *Journal of Clinical Ethics*, 4 (1991), 41–46.
6. L Emanuel, "Advance Directives: What Have We Learned So Far?" *Journal of Clinical Ethics*, 4 (1993), 8–16.
7. LL Emanuel, "Advance Directives: Do They Work?" *Journal American College of Cardiology*, 25 (1995), 35–38.
8. WA Knaus, FE Harrell, J Lynn, L Goldman, RS Phillips, AF Connors, NV Dawson, WJ Fuklerson, RM Califf, N Desbiens, P Layde, RK Oye, RPE Bellamy, RB Hakim, and DP Wagner, "The SUPPORT Prognostic Model: Objective Estimates of Survival for Seriously Ill Hospitalized Adults," *Annals of Internal Medicine*, 22 (1995), 191–203.
9. JM Teno, J Lynn, RS Phillips, et al. "Do Formal Advance Directives Affect Resuscitation Decisions and the Use of Resources for Seriously Ill Patients?" *Journal of Clinical Ethics*, 5 (1994), 23–30.

Chapter 12

May the Doctor–Patient Relationship Heal Itself

> For some patients, though conscious that their condition is perilous, recover their health simply through their contentment with goodness of the physician.
>
> —HIPPOCRATES, c. 460–400 B.C. (in *Precepts*, Ch. 6)

As we have noted in previous chapters, a meaningful doctor–patient relationship is an imperative in order for patients, physicians, and society in general to deal with the enormous problems of end-of-life issues. Before I delve into this discussion any further, I would like to cite a doctor's perspective about the practice of medicine in past years as compared to the practice in contemporary times.

In his book, *Inside Medical Washington*, Dr. James Sammons, an influential physician who presided over the American Medical Association, describes his practice of 30 years ago in Baytown, Texas.

> It was a wonderful time to be a doctor in these United States. It was what I like to think of as the golden age of American medicine, a time when we were conquering disease and no advancement seemed out of the question or beyond our

> reach.... Unfettered by regulation that told us what we could or could not do, physicians simply went out and did it. In return, our patients had a strong degree of faith in their family physicians, and that made it sheer pleasure to be a physician. There was very little government (or insurance company) interference in the practice of medicine.[1]

In a recent editorial, "Case Management: A Disastrous Mistake,"[2] which appeared in a leading medical journal, *Lancet*, the editor describes the ever-present peril of implementing a yet untested and hardly tried health-care system in the United Kingdom:

> Imagine a school which has been through some rocky times but whose staff are beginning to pull together at last. Suddenly, in an arbitrary attempt to raise standards and without prior testing, they are split up into teachers, who continue to provide education, and teaching assessors, who decide what should be taught and whether it is being provided effectively. The assessors are specialists in one subject only and yet they are put in a position of judging all their colleagues; their verdicts have no right of appeal. Any school that adopted a system like this would disintegrate in rowdy rancor within weeks (p. 399).

The article further describes the managed-care system as an unworkable system that will only alienate the medical profession from patients. Managed care's sole objective is cost-savings. Care for the elderly is a prime target for reduced health-care resources. In the name of futility, or better still, marginal utility, many medical services are expected to be cut. No doubt, there is ample waste in our current health-care system. But one should fear the fraudulent representations of much useful care as futile by health-care professionals, whose only criterion for care is cost-effectiveness. And the greater fear is that the traditional trust between patient and doctor will become irretrievably eroded. That would create a tense and hostile environment in which a once noble and esteemed profession falls in disgrace.

Unfortunately, the weighty issue of how these new health-care deliveries will affect care for the elderly has been conspicuously left out of national deliberations about health-care reform. A health-care system that rewards physicians for providing less medical care for their patients is a corrupt system. The motivation of even a well-intentioned practitioner who asks a patient to forsake a futile therapy may become suspect under such a system. Decisions to limit care must be based totally on the doctors' professional judgment and their unwavering devotion to the best interests of their patients. The moral weight of the doctor–patient relationship should be taken seriously at all times.

HOW IS THE CHANGING WORLD OF MANAGED CARE CHANGING THE PRACTICE OF MEDICINE?

An article entitled "California's Anguished Doctor Revolt," by Harry Nelson, recently appeared in *Lancet* (vol. 345, 1995):

> California's doctors are so aggrieved with their lot ... with health care organizations and other intermediaries. These bodies have the power to pick and choose doctors and to determine which services will be provided. Contracts have been terminated suddenly, "gag" clauses in the contract prevent doctors from criticizing their employers, organization, and there are fears that a high proportion of doctors will find themselves out of a job in the next few years. (p. 716)

As one of the doctors put it to a reporter, "We are just guppies in a tank of sharks that already control the market." Indeed, in today's medicine the doctor is different, the patient is different, and society is different. The more important question, however, is whether medicine's core values ought to change with the change of society. And how would that affect the treasured doctor–patient relationships and medical care at the end of life? The essence of medical practice is captured in the oath formulated by Hippocrates (c. 460–400 B.C.), an oath that physicians take upon graduation from medical school:

> I will use treatment to help the sick according to my ability and judgment, but never with a view to injury and wrongdoing. I will keep pure and holy both my life and my art.... In whatsoever houses I enter, I will enter to help the sick and I will abstain from all intentional wrongdoing and harm especially from abusing man or woman, bond or free. And whatsoever I shall see or hear in the course of my profession in my intercourse with men, if it be what should not be published abroad, I will never divulge, holding such things to be holy secrets ...

Furthermore, the Hippocratic oath's instructions include the following:

> Sometimes give your services for nothing, calling to mind a previous benefaction or present satisfaction.... For where there is love of man, there is also love of the art.... For some patients, though conscious that their condition is perilous, recover their health simply through contentment with the goodness of the physician ... and it is well to superintend the sick to *make them well*, to care for the healthy to *keep them well*, also to care for one's own self, so as to *observe what is seemly*.

The essence of the art of medicine derives from the pursuit of preserving health for those who are well, care for the sick and suffering, and comfort for the dying. Its values are guided by moderation, self-restraint, compassion, patience, understanding, discretion, and prudence. It demands truthfulness, sharing information with patients, compassion, encouragement, and fostering an appropriate measure of hope.

Leon Kass, Professor at the University of Chicago, in an article entitled "Neither for Love nor Money: Why Doctors Must Not Kill,"[4] eloquently describes a professional:

> Professing oneself a professional is an ethical act for many reasons. It is an articulate public act, not merely a private and silent choice—a confession before others who are one's witnesses. It freely promises continuing devotion, not merely announces present preferences, to a way of life, not just a way of livelihood, a life of action not only of thought. It serves

> some high good, which calls forth devotion because it is both good and high, but which requires such devotion because its service is not demanding and difficult, and thereby engages one's character, not merely one's mind and hands. (p. 30)

The doctor–patient relationship must be one of trust, predicated upon the patient's faith that his or her doctor's devotion to the patient's best interests is unconditional and unwavering. The patient expects his or her doctor to uphold the principles of devotion, respect, confidentiality, and beneficence. To quote from Plato's *The Republic*,[5] "No physician in-so-far as he is a physician, considers his own good in what he prescribes, but the good of his patient; for the true physician is also a ruler having the human body as a subject, and is not a mere money-maker."

Will this sacred bond between patient and doctor endure in a society in which the rights of man became the rights of consumers? Will it survive in the new schemes of managed care with their relentless focus on limiting expenditure rather than on diverting resources to the severely ill?

Despite medical advances on an unprecedented scale, despite changes in societal and institutional methods of health-care delivery, the essence of medicine remains unaltered since the days of Hippocrates: Healthy people desire to maintain their health, the ill desire to be whole, and the terminally ill seek comfort and encouragement. The contract between patient and doctor is one that seeks to promote wellness for the healthy and wholeness for the one who is ailing. Wholeness, it must be emphasized, means that the body is working sufficiently well, and its powers to sense, think, feel, desire, move, and maintain self are intact. Again, since the time of Hippocrates, the healer was advised to refrain from advising treatment that is not aimed at a degree of wholeness as expressed in the Hippocratic Corpus: "Whenever the illness is too strong for the available remedies, the physician surely must not expect that it can be overcome by medicine. To attempt futile treatment is to display an ignorance that is allied to madness."

Also, Plato reminds us in *The Republic*: "For those whose lives are always in a state of inner sickness, Ascalepius (the divine physician of ancient Greece) did not attempt to prescribe a regime that will only make their life a prolonged misery."

We live in an era when this sacred bond between doctor and patient is threatened to be separated by delivery systems that link "providers" to "consumers."[6] Our nation is in the process of revitalizing previously treasured values of devotion toward family, country, and each other. We need to reevaluate whether to let go of the treasured value of doctor–patient relationship to give room to some untested and untried profit-driven systems.

A RELATIONSHIP WITH A PHYSICIAN SPECIALIZING IN PATIENTS, NOT JUST DISEASE

Why should we hold on to this quaint, labor-intensive, component of health care? What is the danger of replacing it with a cold, impersonal, novel system? And in what way would the change of health-care systems affect treatment near the end of life? To illustrate how a strong doctor–patient bond is ensuring that one's wishes are honored, I would like to share with the reader two case histories that I presented to my medical ethics class.

The first case involves Mr. Smith, a 57-year-old gentleman who smoked three packs of cigarettes a day for 40 years. Mr. Smith developed severe emphysema and chronic inflammation of the airpipes. He continued to smoke in spite of his doctor's advice. The lung condition continued to deteriorate until he could hardly engage in any physical effort without becoming short of breath. He became vulnerable to a recurrent lung infection (i.e., pneumonia). In the year before his death, he was hospitalized four times to receive intensive-care therapy with antibiotics, treatments to facilitate breathing, and various other drugs for other conditions. The last of these hospitalizations required Mr. Smith to be placed on assisted ventilation (a mechanical breathing machine) for almost two weeks, and it took great efforts to wean him from the ventilator. Mr. Smith received oxygen from an oxygen tank day and night. He became chair-bound and could not sleep flat on his back in bed anymore. Prior to discharge from the hospital, the treating physician had a long conversation with Mr. Smith in the presence of Mrs. Smith. The gist of the conversation went as follows: "Mr. Smith, you know we have been lucky this time. It was a close call."

"I know it. It is nice to come back from the ashes ... the raising of Lazarus, sort of ..."

"Not quite ... modern medicine can produce miracles but rarely the kind of 'Pick up thy bed and walk.' On a serious note, you will feel quite weak for a long time, several weeks, maybe several months. Rehabilitation will be very slow. I arranged for a home nurse to visit you once a week to monitor your progress."

"O.K."

"And you will be on oxygen therapy at 2 liters per minute all the time, around the clock."

"How much will he be able to do?" asked Mrs. Smith.

"Not much. He will be almost chair-bound. We'll arrange for him to have a chair that he can use as a bed during the night. This time we prevailed. But now you will have to stop smoking. It is killing you. If you continue to smoke, we may not have another chance."

Mr. Smith leaned over with his head between his hands as if pondering a thought. He looked up and said: "Look doc, I have known all along that cigarettes will kill me one of these days. I also know that I do not have much longer to live. I shall be weak and limited but nevertheless, smoking is one of very few pleasures that I look forward to. If I have a choice between a slightly longer but more miserable life without a cigarette, I choose the shorter life. I will continue to smoke." He paused while struggling for a few more breaths and continued, "I want you to know, I do not want to go through this again, never again would I want to be on a ventilator. If this happens to me again, make me comfortable but let me die."

"I understand and I promise you that we will see to it that your wishes are honored."

Mr. Smith continued to smoke and was cared for at home. As expected, he had a recurrence of lung infection a few weeks later and was brought to the emergency room in severe distress. Mr. and Mrs. Smith were met by the treating physician. Mrs. Smith pleaded, "Please do something to help my husband breathe. Don't let him suffocate to death. He needs to be placed on the breathing machine."

The doctor turned to Mr. Smith, who was in obvious distress, fighting for his breath, half-conscious and drenched in sweat. The doctor asked, "Do you want me to put you on the machine to breathe for you?" The breathless patient nodded as if to say, "Please save me, I am drowning."

I had related this case to my medical students. I asked them: "Who of you would place Mr. Smith on the ventilator?" To my surprise, the response was unanimous. Not one student had any hesitation. The attending physician had made the same decision and Mr. Smith was placed on the ventilator.

The next day, it was discovered that Mr. Smith had suffered a heart attack. Thirty years of heavy smoking not only destroyed his lungs but took a heavy toll on the blood vessels that provide the heart muscle with necessary oxygen. Excessive smoking causes these blood vessels to narrow, and a major coronary artery became totally clogged up. Part of the heart muscle died, and the already severely damaged lungs became flooded with water.

Tedious adjustments in the ventilator machine became necessary. A small plastic tube was placed in Mr. Smith's heart to monitor its pumping function and pressures. Multiple medicines had to be given through multiple tubes, placed in multiple veins, located in multiple places. A tube placed in the bladder monitored urine flow, and another, placed in the stomach, enabled feeding.

Disorders of his heart rhythm required multiple electric shocks and frequent changes in medicines. A clot formed inside Mr. Smith's heart, traveled to his brain vessels and caused a stroke. Bacteria invaded his lungs and from there found their way into his bloodstream. His vital organs failed one after the other: lungs, heart, kidneys, liver, and finally his brain ceased to function.

Three weeks of unrelenting fighting culminated in the realization that the effort had been futile. Mrs. Smith asked that the doctors allow her husband to die without further "heroic" efforts.

I engaged in a "postmortem" discussion with my medical students about this patient. Was Mrs. Smith wrong in asking that her husband be placed on a ventilator? Of course not. She could not bear to see him suffer. An objective, well-reasoned evaluation of the situation, however, would lead to the conclusion that such intervention was doomed to be futile. It is one thing to evaluate the situation from a distance, dissociated from the immense feeling of helplessness, and another matter when you are driven by the gravity of the moment and the passion to hold onto a loved one. Were the doctors at fault? My students justified the doctor's intervention on two grounds: First, they felt that the patient revoked his previous health-care directive by asking the doctor to place him on the ventilator. Second, they felt that the physician would be setting himself up for legal liability had he not intervened as asked. I challenged them on both counts. "Asking a smothering, half-conscious patient whether he wants to be afforded relief is an inappropriate question," I said. "It is a given. This unquestioned duty of the medical profession could be extended with the aid of medicines rather than through a tube connected to a breathing machine. When you give the suffocating patient one option for relief and the patient elects to opt for it, this is not consent. Also, pretending that a half-conscious patient fighting hard for breath is able to think, evaluate, and rationally choose and consent is ridiculous," I added. Unfortunately, what happened with this patient exemplifies an everyday occurrence in intensive-care units and emergency room settings, and in my view, degrades the solemnity of a life near its close.

Had this patient had a really meaningful relationship with his physician, he would have been spared the indignity, travail, and cost of the last three weeks. The treating physician should have made every effort to make Mr. Smith comfortable with oxygen and morphine. If asked, he should have reminded Mrs. Smith of the patient's explicit desire of not wanting to endure such an ordeal. The doctor should never have asked Mr. Smith such a direct and leading question as "Do you want to be placed on a machine to relieve you?" while the patient was half-conscious and in dire distress. Patients in this state of mind are not able to reason; they need relief. Instead, the doctor should have said, "I will do everything to make you comfortable." That is what Mr. Smith explicitly asked for and was promised just a few weeks earlier. After all, in the words of the philosopher, Hegel, life has value only when it has something valuable as its object. I told my students: "Life can be revered not only in its preservation, but also in the manner in which we allow a given life to reach its terminus."

I proceeded to share with my students the story of another of my patients to illustrate the point.

Mrs. Williams, a very kind, 62-year-old lady, lived a life of pain and physical incapacity because of her intractable medical problems. She had a form of psoriasis, a scaly skin condition that was so extensive and so severe that almost all Mrs. Williams' body was covered with dry scales. The skin bruised and bled upon the least contact. Sloughed portions of the skin formed scabs, under which bacteria found a fertile field that enabled them to produce numerous little abscesses. Furthermore, psoriasis is associated with joint disease; Mrs. Williams' psoriasis afflicted all her joints with a vengeance, destroying her knees, hips, and the small joints in her hands and feet. She could not open a jar or squeeze a lemon without pain and she could hardly write her name. In spite of her enormous incapacity, she displayed courage, optimism, kindness, and love for her family. She had been married to her husband for 45 years and had two loving daughters, aged 40 and 38. Mrs. Williams received a multitude of treatments all her life. A year earlier, she had updated her living will and instructed her family to abstain from heroic measures at the close of her life. Recently, she was hospitalized for a stroke that involved the area of the brain responsible for the coordination of body movement. All of a sudden, she was seeing double images, could not speak intelligibly or hold herself up in bed, and was no longer able to feed herself.

I was asked to see her in consultation to evaluate whether the stroke was caused by a blood clot that originated in the heart. I examined Mrs. Williams and obtained an ultrasound image of her heart. It became clear that Mrs. Williams had developed an infection in a heart valve: the mitral valve on the left side of the heart. The infection rendered the valve leaky. Also, the mitral valve developed a large "vegetation," a nest of material infected with bacteria. It was clear that the valve infection arose from one of the many skin abscesses that had plagued her over the years; the same bacterial organism was found in bacterial cultures obtained from her skin and blood.

Under ordinary circumstances, a physician should treat the heart valve infection with antibiotics administered intravenously. After the infection is brought under control, surgical removal of the infected valve and its replacement with a mechanical valve would have been the proper course. A prosthetic heart valve would bring two distinct, new problems, however. First, it is more likely than a normal valve to pick up infection from the blood. Second, it would require treatment with anticoagulants (medicines that prevent blood clotting). In Mrs. Williams's case, these would represent big problems since she already had a high propensity to bleed and would risk the real danger of experiencing another infection in the new valve from bacteria invading her blood from abscesses in her skin. When I considered these problems, in addition to a recent crippling stroke on top of extensive joint deformity, not to mention the punishment of major heart surgery, I decided to recommend against surgical valve replacement. I discussed with Mr. and Mrs. Williams the treatment options and my reasons for my recommendation, in spite of the dangers of not removing the infected valve. These included the risk of heart failure and further clots traveling from the heart valve to vital organs, including the brain. Mrs. Williams accepted my recommendation and declined surgery. That same evening, I received a call through the answering service. One of Mrs. Williams's daughters was on the line, and she was literally livid. I asked the daughter to see me at the hospital the next morning.

"Why do you want my mother to die?" she asked. "Dr. X, the heart surgeon, was here yesterday and said that the only way to save mother is by replacing the infected valve with a mechanical one." The daughter went on to tell me, "I have convinced mother to have the operation as soon as possible."

I told her that surgery would have been the rational choice had her mother been otherwise healthy. "Your mother's other health problems will impose enormous challenges after surgery." She made it clear to me that they were ready to face the consequences.

As expected, surgery proved to be a big mess. The breastbone was so fragile that it fell to pieces while the surgeon was attempting to split it with a saw. Bleeding could not be controlled and the tissues broke down like toilet paper. After six long hours in the operating room, Mrs. Williams was transferred to an intensive-care-unit bed and was connected to a multitude of tubes and machines. The next few days were a series of punishments with bleeding, disordered heart rhythm, lung infection, and sluggish kidneys. On the 10th day after surgery, with Mrs. Williams still in intensive care, the daughter, choked with tears, told me, "My mother doesn't want to live anymore."

I asked, "What makes you think so?"

"Whenever I try to talk to Mother, she turns her head away from me. She wants to tell me that I caused her all of this suffering," she said. I squeezed her shoulder for encouragement. Mrs. Williams continued to deteriorate and died in the intensive-care unit.

Two weeks later, upon entering my office, my secretary informed me that a lady was waiting for me in my office. Mrs. Williams's daughter told me, "I came to apologize to you. I wish I had listened to your advice. My mother's image in the intensive-care unit with all of those bottles, tubes, and machines and with her body exposed, keeps haunting me in my sleep. I know I made a mistake by putting her through this ordeal."

I shared with her that many other well-meaning and loving people go through what she had been through. I showed her a recent survey published in *Social Science and Medicine*, showing that of 5,700 relatives and friends of people who had just died, 28% of the respondents had expressed the view that an earlier death would have been preferable.[7] We agreed that patients' families, when considering choices, often do not entertain the most plausible and realistic scenarios, but the most favorable one, even if that one is quite remote and unrealistic. They do so because they are motivated by noble feelings of love and caring, as well as by fear of loss and separation. I admitted that physicians inevitably make mistakes. That practice of medicine is not an exact science is unarguable. The art of medicine is based on weighing probabilities and derives from the theories of Thomas Baye,[8] an 18th-century English clergyman. His first theorem proposes, in horse-racing terms, that the likelihood of picking a winner from the field is proportional to the prevalence of favorable characteristics in the horse (past performance preferences for hard or soft going, handicaps) and the jockey. Just as there is not "one horse in a race," dealing with odds in the management of a patient poses a similar dilemma. It depends on the characteristics of the patient and the physician. It is uncommon for a treatment option to be the only possible one. There is usually an outsider in the competition, and sometimes the outsider wins.

With a sense of some relief, Mrs. Williams's daughter paused and then asked, "But why did the surgeon not present the options to us objectively. Why did he recommend surgery?"

"Bias and passion for surgery are not unethical so long as the motive is the well-being of the patient. Physicians presenting the facts, and individuals analyzing them, base their decisions not only upon the facts but also upon the way they are presented and the complex human emotions and experiences that shape them," I said.

I gave her the following example. Suppose the surgical intervention in your mother's case had a 5% chance of success. Any one of the two following presentations would be accurate, honest, and ethical.

Scenario 1: "As you know, your mother has enormously complex health problems. With medical treatment, we have a good chance of eradicating the infection from the heart valve. The risk of having a recurring stroke will not be obviated and, likely, your mother will develop heart failure. The latter will be made better with medication, and hopefully we will achieve enough improvement to allow her to engage in a rehabilitation program to deal with her stroke. I cannot recommend valve replacement surgery since her chances to survive surgery are less than 5%. Also, surgical intervention in her case will be attended with enormous logistical difficulties with bleeding, infection, pneumonia, and worsening of her stroke."

Scenario 2: "You mother's heart valve has been chewed up by organisms. It is leaking and soon will throw her into heart failure. The hazard of recurring stroke with this valve is real. Any additional stroke will likely kill her. We have a 1 in 20 chance to save her with surgery. It is not a big chance, but it is the only one."

Both scenarios are sincere but they are likely to result in two different decisions.

She pondered the thought and said, "But how can we, the laypeople, make the right decision about ourselves and our loved ones?" I gave her a long-winded answer, as if I were lecturing to my students: "Ethicists will tell you about the right of the patient to shared decision making. Notwithstanding, proper medical decisions are often complex, multifaceted, and emotionally charged. Your mother's predicament, if any, came about because the physician primarily responsible for her hospital care did not know her as a person long enough and was not attuned to her personal values. He was more knowledgeable about her disease than about the patient herself. She had a living will, but the document had little relevance to her final illness. The essence of medicine is not just to combat disease and carry out procedures. That would reduce medical practitioners into a bunch of slavish technicians without intelligible goals. A *doctor*, according to the dictionary, is 'a teacher, one who is skilled in healing.' Attending to the patient's individual perception of what constitutes the meaning of life and how it is affected by crippling illness is an important component of the healing profession."

She straightened up in the chair and said, "But Mother did not have a primary physician. She was seeing a skin specialist and an arthritis specialist before all this happened."

I told her that any of these specialists could have been her primary physician, especially the arthritis specialist. He knew her limitations, helped her with her disability, and assisted her in dealing with her pain. I am a cardiologist, and in my practice, over 5,000 patients identified me as their primary physician. Your primary physician is the one you have come to trust, the one with whom you share your values and preferences when it comes to decisions of when to wage a fight and when to die. There is no substitute for having a meaningful doctor–patient relationship.

THE TYPE OF MEDICAL PRACTICE MAY INFLUENCE PATIENT–PHYSICIAN COMMUNICATION

A study entitled "Discussion of Preferences for Life-Sustaining Care by Persons with AIDS" was published in the *Archives of Internal Medicine* in May 1993.[9] Dr. Jennifer S. Haas and collaborators collected data from patients in the Boston area at Massachusetts General Hospital, Harvard University, and Boston University Hospital. These authors assessed the determinants of communication about resuscitation between persons with Acquired Immune Deficiency Syndrome (AIDS) and their physicians. The study involved three groups of patients, one at a staff-model health maintenance organization (HMO), one at an internal medicine group practice at a private teaching hospital, and one at an AIDS clinic at a public hospital. The study found that 72% of all patients desired to discuss preferences for life-sustaining care with their physician. Such desire was not dependent upon race, severity of illness, place of care, or medical treatment. Patients were less likely to have had an open discussion about their illness if they were cared for by a HMO rather than a clinic. However, the authors emphasized that better patient–physician communication is needed across the board.

Managed care is now becoming a fixture in the delivery of health care. It is exigent that this type of care delivery not stifle patient–physician communication, for this unique, intimate dialogue is still the best assurance for quality of health care, quality of life—and quality of death.

NOTES

1. JH Sammons, *Inside Medical Washington*. (Knoxville, TN: Whittle Direct Books, 1991), pp. 5–6.
2. Editorial, "Case Management: A Disastrous Mistake," *Lancet*, 345 (1995), 399–401.
3. *Hippocrates* (6 vols.), translated by WHS Jones. The Loeb Classical Library. Cambridge, MA: Harvard University Press, 1988. (Originally published in 1923)
4. LR Kass, *Neither for Love nor Money: Why Doctors Must Not Kill* (Public Interest, published by National Affairs, Washington, DC, 1989), pp. 25–46.
5. Platos, *The Republic* (Hackett Publishing Co., 1974).
6. "Specialization, Centralized Treatment, and Patient Care," *Lancet*, 345 (1995), 1251–1252.
7. M Dean, "Politics of Euthanasia in UK," *Lancet*, 345 (1995), 714.
8. M Chiswick, "The Science of Making Mistakes," *Lancet*, 345 (1995), 871–872.
9. JS Hass, JS Weissman, and PD Cleary, "Discussion of Preferences for Life-Sustaining Care by Persons with AIDS: Predictors of Failure in Patient–Physician Communication," *Archives of Internal Medicine*, 153 (1993), 1241–1248.

Chapter 13

A Practical Living Will

Lessons from Denmark

> To die well is the height of wisdom of life.
>
> —SÖREN KIERKEGAARD (1813–1855)

In the process of writing this book, I came across the Danish living will, a practical, concise, and clear living will. I read about the will in an article by Richard Smith, an editorial writer, that appeared in the *British Medical Journal*, in February 1993. What impressed me the most was the way the Danish citizens reacted to the will, with large numbers of persons 55 years and older executing it. (This is in sharp contrast to the situation in America.) In fact, there was so much enthusiasm that three times the expected number of Danish citizens executed the will.[1]

Recently, I took a trip to Copenhagen, the Netherlands, and to other European countries to study firsthand the way these societies are dealing with the difficult issues pertaining to medical treatment at the end of life. I spent a whole day talking to various members at the Danish Department of Health: Dr. Maria Jensen, its director; Ms. Ulcpsen, the chief nurse; and Ms. Uspfesen, who is in charge of the register. I was favorably impressed by the Danish approach.

DANISH HEALTH CARE: A FINANCIALLY AND MEDICALLY SOUND SYSTEM

An understanding of how medicine is practiced in Denmark is essential before I review the Danish living will.

In Denmark, there is universal access to health care for all citizens. The government picks up the tab, paying doctors a range of salaries that are negotiated every few years. There is no incentive for health-care providers to perform more procedures or to limit care. They are rewarded a fixed fee and are expected to provide appropriate and optimal medical care. Unlike our American health-care system, doctors and hospitals are not rewarded for performing procedures. There do exist a few privately owned, for-profit, small, and highly specialized hospitals, but these provide care to a small minority of Danish citizens. The few complaints about medical negligence or inadequate treatment are reviewed by a grievance medical committee, appointed jointly by the Department of Health and the Danish Medical Association. Some complaints are dismissed. For the few that are deemed valid, the committee suggests the awards or punitive measures to be assessed against the health-care professionals. Only exceptional cases are litigated in court and only after they have been thoroughly reviewed by the appropriate committees.

In Danish hospitals, the intensive-care-unit beds constitute 1–2% of all hospital beds, compared to 5–10% in America. In 1985, the National Board of Health in Denmark implemented guidelines for treatment at the end of life. These guidelines were developed by the Department of Health in conjunction with various medical groups and were widely disseminated and adopted by treating physicians. These guidelines are reviewed periodically.

For example, in 1985, it was noted that over 55% of the elderly died in Danish hospitals. This was felt to be a high percentage. Over the past nine years, the percentage has been brought down to 50%. This was accomplished through an agreed-upon policy between the Department of Health and Danish Medical Association, a concerted effort for public education, and promotion of home and hospice care. (In the United States, over 60% of elderly die in hospitals.)

The guidelines call for no resuscitation efforts for patients in nursing homes. The appropriateness of CPR on patients treated in the hospital are reviewed by the treating team on a case-by-case basis. When in doubt, the question is settled by the most senior physician. Patients with end-stage disease or infection (such as advanced AIDS complicated by extensive brain damage, systemic infection, and evidence of very low immune-cell count) are not placed on a ventilator when they develop pneumonia, a common practice in the United States. Intensive-care-unit beds are used exclusively for those who have the potential of a decent medical recovery. Otherwise, patients are treated at home or in nursing homes and never in an intensive-care unit. Like in all other European countries, very few citizens in Denmark used to execute living wills. Europeans have trusting relationships with their physicians, who are expected to take their moral authority very seriously. It is extremely rare that the professional integrity of a physician is brought into question. The medical practice in Europe is not as high-tech driven as it is in the United States, and citizens there accept death much more readily. In most European countries, the per capita expenditures for health care are about half what they are in the United States.

In all circumstances, the patients and their families are involved in the medical decision-making process, but disputes with physicians are rare. Most patients and family members have a meaningful relationship with their physician.

Trusting patient–doctor relations aside, there is a multitude of complex and often vexing issues related to the application of high-tech interventions and experimentation.

The Central Scientific Ethics Committee (CSEC) was established in Denmark in 1978. This committee, comprised primarily of scientists, is concerned with ethical issues relating to medical research.

In 1988, the Parliament created another layperson committee, the Danish Council of Ethics, to consider a broader range of biomedical issues and to serve as the primary adviser to the Parliament.[2] This council is perhaps more grassroots than any other in the world: It is comprised of 17 members, mostly laypeople who are not health-care professionals, and is nearly evenly divided by gender.

The council's public education efforts are far-reaching and encompass ethical issues dealing with the definition of life and death. It is this council that, after multiple public debates, television documentaries, and other public-education forums, recommended the adoption of upper-brain death as the end of life. The council also arranges and supervises public health-care discussions, including television debates and discussions of health-related issues, and production of health-education materials for school children and the public. They sponsor award-winning movies and national television shows on timely health topics, as well as annual essay contests among school children on health-care issues. Of note is that while health-care costs continued to climb in all Western countries in 1994, health-care expenditures declined in real terms in Denmark without affecting the quality of care or the patients' satisfaction. The lesson is that an informed public is paramount in dealing with such issues.

THE DANISH LIVING WILL: A VERY VIABLE DOCUMENT

Guided by public opinion polls, news media discussions, and open public debates, the Danish Council of Ethics recommended to the Parliament the adoption of the Danish living will, which was enacted into law in October 1992. The Danish public accepted it instantly and with great enthusiasm. This is surprising in view of the prevailing tradition by which Danish citizens relinquished difficult medical decisions to their physicians.

When discussing the Danish living will with Danish physicians, I got mixed messages. Some Danish physicians enthusiastically endorse the legislation as a progressive and much needed move. A few other practitioners believe that they should not have been left out of the debate prior to the legislation. Many argue that the living will has not changed their way of practicing medicine, since they never used high-tech medicine for the treatment of those conditions proscribed by the living will anyway. The Danish Medical Association expressed its worries about certain definitions in the living will. Initially, the association opposed the legislation to enforce the living will.

Eventually, physicians accepted the new living will and now do not question the patient's directives. All living wills executed by patients are entered into a central registry, and all health-care providers have immediate access to them. Health-care professionals are required by law to check the registry before applying life-prolonging treatment to their patients.

There are two components to the will: (1) the legal document executed by the patient and (2) a brochure giving medical scenarios to which the will applies. This medical brochure is disseminated among physicians and provides a reference that helps preclude possible misinterpretation and misapplication of the spirit of the legislation. Following is a translation of the Danish medical brochure and the Danish living will, performed at my request by Rene Kronvold at the School of Business at the University of Tampa, Florida. A translation of the physician's brochures is found in Appendix B. The translations are from original documents, which I obtained from the Registry of the Ministry of Health. A summary of the advantages of the Danish document compared to the American living will is seen in Table 6.

LIVING WILL (FROM DENMARK)

The Choice Is Yours

From early on, there has been no doubt that a doctor's mission is to preserve life as long as possible. With today's opportunities for preserving life, a problem has arisen for many people.

Table 6
Differences between American Living Wills and the Danish Version

	Contemporary American living will	Danish living will
Scope	Terminal illness and when death is imminent	Terminal illness, end-stage organ disease, permanent mental and physical disability
Uniformity	Varies from state to state	One form
Brevity	Often lengthy legal document	Concise and to the point
Language	Legal jargon	Layperson's language
Appointment of surrogate	Optional	Not necessary
Legally binding	No	Yes
Central registry	No	Yes
Immediate access	No	Yes

The thought of living without being conscious or without hope of healing is unpleasant—if not scary. This has led many to say to their loved ones, "If I get in a situation like that, I would rather die in peace." Today's technological possibilities of keeping people alive are so advanced that it is fair to consider whether one should have a "say so" in a situation like this. As a result of this the government has passed a law that makes it possible for individuals to write a living will.

Living Will

By writing a living will while we are well, we can make sure that our wishes are honored. In the living will, we can inform doctors that if death is unavoidable, we do not wish to receive treatment in order to prolong life. We can also say that if we are to lie helpless and hope of improvement is "zero," then we do not wish to receive treatment in order to prolong life.

Inactive Death-Help

One does not sign an agreement that says one wishes to actively encourage death. One makes a wish (for the future) to choose not to be kept alive in a situation where one cannot voice an opinion and where hope of healing has withered away. If one is conscious and can voice a personal opinion, naturally this request will be honored. The living will only becomes "activated" when doctors and loved ones cannot reach the individual and will never again be able to establish contact.

The Living Will Must Be Registered

The living will is made up of the form duplicated at the end of this chapter. After it is filled out, it should be mailed to Rigshospitalet's Living Will Registrar's office—the address is on the bottom of the form. When Rigshospitalet (hospital) receives the form, a confirmation and a request for registration fee of 50 kroner ($10.00) are mailed. If the fee is not paid within 30 days, the registration will be canceled.

If the Will Becomes an Issue

Doctors in medical institutions will contact Rigshospitalet if it is important to find out whether or not the patient has written a living will. There are differences in the way the doctor must honor the patient's wishes. If a patient's living will makes it clear that he or she does not wish to receive treatment if death is unavoidable (section 1) then the doctor has no choice but to honor the request. If a patient does not wish to receive treatment to prolong life, if he or she lies helpless without hope or improvement (Section 2), then the doctor needs to take this into consideration about treatment.

Do Others Need to Know?

It is not necessary to inform anyone else besides the Registrar at Rigshospitalet that one has written a living will. However, it might be a good idea to inform the family about the choice. Otherwise it can be a very difficult situation for the family when it arises. It might also be a good idea to talk to the doctor about the decision.

Changing the Decision

If a patient regrets the decision, he or she can cancel the will by writing the Registrar. If he or she becomes involved in a situation where it becomes an issue, there also is the opportunity to cancel the will by informing the treating physician.

LIVING WILL (THE FORM)

1. I do *not* wish to receive life-prolonging treatment if I am in a situation where death is unavoidable.
2. I do *not* wish to receive life-prolonging treatment in case of advanced severe disability, severe weakness due to old age, accident, advanced heart failure, or a similar illness that has resulted in such a severe state of invalidism that I never will be able to take care of myself physically and mentally.
3. I wish, in the situation mentioned in Section 1, to be spared from pain with the use of medication (painkillers), even though it could result in early death.

COMMENT

The Danish living will (LW) differs in many respects from those currently used in the United States. The Danish document is simple and is written with the common citizen in mind. The document does not need to be witnessed or notarized. This contrasts sharply with the legal language and various requirements that characterize LWs in America. Lack of uniformity and portability provide major impediments to the use of LWs in the highly mobile American society. Whereas the Danish LW is always available by direct access to one central registry, the American LW is often unavailable at the time of need. The Danish LW is legally binding to physicians, who are fully informed about the spirit of the legislation. In America, the LW is often ignored by physicians or overridden through instructions from family members and from surrogates.

The Danish living will has an obvious shortcoming that would stand in the way of its implementation in the United States. The Danish document provides lay individuals with limited information about possible medical scenarios near the end of life. This would not be problematic in Denmark, where the traditional patient–physician trust and physician freedom from the fear of litigation prevail. In the United States, for a Danish-style living will to have effect, it would have to include sufficient details about medical scenarios that cover severe disabilities, severe weakness due to senility, and end-stage organ disease. Nevertheless, the Danish document is an excellent template with which to adapt a viable document for American citizens. The "Universal Living Will" proposed in the next chapter is such a document.

NOTES

1. Editorial, "Public Uses Denmark's Living Will," *British Medical Journal*, 306 (1993), 413–415.
2. *Denmark*. Biomedical Ethics in Biolaw (Bethesda, MD: University Publications of America, 1993), pp. 43–44.

Chapter 14

The Universal Living Will

An American Solution

> Let no one pay me honor with tears nor celebrate my funeral rites with weeping.
> —Quintus Innius, 239–169 B.C. (in Cicero, *De Senectute* XX)

Recent reports suggest that the living will in its present form is practically useless; it is almost irrelevant in guiding treatment near the end of life. This pertains to decisions for CPR as well as other medical interventions for the terminally ill. By executing a living will, many in the Western World intend to assert that they value life only so long as it confers its perceived pleasures and dignity; when they are no longer able or competent to make decisions about medical treatment choices, they resent being enslaved to high-tech machines, and they wish to spare themselves and their loved ones the emotional and financial burdens that come with a meaningless prolongation of a life deemed by them to be not worth living.

As discussed earlier, the idea of a "living will" was proposed in the late 1960s during one of the meetings of the Euthanasia Society of America, and a pioneer will had been distributed by the Euthanasia Educational Council since 1969. This pioneer document found immediate acceptance among the public at large because of its simplicity, brevity, and personalized wording. Its overriding purpose was to guide the withholding and/or withdrawal of treatment in the event of "... physical and mental disability without a reasonable expectation of recovery."

Unfortunately, this "first-generation" document was judged to be ambiguous by physicians, unacceptable by lawyers, and problematic to ethicists, particularly in regard to definitions of "permanent disability," "heroic measures," and "artificial means." As a result, advance directives underwent transformation into "second-generation" documents. Unfortunately, in the process, advance directives became complex, lengthy, confusing, and often intimidating legal documents, encumbered by several requisites and a very limited scope of applicability. Typically, second-generation "living wills" pertain exclusively to cessation of futile medical care when the patient is *in extremis* and when death is imminent, a fact unrevealed to many who execute the documents (and to the dismay of many families and would-be patients). In this regard, current "living wills" fail to express the wishes of those who execute them and loath the torment of dependence and indignity.

In addition to their limited scope, conventional living wills suffer from many other shortcomings, among which are infrequent utilization by citizens, unavailability when needed, lack of specificity, impersonal nature, discordant interpretation of the patient's wishes by the patient-appointed surrogate, unbinding nature with regard to health-care professionals, and inconsistencies in advance directive legislation among different states, to name a few. Table 7 summarizes the main deficiencies of most current advance directives.

Only recently, have all states adopted some form or another of advance directive legislation, and most states have surrogate (health-care proxy) ordinances. For these and other reasons, I propose a short, clear, and all-encompassing "third-generation" advance directive, in an attempt to correct most of the limitations

Table 7
Advantages of the Universal Living Will Compared to the Current American Living Will

	Current American living will	Universal living will
Format	Impersonal	Personal
Language	Legal jargon	Plain English
Applicability	Terminal illness *in extremis*	End-stage disease, as well as terminal illness
Conformity between patient and surrogate	Discrepancy between patient's wishes and that of surrogate	Workbook enables patient to share wishes clearly with surrogate
Portability among states	Nonportable from state to state	Uniformity among all states (with the new act)

of current second-generation living wills (copyright, Library of Congress, 1995).

What makes this proposal even more timely is the Uniform Health-Care Decisions Act that was approved by the Uniform Law Commissioners in August 1993. This legislation proposed to enable all American states to replace their existing legislation on the subject with a single statute, therefore enhancing the utility of the "living will." The proposed act further removed the unnecessary impediments to the use of a living will and widened the scope of the advance directive to encompass not only terminal illness but also end-stage disease when death is expected in a few months. The act was approved by the American Bar Association in February 1994. It is hoped that this much-needed legislation becomes adopted by most or all states in the new few years. The prefatory note cites major weaknesses in current Advance Health-Care Directive legislation, including the fragmented, incomplete, and sometimes inconsistent set of rules and conflicts between statutes in different states, including the lack of portability of a living will from state to state.

The act encompasses the following concepts:

1. The right of a competent person to choose or refuse any or all medical treatment in all circumstances. The patient may extend all or some defined part of this power to one or more specified individuals under specified circumstances articulated by the individual.
2. The act is comprehensive and is designed to replace any and every preceding legislation regarding refusal of medical care by patient or surrogate.
3. The act is designed to simplify and facilitate the making of a living will, which may be either written or oral. A power of attorney for health care must be written but need not be witnessed or notarized.
4. The surrogate must act in accordance with the individual's expressed instructions. Otherwise, he or she should apply the patient's best-interests standard in the decision.
5. The act requires compliance from health-care providers and institutions so long that the directive meets applicable health-care standards. Furthermore, an optional form is suggested for general use. The form has entries for
   a. Choice not to prolong life in case of (1) incurable and irreversible conditions that will result in death in a short time, (2) unconsciousness that is irreversible within a reasonable degree of certainty, or (3) when the likely risks and burdens of treatment would outweigh the expected benefits.
   b. Choice to prolong life within the limits of generally accepted health-care standards.

There are shortcomings in the aforementioned legislation. I believe that the medical scenarios lack the specificity to make them binding to health-care providers. Also, it implies that medically unnecessary treatment would be automatically provided for those who do not execute a living will. For these reasons, and in order to strengthen the proposed legislation, I propose the universal living will. The benefits of the universal living will over the contemporary American living will are summarized in Table 7.

In my view, the utilization of one simplified form of "living will" (that encompasses not only terminal illness but also end-stage disease) will go a long way to encourage the use of the advance directive. Furthermore, the establishment of one central, computerized registry of all those who execute "living wills," to which health-care professionals can have immediate access, will make the "living will" more meaningful and effective in the United States.

The "universal living will" was designed to consist of two parts: a workbook and the document itself. The two sections are found in Appendix C.

SUMMARY

Many problems undermine the utility and effectiveness of current living will forms. We propose a new "universal living will" that has the following distinct advantages:

- Written in plain, simple, easily understood English.
- A workbook is provided, by which the patient becomes familiar with end-of-life medical scenarios and therefore can make informed choices.
- Focused yet encompasses a wide range of medical scenarios not only limited to terminal illness, but also covering other medical conditions when death is near but not imminent, or when the patient has become totally dependent.
- Should be binding to physician, health-care professionals, and relatives; dispels fear of litigation that derives from ambiguities.
- Can be easily stored in the data bank of a central registry.
- Has provisions for a patient's special wishes and can be personalized.

- Allows for decisions regarding cardiopulmonary resuscitation.
- Obviates the possibility of an appointed surrogate acting contrary to the patient's desires.

I hope that this simple but all-encompassing, specific document will become universally adopted in place of current living wills. This will conform with the spirit of the recently proposed legislation, the "Uniform Living Act." Furthermore, it will go a long way toward the establishment of a centralized national registry to which health-care professionals will have immediate access. And finally, it can do much to eliminate the needless suffering involved in futile medical care.

Chapter 15

Essays by Physicians on Living and Dying

My Living Will, My Dying Will

LOFTY BASTA, M.D.

This book has been a personal and professional testament. It is my "living will" that the information I have provided will allow the reader to take more control over his or her destiny.

The bulk of this book has been constituted by my professional experience with the issue of dying with dignity. I would now like to end this book with these personal testaments on mortality:

Sooner or later, the clock of my genes will wind down and I shall face the inevitability of my death. I can quote Seneca: "Life, well used, is long enough for me." With contentment and peace, I heed Epicurus: "To a longer and worse life, a shorter and better is by all means to be preferred." Fortunately, the essence of my genes is alive and well in my children—Victor, Steven, and Mona—and continues to replicate vigorously in my grandchildren, Max and Elliott, ensuring my immortality.

A fast replay of my life events flashes through my mind. And so do the words of Benjamin Franklin: "Were it offered to my choice, I should have no objection to a repetition of the same life from its beginning, only asking the advantages authors have in a second edition ... to correct some faults in the first." I wish I could undo the many mistakes I have committed through negligence, inattention, or just sheer stupidity. Throughout my life, I have tried, succeeded and failed, laughed and cried, celebrated and grieved, overcome travails and succumbed to pangs, but I never stopped trying. I have been a musician who played solo in public while learning the instrument as life went on.

Sooner or later, my flesh will be invaded, displaced, overwhelmed, and smothered by cancer cells exploding out of hiding and replicating vigorously. Or I might outlive my cancer to die slowly from a heart ailment or another debilitating condition. At that time, I do not need experts in life prolongation. I need helpers for enduring physical pain and mental anguish.

Don't tuck me in the isolation of the torture chamber called intensive care, where I would be cold, unclad, and invaded. I would like to be kept clean, warm, shaved, and comfortably attended to in my own bed. Spray my face with my favorite fragrance. Open my window so that I can feel God's soothing breeze, see God's uplifting sunshine, and hear God's hymnals through the singing of the birds. Play me Beethoven's *Moonlight Sonata* to enliven my soul. Keep me close to my immensely charming, utterly unselfish, beautifully pure, richly graceful wife, Laila. As she glows in that very special perfume, let me place my hand in hers as she reads me Anna Barlaud's poem:

> Life! We have been long together
> through pleasant and through cloudy weather;
> Tis hard to depart when friends are dear,
> Perhaps it will cost a sigh, a tear;
> Then steal away give better warning,
> Choose thine own time,
> Say not "good night" but in some brighter clime,
> Bid me good morning.[1]

And as I utter my last words, I shall hear Him calling me from heaven: "Well done, thou good and faithful servant; enter now into the joy."

*To Remember Me**

CHARLES ISRAEL, M.D.

The day will come when my body will lie upon a white sheet neatly tucked under four corners of a mattress located in a hospital busily occupied with the living and the dying. At a certain moment a doctor will determine that my heart has ceased to beat and that, for all intents and purposes, my life has stopped.

When that happens, do not attempt to instill artificial life into my body by the use of a machine. And don't call this my deathbed. Let it be called the Bed of Life, and let my body be taken from it to help others lead fuller lives.

Give my sight to the man who has never seen a sunrise, a baby's face, or love in the eyes of a woman. Give my heart to a person whose own heart has caused nothing but endless days of pain. Give my blood to the teenager who was pulled from the wreckage of his car, so that he might live to see his grandchildren play. Give my kidneys to one who depends on a machine to exist. Take my bones, every muscle, every fiber and nerve in my body, and find a way to make a crippled child walk.

Explore every corner of my brain. Take my cells, if necessary, and let them grow so that, someday, a speechless boy will shout at the crack of a bat and a deaf girl will hear the sound of rain against her window.

If you must bury something, let it be my faults, my weaknesses, and all prejudice against my fellow man.

Burn whatever remains of my body and throw my ashes in the wind so that a young bird may become able to sing or a budding flower may grow.

If, by chance, you wish to remember me, do it with a kind deed or word to someone who needs you. If you do all I have asked, I will live forever.

*Written by the author (a physician friend) in 1976, before his untimely death in his thirties from multiple sclerosis.

If I Become Ill and Unable to Manage My Own Affairs ...

EUGENE A. STEAD, JR., M.D.*

This is the first generation in which the majority of persons between 40 and 60 years of age are financially responsible for three generations. Each family *with children* has at least four grandparents and, in this day and age, at least one of the grandparents will survive and become partially or completely senile. This last week, I have been shopping for a very sweet but beginning-to-be-confused grandmother. She is used to doing for herself, and she does not adapt easily to having other people do for her. She tells her house-helper not to do most things. She intends to do them herself. But, alas, she forgets and they are never done. She likes the visiting nurse who helps her with personal cleanliness and gives her advice about cooking, eating, and shopping but, again, she cannot believe that she can't do it on her own.

As I shopped in the community where she has spent her life, I found good will on all sides. The saleswoman in the department store, the assistant manager of the bank, the salesmen responsible for mattresses, pillows, and linens were interested in my problem: how to keep my lady functioning and living in her community. Each of them has faced similar problems. They look on the nursing home as inevitable but each, on the basis of his own experience, hopes that time can be postponed. They have no good answers to old age—nor do I.

What shall we do if Grandmother slips and breaks her hip? What shall we do if she develops pneumonia? Must medical science intervene and keep her breathing but not living?

Our family must face the problem and advise Grandmother's doctor of our feelings. We, as parents, must remember that the patterns we devise for our parents are likely to be followed by our children when they must make similar decisions.

*Previously Distinguished Professor and Chairman of Internal Medicine, Duke University, Durham, North Carolina (published in *Medical Times*, August 1970).

Many years ago, I wrote my own personal physician a letter to guide his hand if I became ill and my mind was not functioning normally. I quote from that letter.

> If I become ill and unable to manage my own affairs, I want you to be responsible for my care. To make matters as simple as possible, I will leave certain specific instructions with you.
>
> In the event of unconsciousness from an automobile accident, I do not wish to remain in a hospital for longer than two weeks without full recovery of my mental faculties. While I realize that recovery might still be possible, the risk of living without recovery is still greater. At home, I want only one practical nurse. I do not wish to be tube-fed or given intravenous fluids at home.
>
> In the event of a cerebral accident, other than a subarachnoid hemorrhage, I want no treatment of any kind until it is clear that I will be able to think effectively. This means no stomach tube and no intravenous fluids.
>
> In the event of a subarachnoid hemorrhage, use your own judgment in the acute stage. If there is considerable brain damage, send me home with one practical nurse.
>
> If, in spite of the above care, I become mentally incapacitated and have remained in good physical condition, I do not want money spent on private care. I prefer to be institutionalized, preferably in a state hospital.
>
> If any other things happen, this will serve as a guide to my own thinking.
>
> Go ahead with an autopsy with as little worry to Ev as possible. The Anatomy crematory seems a good final solution.

Now the time has come to write a letter to Grandmother's doctor. He is a wise man and will appreciate the support a family can give in a problem for which there is no wholly satisfactory answer.

Address to the Medical School Class of 1871

Oliver Wendell Holmes, M.D.

The persons who seek the aid of the physician are very honest and sincere in their wish to get rid of their complaints, and generally speaking, the future is painted for them, they are attached to the planet with which they are already acquainted. They are addicted to the daily use of this empirical and unchemical mixture which we call air, and would hold onto it as a tippler does to his alcoholic drinks. There is nothing men will not do, there is nothing they have not done, to recover their health and save their lives. They have submitted to be half-drowned in water, and half-choked with gases, to be buried up to their chins in earth, to be seared with hot irons like galley slaves, to be crimped with knives, like cod-fish, to have needles thrust into their flesh, and bonfires kindled in their skin, to swallow all sorts of abominations, and to pay for all this, as if to be singed and scalded were a costly privilege, as if blisters were a blessing, and leeches were a luxury.

NOTES

1. AL Barbauld. "Ode to Life, 1773." In: *Quotations on Historical Principles from Ancient and Modern Sources*, HL Menchen, ed. (New York: Alfred A Knopf, 1987), p. 263. (Originally published in 1942)

Appendix A

Hospital Policies Regarding Futile Care*

The documents are presented to show the lack of uniformity in the interpretation of futility and the procedure to deal with it in various leading institutions.

Although much valuable thought has been utilized in formulating these procedures, there is great need to debate these issues among the public at a national level.

ALLEGHENY GENERAL HOSPITAL, PITTSBURGH, PENNSYLVANIA

"... When the attending physician believes that life-sustaining treatment may be potentially "futile," that is, physiologically unable to work, then it is not necessary to initiate this treatment. The physician does not need permission to forego such treatment.... Other definitions of futility are ambiguous because they involve

*From D. B. Waisel and R. D. Truog, "The Cardiopulmonary Resuscitation Non-Indicated Order: Futility Revisited." *Annals of Internal Medicine* 122(1995), pp. 304–308.

making value judgments about the quality of life.... Determinations of futility in this context (quality of life), made unilaterally by the physician, are not appropriate."

Allegheny General Hospital endorses a policy that is based on the ability to achieve certain physiological parameters, or physical functions. Although these specific parameters are not defined, the hospital's proposal is clarified by contrasting physiological futility with other kinds of futility, such as a treatment with a high likelihood of failure or one incapable of resolving the patient's underlying condition. Furthermore, the policy notes that "very few life-sustaining treatments are going to meet this narrow definition of futility." Using a physiological basis to define *futility* limits the need for qualitative and quantitative judgments. Allegheny General Hospital's policy is an excellent example of an attempt to appreciate the concerns of potentially futile care while acknowledging the difficulty of implementing a more sweeping proposal.

VETERANS AFFAIRS MEDICAL CENTER, SEATTLE, WASHINGTON

"A medical judgment is made that attempted CPR would be futile when either of the following (are fulfilled): (a) Quantitative futility: ... a very low or rare probability of achieving the return of vital organ function and survival beyond a short period of time or (b) Qualitative futility: CPR might be effective in sustaining life but the patient's quality of life falls well below the threshold considered minimal by general professional judgment. In making a judgment of futility, the physician relies on personal experience, medical literature, and on observations in the context of caring for the individual patient.... When a patient (or surrogate decision-maker) disagrees with the physician's judgment of medical futility and would like to receive CPR, the physician should not write a DNR (do not attempt resuscitation) order until resolution of the disagreement."

This policy attempts to avoid the inherent problems of vague definitions by adopting a proposal by Schneiderman and colleagues; they define a treatment as futile if "physicians conclude (either through personal experience, experiences shared with colleagues or consideration of reported empirical data) that in the last 100 cases, a medical treatment has been useless." This would mean that a clinician would be "95% confident that no more than three successes would occur in each 100 comparable trials." *Useless* is defined as death, permanent unconsciousness, or permanent dependence on intensive medical care. When a situation is judged to be futile, recovery of the patient would be "highly improbable and ... cannot be systematically reproduced."

The precision of quantitative futility is diminished in the Veterans Affairs policy (compared with the proposal of Schneiderman and colleagues). However, "very low or rare" does have the admirable quality of admitting imperfection in the ability to predict outcomes. The process for defining futility is severely hampered by inconsistency, memory, and medical prejudices. For example, relying on subjective and anecdotal information allows physicians to unintentionally make decisions, perhaps through selective recollection, that may not be equitable. Even if an exact definition of quantitative futility were possible, empirical data may not provide the answers. A recent study indicated the difficulty of defining which clinical variables predict survival after CPR: "Successful resuscitation was not associated with gender, comorbidities, age, or interval from admission." Worthwhile comorbid conditions somewhat predictive of survival to hospital discharge in one hospital were not predictive in another hospital. Furthermore, defining what determines a cohort group for treatment analysis of the last 100 patients can be difficult. The qualitative definition of life—"below the threshold considered minimum by professional judgment," and "length of time," "short periods of time," requires value assessment and is open to interpretation. This policy, too, requires the resolution of disagreements among patient, family, and caregiver before a DNR order can be written; it is therefore not a unilateral CPR-not-indicated policy.

BETH ISRAEL HOSPITAL, BOSTON, MASSACHUSETTS

"The attending physician may enter the 'CPR Not Indicated' order only in the following circumstances: (a) The patient is dying with no chance of recovery; or (b) there is no reasonable likelihood that CPR efforts would be successful in restoring cardiac and pulmonary function ... and no therapeutic alternatives could reverse or significantly slow the downhill course of illness ... and the proposed treatment would increase or prolong the patient's suffering and cannot be justified on medical grounds. The attending physician should discuss with the patient or family the medical basis for not attempting resuscitation.... *The discussion is not for the purposes of securing permission* (emphasis added) but rather an opportunity to develop as full an understanding of the patient's situation...."

Although the policy states "dying with no chance of recovery," Beth Israel Hospital uses Schneiderman and colleagues' definition of quantitative futility; this is stated in a footnote. This policy also asks for "concurrence by other involved physicians." Although they do not define qualitative futility directly, they imply that when the physician believes that the patient's suffering outweighs the advantage of being alive, the treatment is qualitatively futile. This qualitative assessment is broad and certainly subject to personal or institutional biases. This policy places the question of "whose values" squarely in the physician's corner. In this sense, Beth Israel Hospital has an unequivocal CPR-not-indicated policy, implying that the offering of CPR can, in some circumstances, be an absolute medical decision.

JOHNS HOPKINS HOSPITAL, BALTIMORE, MARYLAND

"Any course of treatment may be regarded as futile if it is highly unlikely to have a beneficial outcome, or if it is highly likely merely to preserve permanent unconsciousness or persistent vegetative state or require permanent hospitalization in an intensive care unit.... Substantiation of (the reasons why requested options are futile) through recording in the chart literature references and the options of medical consultants is encouraged.... It is the policy of the Johns Hopkins Hospital that attending physicians are not required to offer life-sustaining intervention, and may refuse a request for the same, if the intervention is medically futile and will not offer meaningful benefit to the patient. When conflicts arise ... attempts at resolution should proceed.... If the conflict remains irreconcilable, the attending physician or the patient may seek an alternative attending physician."

Drs. Waisel and Truog of Massachusetts General made the following observation: This policy uses "highly unlikely" and "beneficial" to define quantitative and qualitative futility, but, more importantly, this policy defines *quality of life* as a function of location. This presupposes that any patient who is permanently hospitalized in the intensive-care unit has a poor quality of life. Although it is unlikely that they intended to cut such an extensive swath, precision in policies is important. Until these concerns can be answered, qualitative definitions that hinge on location are questionable. Such a proposal gives a physician exceedingly broad rights.

The Johns Hopkins policy solves the value-orientation problem by allowing the patients or surrogates to seek out alternative physicians whose views may be similar to their own. This is consistent with the fact that patients and surrogates have always been free to go to another physician if they choose. By allowing the patient to control options by choosing a physician with similar values, this policy permits the patient's values to be honored without subjugating the physician's values.

Appendix B

Danish Medical Brochure*

DOCTOR'S INSTRUCTIONS, BOOK I

In virtue of section 2 and 5 in the Health Department's publication/official notice about living wills the stipulations are as follows:

Living Wills

Section 1

Point 1. A living will is a written certificate in which a person notifies that he or she does not wish to receive life-prolonging treatment in a situation where death is inevitable or in a situation where incurable and extremely disabling suffering causes a person to be permanently incapable of taking care of him/herself physically and mentally.

Point 2. Life-prolonging treatment is treatment that effects a certain extension of life, but there is no hope of healing, recovery, or relief. Please see section 6, point 4.

*This brochure contains instructions for physicians and is disseminated to all physicians licensed to practice medicine in Denmark. The brochure explains the intent and scope of the Danish Living Will legislation. It was translated by René Kronvold of the University of Tampa.

Point 3. The Health Department has, in its publication official notice of the 18th of September 1992 about living wills, stipulated rules/laws concerning establishing, making, registering, and canceling living wills.

Section 2. The Health Department has developed a formula/form which must be followed when establishing and registering a living will.

Point 2. This formula/form contains the following possibilities for stating one's wishes:

1—that one does not wish to receive life-prolonging treatment in a situation where the testator is inevitably going to die;

2—that one does not wish to receive life-prolonging treatment where sickness, advanced weakness due to aging, accident, heart failure or the like has resulted in such a severe condition that the testator will never again be able to take care of him/herself physically and mentally;

3—that the testator, in the situation mentioned in 1 wishes to be spared from pain with the use of medication (painkillers) even though it could result in early death.

Section 3. A living will becomes active from the moment where the patient no longer is able and therefore in a situation where he/she cannot exercise his/her right to decide what he/she wants and when a doctor has substantiated that the patient is in a condition described in the living will formula/form. Please see section 2, point 2, numbers 1 and 2.

The Registrar of Living Wills at Rigshospitalet

Section 4. A Registrar's office of Living Wills has been instituted at State Hospital and every citizen has the privilege to register a living will. Please see the Health Department's publication/official notice of the 18th of September 1992 about living wills, section 6.

The Doctor's Estimate

Section 5

Point 1. The doctor must always estimate the condition of the patient and the possibility of recovery along with the possibilities for treatment.

Point 2. The doctor estimates whether or not death is unavoidable; see the living will form number 1. If the patient is in a condition where incurable and extremely disabling suffering causes the person to be permanently incapable of taking care of him/herself physically and mentally; see the living will formula/form point 2.

Point 3. In every case where the patient is in a condition described in the living will form, (see section 2, point 2, numbers 1 and 2) the doctor must check to find out whether or not a living will has been registered. However, see section 7, point 1, about cancelling a living will.

The Doctor's Duties

Foregoing Notification (Living Will)

Section 6

Point 1. If the patient has a registered living will and he/she does not wish to receive life-prolonging treatment in a situation where death is unavoidable (living will form 1) then the doctor must honor this wish.

Point 2. If the living will contains other wishes/choices than those described in point one (form) then the doctor has to include them in his/her evaluation about further (future) treatment.

Actual Notification

Section 7

Point 1. A living will can be cancelled by unequivocal notification in case of sickness; see the Health Department's official notice of the 18 of September 1992 about living wills, section 7, point 2.

Point 2. A patient also has the opportunity to invoke the Law of Doctors section 6, point 3, number 1 in a situation of sickness and make it known that he/she does not wish to receive life-prolonging treatment. The doctor will then be obligated to honor the patient's wishes. This obligation/duty also applies where disqualification of the patient (i.e., unconsciousness) occurs later.

No Notification

Section 8

Point 1. In case the patient does not have a registered living will and has not specified his/her wishes about treatment (see section 7, point 2) the doctor has the right to, after he/she has evaluated whether or not the patient inevitably is going to die, make a decision as to whether or not to begin or continue treatment that can only postpone the time of death. See the Law of Doctors section 6, point 5, number 1.

Point 2. Under the same circumstances, the doctor can administer the necessary pain medicine in order to relieve the patient even though this can accelerate/expedite the time of death; see the Law of Doctors section 6, point 5, number 2.

Keeping Journal

Section 9

Point 1. Accurate descriptions of the doctor's evaluations of the condition of the patient must be, in each case, kept in the journal.

Point 2. Furthermore, detailed descriptions of whom has contacted the Office of the Living Will Registrar, when this took place, and the result thereof must be kept in the patient's journal.

Point 3. In addition to these requirements, descriptions of the patient's notifications must be included in the journal.

Responsibility

Section 10

Point 1. The doctor who is going to or already has treated the patient is responsible for seeing that the circular complies with the stated criteria.

Section 11. The Health Department has made guidelines, of September 1992, about doctors' obligations in relation to the content of a living will.

In Effect

Section 12. The circular becomes effective October 1, 1992.

The Department of Health, September 22, 1992

Doctor's Instructions, Book II

(To the country's doctors)

1. Introduction

Based on the Law of Doctors' section 6, point 3, a law has been made active October 1, 1992, about principles concerning a person's right to decide for him-/herself as well as rules concerning the lawful meaning of living wills.

The Law of Doctors section 6, point 3, number 1 concerns the able patient and determines that the doctor cannot begin or continue treatment if it is against the will of the patient, unless something else has been agreed upon.

The Law of Doctors section 6, point 3, number 2 concerns the unable patient. By writing a living will, a patient can express his/her wishes about treatment in a case where he/she cannot voice a personal opinion.

Furthermore, with the Law of Doctors section 6, point 5, a law has been passed to enable a doctor to choose not to begin or continue treatment in a situation where the patient inevitably is going to die, and where treatment only postpones the time of death. The doctor also has the right to give "painkillers" even though it can speed up the time of death. The Law of Doctors sections 6 and 6a serve as an appendix for guidance.

2. The Aim of This Guidance

The guidance is concordant with the Health Department's circular of September 22, 1992, about a doctor's obligations concerning living wills.

It should be made known that a living will only becomes active in a situation where a patient no longer can voice a personal opinion.

The guidance describes the two situations, included in the Health Department's living will form/formula, in which there is no wish for life-prolonging treatment. The guidance also describes the practical way/method a doctor should follow when he/she investigates whether or not the patient has registered a living will.

3. The Registrar of Living Wills

The main hospital in Denmark has established a Living Will Registrar's Office where an individual can register a living will.

If the doctor estimates that a patient is in a condition described in the living will form, he/she must first check to see whether or not the patient has registered a will.

The doctor does not, however, have to contact the Living Will Registrar, if the patient, in case of illness, has made it known that he/she wishes to cancel a living will.

4. Inevitably Dying

According to the circular's section 2, point 2, number 1, a person can, in a living will, make it known that he/she does not wish to receive life-prolonging treatment in a situation where the testator is going to die.

Prolonging treatment is treatment where there is no hope of healing, recovery, or relief, but only of a certain extension of life.

Generally, it is not possible to define in which situations and time frames a patient is inevitably going to die. In relation to the content of a living will, it is the Health Department interpretation that a patient is inevitably dying when death, with a very high probability, is expected to occur within days or weeks in spite of the use of the available treatment opportunities and knowledge about the disease.

As examples the following can be mentioned:

a) Patients who are in the end-phase of a cancer disease and do not show any sign of recovery or relief in response to treatment;
b) Patients with irreparable failure of several organ-systems (i.e., heart, lungs, kidney, liver) where, in spite of maximum treatment, the physiological functions continue to deteriorate.

5. Severely Disabling Suffering

According to the circular's section 2, point 2, number 2, a person can make it known that he/she does not wish to receive life-prolonging treatment in case of sickness, advanced weakness due to aging, accident, heart failure or the like has resulted in such a severe condition that the testator never will be able to take care of him-/herself physically and mentally.

It includes the most hopeless forms of incurable and severely disabling sufferings. As examples, the following can be mentioned:

- Severe dementia's (Alzheimer's disease, etc.) disabling consequences of stroke or coma on those who have lost their ability to recognize self and surroundings, become unable to communicate with others, or are unable to care for themselves to the extent of having become totally dependent.
- Terminal pulmonary insufficiencies: Patients who suffer from advancing weakness of the lungs, without accompanying treatable disease, where the lung suffering is so advanced that only respirator treatment can prolong life.
- Patients who, because of severe injury or disease of the spinal cord are totally lame (palsy) and unable to negotiate movement in their surroundings.

6. The Doctor's Estimate/Evaluation

It is a doctor's prerogative, based on knowledge of the patient's actual condition, to determine whether or not a patient is inevitably going to die or is in a condition where sickness, advanced weakness due to aging, accident, heart failure or the like has resulted in such a severe condition that testator will be unable to take care of him-/herself.

In some cases the doctor can, because he/she knows the patient, estimate that the patient is in a condition described in the above; see point 1, and point 2 in the living will form.

In other cases, a doctor has to study the patient's situation in order to estimate his/her condition. If the doctor has any doubt about the condition of the patient, he/she must treat the individual until the condition is known.

7. The Doctor's Duties

7.1. Future Announcement (Living Will)

7.1.1. Inevitable Dying

If the doctor estimates that a patient is going to die and the patient has registered a living will, where he/she does not wish to receive life-prolonging treatment (living will form point 1), the doctor must stop treatment of the patient. The living will is in this situation binding to the doctor.

If the patient, in the living will, has made it known that he or she does not wish to receive medicine in a situation where the patient inevitably is going to die (living will form point 3) the doctor has to honor this request.

7.1.2. Severely Disabling Sufferings

If the doctor estimates that the patient is in a condition where severely disabling suffering has resulted in a situation where the patient will be unable to take care of him-/herself physically and mentally, and the patient has registered a living will in which he/she does not wish to receive treatment in a situation like this (living will form point 2), then the doctor has to honor this request. The doctor must therefore include the wish/request in his/her evaluation about further treatment.

7.2. Actual Notification

If a patient has made it known that he/she, in case of sickness, does not wish to receive life-prolonging treatment then the doctor has to honor the request/wish.

If the actual notification is a cancellation of the will then the doctor has to honor this request.

7.3. No Notification

In a situation where the patient inevitably is going to die and where there is no notification from the patient in form of a living will or verbal notification that prolonging treatment is desired, then the doctor can decide not to begin or continue treatment that only prolongs the time of death.

The doctor can, in this situation, give the patient pain medicine needed to ease the painful condition of the patient, even though this could speed up or accelerate the time of death.

8. Practical Procedure

Contact to hospital can be made seven days a week, twenty-four hours a day, but if possible should be made during the week within normal hours. The telephone number is ______________.

When the doctor contacts the Registrar of Living Wills, he or she must give his/her name and a telephone number, so a reverse call can be made, along with the name and social security number of the patient. The doctor will also be asked to give his/her social security number.

The Living Will Registrar will then call the doctor. He or she must confirm the information about the patient's name, address and social security number. Registered information about the treatment will be communicated to the doctor and he/she will be asked to repeat what was communicated to him/her.

This telephone message to the doctor is the final message and must enter a journal; see the Health Department's circular about a doctor's duties/responsibilities concerning living wills and the like of September 22, 1992, section 9.

Appendix C

Universal Living Will*

Lofty Basta, M.D.

This Living Will form is a simple yet comprehensive document written in plain English. It is accompanied by a workbook describing various medical scenarios near the close of life.

We have designed this workbook to assist you in completing your living will. The last page of this book is the "Universal Living Will" document. *Do not fill this page and do not sign before you have completed the workbook.* Feel free to make notes or comments in the workbook pages.

In the workbook, specific scenarios of medical conditions are provided, followed by a list of treatment options.

After completion of the workbook, if you agree with its provisions, execute the "Living Will." If you have any additional comments, provide them in the appropriate space provided. The Living Will document *should be discussed with your physician and health-care proxy,* the person you have chosen to make medical decisions on your behalf if you are unable to do so. Then have the document signed, witnessed, and notarized. Upon registration, an individual card will be mailed to you. A yearly update is expected from participants.

Common questions about the living will:

- *What is a "living will"?*

A "living will" is a legal document in which a competent person expresses his/her preferences for medical treatment at the end of life. Its purpose is to guide the choice of treatment if the patient is unable to communicate his/her wishes or unable to make those decisions.

- *Who should have a "living will"?*

Every adult citizen (18 years and older) should execute a "living will." Although the older members of society are at a higher risk of a life-threatening condition, a crippling accident or illness could afflict anyone at any age.

- *Why should one execute a "living will"?*

Advances in medical technology have enabled physicians to sustain life by machines even when the prospects of recovery are remote. Many individuals in our society feel that advances in medical technology have interfered with the natural process of death and in so doing have dehumanized life, undermined dignity, and caused protracted suffering for patients and their families at the end of life. Also, physicians, fearful of legal repercussions, are hesitant to withhold or stop treatment as long as there is a remote chance for a limited improvement unless they have a clear directive from the patient's representative. Many individuals would rather spare themselves, their loved ones and society the burdens of suffering, indignity, and the expense of protracted, painful, useless care.

- *Which form of "living will" should I consider?*

There are several standard forms of living wills. Some states have adopted specific forms. However, most available "living wills" apply only to the last moments of life and are lacking in specifics. The "Universal Living Will" proposed in this book is designed to encompass several specific medical scenarios. Therefore, it enables the person to evaluate and choose among treatment options in specific scenarios near the end of life.

- *How do I complete a "living will" that reflects my wishes?*

In the attached workbook we provide various medical scenarios in a clear and concise manner. After reading each scenario, you can indicate in the workbook how you would want to be treated, under these specific circumstances. A summary page is provided in which your wishes can be summed up.

- *When do I renew a "living will"?*

In order to stay current, it is best to renew your will *annually*. Medical progress and other circumstances may influence one's wishes. Also, a current living will is the best guarantee that one's wishes will be carried out. However, the "living will" can be modified by you, if need be, at any time.

- *Whom should I choose as a health-care proxy, a person who will have the power to make medical decisions on my behalf in the event that I have lost the ability to make medical care decisions?*

Choose the person you trust will carry out your wishes. Ordinarily one chooses one's spouse or daughter or son. Those who have had a long, trusting relationship with their doctor may designate the physician as their attorney for health-care issues. Most importantly, *you have to discuss your wishes clearly and specifically with your designee*. You may wish to use this workbook format for that purpose.

- *Where should I keep my "living will"?*

The last page of this booklet is your legal document. Once you have completed the last page of this booklet, you need to sign and notarize your signature with two witnesses. Keep a copy in your safe, give one copy to each of your treating physicians and one to your appointed health-care proxy. If you wish to maintain your will in a central registry, please fill out the stub from the last page. Detach the stub along the dotted line and send the completed stub to the address shown. You will receive a plastic card specifying your wishes (similar to your driver's license). By registering your "Universal Living Will," the information will be stored permanently unless otherwise requested by you. Any health-care provider will have access to the registered, updated will when the need arises.

MEDICAL SCENARIOS COVERED BY THIS WILL

The first three scenarios apply to conditions of *terminal illness* or *severe brain damage*:

Scenario I: Terminal Illness

- Death is expected to occur with or without intervention in a few days, maximally in two weeks;
- The disease is irreversible; no intervention is expected to materially change the course of events;
- The condition is irreparable, treatment interventions will not improve the quality of remaining life.

Scenario II: Coma

Refers to permanent unconscious deep sleep from which the patient cannot be aroused. There is brain damage, severe enough to render the individual unresponsive and unable to feel or communicate in any way. There is no reasonable chance for recovery.

Scenario III: Persistent Vegetative State

There is permanent brain damage, severe enough to render the individual unaware of self or the environment. In this case there are periods during which the patient appears to be awake. The patient opens and moves the eyes but does not fix the gaze. The patient may react to light, or sounds or painful stimuli but the patient does not see, does not hear, and does not suffer. The patient has irretrievably lost the ability to appreciate, understand and communicate. There is no reasonable chance for significant improvement.

Choices for Scenarios I, II, and III (terminal illness, coma, vegetative state)

○ By filling in the small circle, you mean:

- Stop all interventions including, but not limited to antibiotics, blood transfusion, endoscopy, surgery, and feeding and hydration;
- Apply merciful treatment that preserves my dignity and brings peace and comfort, including pain treatment;
- Order not to resuscitate in the event of arrest of heartbeat and/or breathing.

MEDICAL SCENARIOS OF ADVANCED, INCURABLE, CRIPPLING DISEASE

The next three scenarios apply to conditions that *do not* qualify as terminal illness or extensive brain damage. In these conditions the end of life is *near* but *not imminent* and may last for several months or even longer. Active intervention is *unlikely* to significantly improve the length or quality of life.

Scenario IV: Severe Dementia

In this case, brain damage has been present for a while, such as with severe Alzheimer's disease or multiple strokes. The brain damage is *severe enough* to make the individual lose his or her ability to recognize others, interact with them, or make intelligent decisions. The individual is conscious but often confused and is totally dependent. The individual has irretrievably lost the qualities that characterized the individual as a person.

Scenario V: End-Stage Disease

Death is expected in a few weeks or months with or without treatment:

- Disseminated cancer *not responsive to treatment;*
- End-stage heart or lung disease provided heart–lung transplantation is *not* indicated or feasible (end-stage heart disease when there is loss of response to maximum medical therapy and requiring repeated hospitalizations over the last 3 months; end-stage lung disease rendering the patient chair-bound and needing oxygen around the clock);
- End-stage infection such as with terminal stages of AIDS when several organs are affected;
- Disseminated infection with an organism resistant to all available antibiotics;
- End-stage liver disease when liver transplant is not indicated or not feasible;
- End-stage kidney disease in conjunction with advanced heart, lung, or liver disease; Dialysis is either not indicated or unlikely to improve the quality or length of life;
- End-stage nervous disorder with near complete total body paralysis, total dependence with no hope for improvement.

Scenario VI: Advanced Senility

Associated with severe weakness, total dependence, and pain from arthritis and/or osteoporosis.

In this condition, the individual is still able to recognize self, some people, and surroundings, but has become so senile and frail that he or she has become totally dependent—and immobile; minor movement causes immense pain.

These individuals are particularly susceptible to bone fractures, pneumonia, heart attacks, and strokes.

CHOICES FOR SCENARIOS IV, V, AND VI (SEVERE DEMENTIA, END-STAGE DISEASE, OR ADVANCED SENILITY)

○ By filling the circle you mean:

- Do not interfere with the natural process of dying.
- No placement on ventilator.
- No surgical procedures, no chemotherapy, no blood transfusion, except as needed to prevent or alleviate suffering.
- No resuscitation efforts in the event of arrest of the heart or breathing.
- No placement in intensive-care unit except for absolute necessity to relieve suffering.
- No active treatment of a new, reversible condition such as a newly discovered cancer, heart attack, or pneumonia.
- As much as possible, treat at home or in a comfortable bed in comfortable surroundings with family and/or hospice care.
- Use pain medications fully to maximally alleviate pain, even if it hastens the moment of death.

Addendum

○ Other:

For *other* in the living will, indicate in writing any specific instructions that you wish to add. For example, someone may *not* want to be resuscitated in the event of sudden heart–lung death under certain circumstances (e.g., above age 80 years). Some would want feeding and hydration to be continued until the very end. Others may not want to have blood transfusion under any circumstances.

THE UNIVERSAL LIVING WILL

I, ________________, while competent and able, hereby express my wishes regarding my medical care near the end of life. I have chosen the universal living will, reviewed various medical scenarios presented in the living will workbook and I choose:

○ (yes) for scenarios I, II, III, which relate to terminal illness, permanent unconsciousness or persistent vegetative states: under these scenarios, I choose to have treatment that brings peace and comfort only. I do not wish to have any intrusive medical interventions (including feeding and hydration) that will serve only to delay the moment of death. I instruct to withdraw any interventions already in place.

○ (yes) for scenarios IV, V, VI, which apply to severe dementia or end-stage disease that is expected to cause death in a few months, or advanced senility with severe weakness and total dependence. I instruct my treating physicians *not* to interfere with the process of dying. I prefer to die in a comfortable bed, preferably at home, and certainly not in an intensive-care unit. Medical interventions are allowed only to the extent that they preserve my dignity and keep me clean, warm, and free from severe pain. When my heart stops beating or I stop breathing, I direct that no efforts be undertaken to resuscitate me.

○ Other

____

____

____

I appoint ________________, or ________________ to carry out my wishes should there by *any* further questions about my medical care. I have discussed the contents of my will with these individuals in detail.

Signed ______________________________________

Date ____

Witness ______________________________________

Notary ______________________________________

PLEASE DETACH AT PERFORATION BEFORE MAILING

UNIVERSAL LIVING WILL REGISTRY

Please fill in block letters or type:

Name ____
First Middle Last

Social Security Number _________ Male __ Female __

Address: Street ______________________________________

City ____________________ State ______________

Zip Code ________________

Telephone (___) _______

○ Scenarios I, II, III Initial ____________

○ Scenarios IV, V, VI Initial ____________

○ Other Initial ____________

I hereby authorize the Universal Will Registry to release this information to my health insurance company, hospital, and treating physicians and health-care professionals. Also, I consent that it be used for statistical or research purposes.

Signed ____

Date ____

Witnessed by ____________________________________

and ____

Notary ____

Bibliography

CHAPTER 1

Aristotle. Ethica Nicomachea: *Masterpieces of World Philosophy*. FN Magill, ed. (New York: HarperCollins, 1990), p. 73.

D Avila. "Saying No to Life: Reflections on Death and Justice," *Issues in Law and Medicine*, 9(1993), 227–254.

SE Baldwin. "The Natural Right to a Natural Death," *St. Paul Medical Journal*, 1 (1899), 875–889.

DJ Boorstin. *The Amateur Spirit. Living Philosophies: The Reflections of Some Men and Women of Our Time*. C Fadiman, ed. (New York: Doubleday, 1990), pp. 23–29.

LR Churchill. "Reviving a Distinctive Medical Ethic," *Hastings Center Report*, 19(3)(1989), 28–34.

I Kant. Critique of Practical Reason *and Other Writings in Moral Philosophy*. LW Beck, trans. (Chicago: University of Chicago Press, 1949).

SB Nuland. *How We Die: Reflections on Life's Final Chapter*. (New York: Knopf, 1993).

Plato. *The Dialogues of Plato*. B Jowett, Ed. 4th ed., rev. by DJ Allan and HE Dole. 4 Volumes. (London: Oxford University Press, 1953).

S Spender. *What I Believe. Living Philosophies: The Reflections of Some Eminent Men and Women of Our Time*. C Radiman, ed. (New York: Doubleday, 1990), pp. 200–212.

EA Stead. "If I Become Ill and Unable to Manage My Own Affairs," *Medical Times*, 98(1970), 191–192.

EA Stead. *What This Patient Needs Is a Doctor*. (Durham, NC: Carolina Academic Press, 1978).

The Chiron Dictionary of Greek Roman Mythology. E Burr, trans. (Wilmette, IL: Chiron Publications, 1994), pp. 204–295.

Tithonus by Lord A. Tennyson—Immortal Poems of the English Language. O Williams, ed. (New York: Washington Square Press, 1952), pp. 381–383.

CHAPTER 2

American Thoracic Society. "Withholding and Withdrawing Life-Sustaining Therapy," *American Review of Respiratory Disease*, 144(1991), 726–731.

DW Amundsen. "The Physician's Obligation to Prolong Life: A Medical Duty Without Classical Roots," *Hastings Center Report*, 8(1978), 23–30.

Bishops of Texas and the Texas Conference of Catholic Health Facilities. "An Interim Pastoral Statement on Artificial Nutrition and Hydration." (March 28, 1990).

E Braunwald. "The Golden Age of Cardiology," *American College of Cardiology*, (1991), S1–S4.

D Callahan. "Medical Futility, Medical Necessity: The Problem-Without-a-Name," *Hastings Center Report*, 21(1991), 30–35.

LH Cohn. "The Paradox of High-Tech Health Care: Has Our Technology Outstripped Our Ability to Be Ethical, Cost-Effective and Timely in Its Delivery?" *Chest*, 98(1988), 864–867.

MJ Edwards and SW Tolle. "Disconnecting the Ventilator at the Request of a Patient Who Knows He Will Then Die: The Doctor's Anguish," *Annals of Internal Medicine*, 117(1992), 254–256.

A Einstein. *From Living Philosophies (1931)*. C Fadiman, ed. (New York: Doubleday 1990), pp. 3–6.

A Einstein. *Out of My Later Years: The Scientist, Philosopher and Man Portrayed Through His Own Words*. (New York: Wings Books, 1956).

R Felknor. "The CHF Gap: Knowledge vs. Practice," *Cardiology World News*, 10(1994), 10–15.

LW Foderaro. "Death Wishes: All of a Sudden the Subject of Dying Is No Longer Tabu," *New York Times* (April 3, 1994), Section 9, p. 1.

JP Kassirer. "Academic Medical Centers Under Siege," *New England Journal of Medicine*, 331(1994), 1370–1371.

R Macklin. *Enemies of Patients.* (Oxford: Oxford University Press, 1993).

RL Martensen. "The Allure of the Permanent Cure," *Journal of the American Medical Association*, 273(1995), 1243.

EH Morreim. "Fiscal Scarcity and the Inevitability of Bedside Budget Balancing," *Archives of Internal Medicine*, 149(1989), 1012–1015.

EH Morreim. "Profoundly Diminished Life. The Casualties of Coercion," *Hastings Center Report*, 24(1994), 33–42.

LS Murray, GM Teasdale, GD Murray, et al. "Does Prediction of Outcome Alter Patient Management?" *Lancet*, 341(1993), 1487–1491.

SB Nuland. *How We Die: Reflections on Life's Final Chapter.* (New York: Knopf, 1993).

SB Nuland. "The Day I Discovered Death," *Hypocrites*, June(1994), 22–23.

D Orentlicher. "The Illusion of Patient Choice in End-of-Life Decisions," *Journal of the American Medical Association*, 267(1992), 2101–2104.

RA Pearlman. "Forgoing Medical Nutrition and Hydration: An Area for Fine-Tuning Clinical Skills," *Journal of General Internal Medicine*, 8(1993), 225–227.

R Peatfield. "Toward More Selective Resuscitation," *American Heart Journal*, 96(1978), 698–699.

President's Commission for the Study of Ethical Problems in Medicine and Biomedical and Behavioral Research. *Making Health Care Decisions*, Vol. 2. (Washington, DC: U.S. Government Printing Office, 1982), pp. 254–262.

LJ Schneiderman, NS Jecker, and AR Jonsen. "Medical Futility: Its Meaning and Ethical Implications," *Annals of Internal Medicine*, 112(1990), 949–954.

JE Spicher and DP White. "Outcome and Function Following Prolonged Mechanical Ventilation," *Archives of Internal Medicine*, 147(1987), 421–425.

RM Veatch. "The Definition of Death: Ethical, Philosophical, and Policy Confusion," *Annals of the New York Academy of Sciences*, 315(1978), 307–321.

"Who Owns Medical Technology," *Lancet*, 345(1995), 1125–1126.

CHAPTER 3

Aristotle. Ethica Nicomachea: *Masterpieces of World Philosophy*. FN Magill, ed. (New York: HarperCollins, 1990), p. 73.

SE Baldwin. "The Natural Right to a Natural Death," *St. Paul Medical Journal*, 1(1899), 875–889.

AJ Bennett. "When Is Medical Treatment 'Futile'?" *Issues in Law and Medicine*, 435(1993), 35–45.

TA Brennan. "Practice Guidelines and Malpractice Litigation: Collision or Cohesion?" *Journal of Health Politics, Policy and Law*, 16(1)(1991), 67–85.

D Callahan. "Medical Futility, Medical Necessity: The Problem-Without-a-Name," *Hastings Center Report*, 21 (July–August 1991), 30–35.

P Carrick. *Medical Ethics in Antiquity: Philosophical Perspectives on Abortion and Euthanasia*. (Boston: Dordrecht, 1985), p. 778.

L Churchill. "Reviving a Distinctive Medical Ethic," *Hastings Center Report*, 19(3) (1989), 28–34.

RE Cranford. "Medical Futility: Transforming a Clinical Concept into Legal and Societal Policies," *Journal of the American Geriatrics Society*, 42(1994), 894–898.

L Edelstein. "The Hippocratic Oath: Text, Translation, and Interpretation," In: *Ancient Medicine: Selected Papers of Ludwig Edelstein*. O Temkin and CL Temkin, eds. (Baltimore: Johns Hopkins Press, 1967).

LW Foderaro. "Death Wishes: All of a Sudden the Subject of Dying Is No Longer Tabu," *New York Times* (April 3, 1994), Section 9, p. 1.

JM Garrett, RP Harris, JK Norburn, DL Patrick, and M Danis. "Life-Sustaining Treatments During Terminal Illness: Who Wants What?" *Journal of General Internal Medicine*, 8(1993), 361–368.

GR Gillett. "Learning to Do No Harm," *Journal of Medicine and Philosophy*, 18(1993), 253–268.

TE Hill. *Autonomy and Self-Respect*. (Cambridge: Cambridge University Press, 1991).

D Humphry. "Hemlock Founder Humphry on Hospice," *Free Inquiry* (Winter 1991/92), 26.

EH Loewy and RA Carlson. "Futility and Its Wider Implications: A Concept for Further Examination," *Archives of Internal Medicine*, 153(1993), 429–431.

D Maass. "Die Methode der Wiederbelebung bei Herztod nach Chloroformeinatmung," *Berliner Klinige Wochenschrift*, 12(1892), 265–268.

RL Martersen. "The Allure of the Permanent Cure," *Journal of the American Medical Association*, 273(1995), 1243.

SH Miles. "Informed Demand for 'Non-Beneficial' Medical Treatment," *New England Journal of Medicine*, 325(1991), 512–515.

EH Morreim. "Profoundly Diminished Life: The Casualties of Coercion," *Hastings Center Report*, 24(1994), 33–42.

JL Nelson. "Families and Futility," *Journal of the American Geriatrics Society*, 42(1994), 879–882.

S Neu and CM Kjellstrand. "Stopping Long-Term Dialysis: An Empirical Study of Withdrawal of Life-Supporting Treatment," *New England Journal of Medicine*, 314(1986), 14–20.

J O'Toole. "The Story of Ethics: Narrative as a Means for Ethical Understanding and Action," *Journal of the American Medical Association*, 273(1995), 1387, 1390.

RA Pearlman. "Are We Asking the Right Questions?" *Hastings Center Report*, 24(1994), S24–S27.

RA Pearlman. "Medical Futility: Where Do We Go from Here?" *Journal of the American Geriatrics Society*, 42(1994), 904–905.

R Peatfield. "Toward More Selective Resuscitation," *American Heart Journal*, 96(1978), 698–699.

LJ Schneiderman, NS Jecker, and AR Jonsen. "Medical Futility: Its Meaning and Ethical Implications," *Annals of Internal Medicine*, 122(1990), 949–954.

CHAPTER 4

HJ Aaron. "Lessons from the United Kingdom," In: *Brookings Dialogues on Public Policy*. MA Strosberg, IA Fein, and JD Carroll, eds. (Washington, DC: The Brookings Institute, 1986), pp. 24–31.

TJ Ackerman. "Futility Judgments and Therapeutic Conversation," *Journal of the American Geriatrics Society*, 42(1994), 902–903.

American Thoracic Society. "Withholding and Withdrawing Life-Sustaining Therapy," *American Review of Respiratory Disease*, 144(1991), 726–731.

DW Amundsen. "The Physician's Obligation to Prolong Life: A Medical Duty without Classical Roots," *Hastings Center Report*, 8(1978), 23–30.

M Angell. "After Quinlan: The Dilemma of the Persistent Vegetative State," *New England Journal of Medicine*, 330(1994), 1524–1525.

GJ Annas. "Asking the Courts to Set the Standard of Emergency Care—The Case of Baby K," *New England Journal of Medicine*, 330(1994), 1542–1545.

R Baker. "The Patient Who Wants to Fight," In: *The Machine at the Bedside: Strategies for Using Medical Technology in Patient Care*. S Reiser and M Anbar, eds. (Cambridge: Cambridge University Press, 1984), pp. 213–220.

Barber v. Superior Court of the State of California, (195 California Report 484 486, 1983).

AJ Bennett. "When Is Medical Treatment 'Futile'? *Issues in Law and Medicine*, 435(1993), 35–45.

LJ Blackhall, J Cobb, and MA Moskowitz. "Discussions Regarding Aggressive Care with Critically Ill Patients," *Journal of General Internal Medicine*, 4(1989), 399–402.

Bishops of Texas and the Texas Conference of Catholic Health Facilities. "An Interim Pastoral Statement on Artificial Nutrition and Hydration." (March 28, 1990).

MM Burgess. "The Medicalization of Dying," *Journal of Medicine and Philosophy*, 18(1993), 269–279.

D Callahan. *The Troubled Dream of Life: Living with Mortality*. (New York: Simon and Schuster, 1993).

RE Cranford. "Medical Futility: Transforming a Clinical Concept into Legal and Societal Policies," *Journal of the American Geriatrics Society*, 42(1994), 894–898.

M Danis, J Garrett, R Harris, and DL Patrick. "Stability of Choices About Life-Sustaining Treatments," *Annals of Internal Medicine*, 120(1994), 567–573.

EJ Emanuel. "A Review of the Ethical and Legal Aspects of Terminating Medical Care," *American Journal of Medicine*, 84(1988), 291–301.

JJ Fins. "Futility in Clinical Practice: Report on a Congress of Clinical Societies," *Journal of the American Geriatrics Society*, 42(1994), 861–865.

D Frankl, R Oye, and PE Bellamy. "Attitudes of Hospitalized Patients toward Life-Support: A Survey of 200 Inpatients," *American Journal of Medicine*, 86(1989), 645–658.

JM Garrett, RP Harris, JK Norburn, DL Patrick, and M Danis. "Life-Sustaining Treatments During Terminal Illness: Who Wants What?" *Journal of General Internal Medicine*, 8(1993), 361–368.

Lord Goff of Chieveley. *Letter in Airedale NHS Trust (Respondents) v. Bland (Acting by* His *Guardian Ad Litem) (appellant)*. Judgement: (February 4, 1993), pp. 5–21.

G Grisez. "Should Nutrition and Hydration Be Provided to Permanently Comatose and Other Mentally Disabled Persons?" *Linacre Quarterly*, 57(1990), 30–43.

MA Grodin. "Religious Advance Directives: The Convergence of Law, Religion, Medicine, and Public Health," *American Journal of Public Health*, 83(1993), pp. 899–903.

W Harmon, ed. *The Top 500 Poems*. (New York: Columbia University Press, 1992).

SW Hawking. *A Brief History of Time from the Big Bang to Black Holes*, (New York: Bantam, 1988).

LL Heintz. "Legislative Hazard: Keeping Patients Living, Against Their Wills," *Journal of Medical Ethics*, 14(1988), 82–86.

In re Browning, 568 So. 2d 4 (Fla. 1990).

NS Jecker. "Knowing When to Stop: The Limits of Medicine," *Hastings Center Report*, 21(3)(1991), 5–8.

Lord Keith of Kinkel. *Letter in Airedale NHS Trust (Respondents) v. Bland (Acting by His Guardian Ad Litem) (appellant)*. Judgment: (February 4, 1993), pp. 1–5.

L Kirkland. "Neuromuscular Paralysis and Withdrawal of Mechanical Ventilation," *Journal of Clinical Ethics*, 5(1994), 38–39.

RA Knox. "Study: Americans Rethinking Effects to Prolong Life," *Boston Globe* (May 21, 1994), p. 1.

RD Lamm. "Columbus and Copernicus: New Wine in Old Wineskins," *Mount Sinai Journal of Medicine*, 56(1989), 1–10.

DKP Lee, AJ Swinburne, AJ Fedullo, and GW Wahl. "Withdrawing Care: Experience in a Medical Intensive Care Unit," *Journal of the American Medical Association*, 271(1994), 1358–1361.

S Lemeshow, D Teres, J Elar, JS Avrunin, SH Gehlbach, and J Rapoport. "Mortality Probability Models (MPH II) Based on an International Cohort of Intensive Care Unit Patients," *Journal of the American Medical Association*, 270(1993), 2478–2486.

M Levetown, MM Pollac, TT Cuerdon, UE Ruttimann, and JJ Glover. "Limitations and Withdrawals of Medical Intervention in Pediatric Critical Care," *Journal of the American Medical Association*, 272(16) (1994), 1271–1275.

PJ Liacos. "Dilemmas of Dying," *Medicolegal News*, 7(1979), 4–7.

B Lo. "The Death of Clarence Herbert: Withdrawing Care Is Not Murder," *Annals of Internal Medicine*, 101(1984), 248–251.

Lord Lowry. *Letter in Airedale NHS Trust (Respondents) v. Bland (Acting by His Guardian Ad Litem) (appellant)*. Judgement: (February 4, 1993), pp. 21–24.

B Lown, R Amarsingham, and J Newman. "New Method for Terminating Cardiac Arrhythmia: Use of Synchronized Capacitor Discharge," *Journal of the American Medical Association*, 182(1962), 548–555.

KG Manton, E Stallard, and HD Tolly. "Limits to Human-Life Expectancy: Evidence, Prospects, and Implications," *POPUP Developmental Review*, 17(1991), 603–637.

A Meisel. "In re Evans v. Bellvue Hospital," In: *The Right to Die*. (Wiley Law Publications, 1989).

SH Miles. "Informed Demand for 'Non-Beneficial' Medical Treatment," *New England Journal of Medicine*, 325(1991), 512–515.

B Miller and M Tousignant. "Mother Fights Hospital to Keep Infant Alive: Court Rules 'Baby with Almost No Brain' Has Right to Treatment," *Washington Post* (September 23, 1993), p. A1.

JS Morris. *Ethics and Scarcity. Brookings Dialogues on Public Policy*. MA Strosberg, IA Fein, and JD Carroll, eds. (Washington, DC: The Brookings Institute, 1986), pp. 11–16.

DJ Murphy. "Can We Set Futile Care Policies? Institutional and Systemic Challenges," *Journal of the American Geriatrics Society* 42(1994), 890–893.

EK Murphy. "US Supreme Court to Hear First 'Right-to-Die' Case," *Association of Operating Room Nurses Journal*, 51(1990), 1391–1394.

LS Murray, GM Teasdale, GD Murray, et al. "Does Prediction of Outcome Alter Patient Management?" *Lancet*, 341(1993), 1487–1491.

D Orentlicher. "Rationing and the Americans with Disabilities Act," *Journal of the American Medical Association*, 271(1994), 308–314.

D Orentlicher. "The Illusion of Patient Choice in End-of-Life Decisions," *Journal of the American Medical Association*, 267(1992), 2101–2104.

JJ Paris, RK Crone, and R Reardon. "Physician's Refusal of Requested Treatment: The Case of Baby L," *New England Journal of Medicine*, 322(14)(1990), 1012–1015.

RA Pearlman, KC Cain, DL Patrick, et al. "Insights Pertaining to Patient Assessments of States Worse Than Death," *Journal of Clinical Ethics*, 4(1993), 33–41.

President's Commission for the Study of Ethical Problems in Medicine and Biomedical and Behavioral Research. *Deciding to Forgo Life-Sustaining Treatment*. (Washington, DC: 1983).

L Rensman. "Notification Procedure for the Medical Termination of Life on Request and Without Request as Laid Down by Order in Council." *Persbericht. Ministry of Justice, Information Department*, (Dec. 22, 1993), 2295.

B Riddick and L Schneiderman. "Distinguishing between Effect and Benefit," *Journal of Clinical Ethics*, 5(1994), 41–43.

DV Schapira, J Studnicki, DD Bradham, P Wolff, and A Jarrett. "Intensive Care, Survival and Expense of Treating Critically Ill Cancer Patients," *Journal of the American Medical Association*, 269(1993), 783–786.

LJ Schneiderman and RG Spragg. "Ethical Decisions in Discontinuing Mechanical Ventilation," *New England Journal of Medicine*, 318(1988), 984–988.

D Teres. "Triage: An Everyday Occurrence in the Intensive Care Unit," *Brookings Dialogues on Public Policy*. MA Strosberg, IA Fein, IA, and JD Carroll, eds. (Washington, DC: Brookings Institute, 1986), pp. 70–75.

JS Tobias and RL Soulami. "Fully Informed Consent Can Be Needlessly Cruel," *British Medical Journal*, 307(1993), 1199–1201.

R Truog and J Burns. "To Breathe or Not to Breathe," *Journal of Clinical Ethics*, 5(1994), 39–41.

Wackwitz v. Roy. In "Death and Dying: State and Federal Courts Agree That Suicide Rules Out Wrongful Death Claim in Virginia. 244 Va. 60, 418 SE 2d 861 (1992)," in *Biolaw* (Copyright by University Publications of America, Bethesda, MD, 1993), U11–U13.

RF Weir and L Gostin. "Decisions to Abate Life-Sustaining Treatment for Nonautonomous Patients: Ethical Standards and Legal Liability for Physicians after Cruzan," *Journal of the American Medical Association*, 264(1990), 1846–1853.

"Behind a Boy's Decision to Forgo Treatment," *New York Times*. (June 13, 1994), p. A12.

Bland v. Trust, Airedale NHS Judgement (February 4, 1993).

Bowers v. Hardwick, 478 US 186, 194-195, 106 S. Court. 2841, 2846, 92 L. Editor 2d 140 (1986).

Camp v. White, 510 So. 2d 166, 168 (Ala. 1987).

Cruzan v. Harmon, 760 SW 2d 408 (Mo. 1988).

Cruzan v. Mouton, Estate No. CV384-9P (Circuit Court, Jasper County, MO, 14 December, 1990). Reported in 6 issues in *Law and Medicine* 433(1991).

Donaldson v. Van de Kamp, 2 California App. 4th 1614, 4 California Reporter 2d 59 (1992).

"Guidelines for Withholding Food and Water: Sustenance Discussed," *Medical Tribune* (October 4, 1990), p. 1.

"Hospital Appeals Decision on Treating Anencephalic Baby," *Hospital Ethics*, 9(1993), 6–7.

In re Busalacchi, No. 73677, 1993 WESTLAW 32356 (Mo. 26, Jan. 1993).

In re Conroy, 98 NJ 321, 486 A. 2d 1209, 1223 (1985).

In re Doe, Civil Action Number D-93064 (Fulton County, GA, October 17, 1991).
In re E.G., 133 Ill.2d 98, Ill. Dec 810, 549 NE 2d 322, 139 (1990).
In re Estate of Greenspan, 137 Ill.2d 1, 146 Ill. Dec. 860,58 NE 2d 1194 (1990).
In re Longeway, 133 Ill, 2d 33, 139 Ill. Dec 780, 549 NE 2d 292, (1989).
In re O'Connor, 72 NY 2 d 517, 531 NE 2d 607, 534 N.Y.S.2d 886 (1988).
In re Spring, 380 Mass. 629, 405 NE 2d 115, 119 (1980).
In re Wanglie, No. PX-91-283 (4th District Court, Hennepin County, MN, July 1, 1991).
In the Matter of Baby "K." No. CIV. A. 93-104-A (E.D. VA, July 7, 1993).
Mack v. Mack, 329 MD. 188, 618 A.2d 744 (1993).
"Nature and Limits of Legal Consensus about Forgoing Life-Sustaining Treatment," *Biolaw*, (1993), U138–U139.
Ragona v. Preate, 11 Fiduc. Rep 2d I (C.P. Lackawanna County PA, 1990) (reported in 2 Biolaw U: 1875) (Dec. 1990).
"The United States Bishops' Committee Statement on Nutrition and Hydration," *Cambridge Quarterly of Healthcare Ethics*, 2(1993), 342–352.
Weber v. Stony Brook Hospital, 95 A.D. 2d 587, 467 NY S. 2d 685.

CHAPTER 5

SE Bedell and TL Delbanco. "Choices about Cardiopulmonary Resuscitation in the Hospital: When Do Physicians Talk with Patients?" *New England Journal of Medicine*, 310(17)(1984), 1089–1093.
SE Bedell, TL Delbanco, EF Cook, and FH Epstein. "Survival After Cardiopulmonary Resuscitation in the Hospital," *New England Journal of Medicine*, 309(1983), 569–576.
S Bedell, D Pelle, PL Maher, and PD Cleary, "Do-Not-Resuscitate Orders for Critically Ill Patients in the Hospital: How Are They Used and What Is Their Impact?" *Journal of the American Medical Association*, 256(1986), 233–237.
LJ Blackhall. "Must We Always Use CPR?" *New England Journal of Medicine*, 317(1987), 1281–1285.
KM Boozang. "Death Wish: Resuscitating Self-Determination for the Critically Ill," *Advances Law Review*, 35(1993), 24–85.
PL Carlen and M Gordon. "Cardiopulmonary Resuscitation and Neurological Complications in the Elderly," *Lancet*, 345(May 20, 1995), 1253.

C Charon. "Resuscitation vs. the Right to Die," *Association of Operating Room Nurses Journal*, 48(1988), 362–364.

PP Chiang and D Schiedermayer. "Getting the CPR You Want: DNR and Alice's Restaurant," *Journal of Clinical Ethics*, 4(1993), 186–188.

CB Cohen and PJ Cohen. "Do-Not-Resuscitate Orders in the Operating Room," *New England Journal of Medicine*, 325(1991), 1879–1882.

JR Curtis, DR Park, MR Krone, and RA Pearlman. "Use of the Medical Futility Rationale in Do-Not-Attempt-Resuscitation Orders," *Journal of the American Medical Association*, 273(2)(1995), 124–128.

M Cushing. "Law for Leaders 'No Code' Orders." *Journal of Nursing Administration*, (April 1981), 22–29.

MH Ebell, DJ Doukas, and MA Smith. "The Do-Not-Resuscitate Order: A Comparison of Physician and Patient Preferences and Decision-Making," *American Journal of Medicine*, 91(1991), 255–260.

MH Ebell, MA Smith, KG Seifert, and K Poisinelli. "The Do-Not-Resuscitate Order: Outpatient Experience and Decision-Making Preferences," *Journal of Family Practice*, 31(1990), 630–634.

M Eisenberg. "Bystander CPR." *Journal of the Royal College of Physicians in London*, 28(6)(1994), 585–586.

"Guidelines for Cardiopulmonary Resuscitation and Emergency Cardiac Care: VIII. Ethical Considerations in Resuscitation: Emergency Cardiac Care Committee and Subcommittees of the American Heart Association. *Journal of the American Medical Association*, 268(1992), 2282–2288.

AI Evans and BA Brody. "The Do-Not-Resuscitate Order in Teaching Hospitals," *Journal of the American Medical Association*, 253(1985), 2236–2239.

D Frankl, R Oye, and PE Bellamy. "Attitudes of Hospitalized Patients toward Life-Support: A Survey of 200 Inpatients," *American Journal of Medicine*, 86(6)(1989), 645–658.

K Gleeson and S Wise. "The Do-Not-Resuscitate Order: Still Too Little Too Late?" *Archives of Internal Medicine*, 150(1990), 1057–1060.

MD Godkin and EL Toth. "Cardiopulmonary Resuscitation and Older Adults Expectations," *Gerontologist*, 34(1994), 797–802.

WA Gray. "Prehospital Resuscitation: The Good, the Bad, and the Futile," *Journal of the American Medical Association*, 270(1993), 1471–1472.

Hastings Center. *Guidelines on the Termination of Life-Sustaining Treatment and the Care of the Dying*. (Bloomington, Indiana: Indiana University Press, 1987).

RL Jayes, JE Zimmerman, DP Wagner, EA Draper, and WA Knaus. "Do-Not-Resuscitate Orders in Intensive Care Units. Current Practices and Recent Changes," *Journal of the American Medical Association*, 270(1993), 2213–2217.

NS Jecker and LD Schneiderman. "An Ethical Analysis of the Use of 'Futility' in the 1992 American Heart Association Guidelines for Cardiopulmonary Resuscitation and Emergency Cardiac Care," *Archives of Internal Medicine*, 153(1993), 2195–2198.

JR Jude and JO Elam. *Fundamentals of Cardiopulmonary Resuscitation*. (Philadelphia: FA Davis, 1965).

JR Jude, WB Kouwenhoven, and GG Knickerbocker. "Cardiac Arrest: Report of Application of External Cardiac Massage in 118 Patients," *Journal of the American Medical Association*, 178(1961), 1063–1070.

WB Kouwenhoven. "The Development of the Defibrillator," *Annals of Internal Medicine*, 71(1969), 449–458.

WB Kouwenhoven, JR Jude, and GG Knickerbocker. "Closed Chest Cardiac Massage," *Journal of the American Medical Association*, 173(1960), 1064–1067.

DKP Lee, AJ Swinburne, AJ Fedullo, and GH Wahl. "Withdrawing Care: Experience in a Medical Intensive Care Unit," *Journal of the American Medical Association*, 271(1994), 1358–1361.

HL Lipton. "Physicians' Do-Not-Resuscitate Decisions and Documentation in a Community Hospital," *QRB Quality Review Bulletin*, 75 (1989), 108–113.

B Lo, GA McLeod, and G Saika. "Patient Attitudes to Discussing Life-Sustaining Treatment," *Archives of Internal Medicine*, 146(1986), 1613–1615.

KM McIntyre. "Failure of 'Predictors' of Cardiopulmonary Resuscitation Outcomes to Predict Cardiopulmonary Resuscitation Outcomes," *Archives of Internal Medicine*, 153(1993), 1293–1296.

KM McIntyre. "Loosening Criteria for Withholding Prehospital Cardiopulmonary Resuscitation," *Archives of Internal Medicine*, 153(1993), 2189–2192.

A Maksoud, DW Jahnigen, and CI Skibinski. "Do-Not-Resuscitate Orders and the Cost of Death," *Archives of Internal Medicine*, 153(10)(1993), 1249–1253.

FH Marsh and A Staver. "Physician Authority for Unilateral DNR Orders," *Journal of Legal Medicine*, 12(1991), 115–165.

SH Miles, R Cranford, and AL Schultz. "The Do-Not-Resuscitate Order in a Teaching Hospital: Considerations and a Suggested Policy," *Annals of Internal Medicine*, 96(1982), 660–664.

SH Miles, J Dirscoll, and M McCusker. "CPR in Nursing Homes: Policy and Clinical Realities," *Minnesota Medicine*, 74(1991), 31–35.

SH Miles and DG Moldow. "The Prevalence and Design of Hospital Protocols Limiting Medical Treatment," *Archives of Internal Medicine*, 144(1984), 1841–1843.

D Miller, D Jahnigen, and M Gorbien. "Cardiopulmonary Resuscitation 'Attitudes and Knowledge of Elderly Population'." *Archives of Internal Medicine*, 152(1992), 578–582.

D Miller, D Jahnigen, and M Gorbien. "Cardiopulmonary Resuscitation: What Factors Influence Physician Recommendations?" *Journal of the American Geriatrics Society* 39(1991), A30.

DL Miller, MJ Gorbien, LA Simbartl, and DW Jahnigen. "Factors Influencing Physicians in Recommending In-Hospital Cardiopulmonary Resuscitation," *Archives of Internal Medicine*, 153(1993), 1999–2003.

J Mittelberger, B Lo, D Martin, and R Uhlmann. "Impact of a Procedure-Specific Do-Not-Resuscitate Order Form on Documentation of Do-Not-Resuscitate Orders," *Archives of Internal Medicine*, 153(1993), 228–232.

AH Moss. "Discussing Resuscitation Status with Patients and Families," *Journal of Clinical Ethics*, 4(1993), 180–182.

DJ Murphy and TE Finucane. "New Do-Not-Resuscitate Policies: A First Step in Cost Control," *Archives of Internal Medicine*, 153(1993), 1641–1648.

DJ Murphy, AM Murray, BE Robinson, and EW Campion. "Outcomes of Cardiopulmonary Resuscitation in the Elderly," *Annals of Internal Medicine*, 111(1989), 199–205.

MT Rabkin, G Gillerman, and NR Rice. "Orders Not to Resuscitate," *New England Journal of Medicine*, 7(1976), 364–366.

M Rosenberg, C Wang, S Hoffman-Wilde, and D Hickam. "Results of Cardiopulmonary Resuscitation: Failure to Predict Survival in Two Community Hospitals," *Archives of Internal Medicine*, 153(1993), 1370–1375.

GA Sachs, SH Miles, and RA Levin. "Limiting Resuscitation: Emerging Policy in the Emergency Medical System," *Annals of Internal Medicine*, 114(1991), 151–154.

RH Schmerling, SE Bedell, A Lillifield, and TL Delbanco. "Discussing Cardiopulmonary Resuscitation: A Study of Elderly Outpatients," *Journal of General Internal Medicine*, 3(1988), 317–321.

Z Scholstralk. "Jewish Ethical Guidelines for Resuscitation and Artificial Nutrition and Hydration of the Dying Elderly," *Journal of Medical Ethics*, 20(1994), 93–100.

DA Schwartz and P Reilly. "The Choice Not to Be Resuscitated," *Journal of the American Geriatrics Society* 34(1986), 807–811.

MJ Shapiro. "The Do-Not-Resuscitate Order in a Teaching Hospital" Letter to Editor. *Annals of Internal Medicine*, 96(1982), 660–664.

GL Snider. "The Do-Not-Resuscitate Order: Ethical and Legal Imperative or Medical Decision?" *American Review of Respiratory Diseases*, 143 (1991), 665–674.

T Tomlinson and H Brody. "Ethics and Communication and Do-Not-Resuscitate Orders," *New England Journal of Medicine*, 318(1988), 43–46.

T Tomlinson and H Brody. "Futility and the Ethics of Resuscitation," *Journal of the American Medical Association*, 264(1990), 1276–1280.

RT Uhlmann, RA Pearlman, and KC Cain. "Physicians' and Spouses' Predictions of Elderly Patients' Resuscitation Preferences," *Journal of Gerontology*, 43(1988), M115–M121.

RT Uhlmann, RA Pearlman, and KC Cain. "Understanding of Elderly Patients' Resuscitation Preferences by Physicians and Nurses," *Western Journal of Medicine*, 150(1989), 705–707.

JM Van Delden, PJ van der Maas, L Pijnneborg, and CWN Looman. "Deciding Not to Resuscitate in Dutch Hospitals," *Journal of Medical Ethics*, 19(1993), 200–205.

National Conference on Cardiopulmonary Resuscitation and Emergency Cardiac Care. "Standards for Cardiopulmonary Resuscitation (CPR) and Emergency Cardiac Care (ECC)," *Journal of the American Medical Association*, 227(1974), 864–866.

Omnibus Budget Reconciliation Act. 1990, Pub L No. 101–508, 4206, 4751.

State v. McAfee, 259 Georgia, 579, 385 SE 2d 651 (1989).

CHAPTER 6

GJ Annas. "Death by Prescription. The Oregon Initiative," *New England Journal of Medicine*, 331(1994), 1240–1243.

GJ Annas. "Killing with Kindness: Why the FDA Need Not Certify Drugs Used for Execution as Safe and Effective," *American Journal of Public Health*, 75(1985), 1096.

MP Battin. "The Least Worst Death," *Hastings Center Report*, 13(1983), 13–16.

MP Battin and TJ Bole. "What if Euthanasia Were Legal? Introducing the Issue," *Journal of Medicine and Philosophy*, 18(1993), 237–240.

K Binding and A Hoche. "Permitting the Destruction of Unworthy Life: Its Extent and Form," *Issues in Law and Medicine*, 8(1992), 231– 265.

JD Bleich. "Life as an Intrinsic Rather Than an Instrumental Good: The "Spiritual" Case against Euthanasia," *Issues in Law and Medicine*, 9(1993), 139–149.

R Boehm. "Arbeiten aus dem pharmakologischen Institute der Universitat Dorpat, XIII; Ueber Wiederbelebung nach Vergiftungen and Asphyxic," *Archives of Experimental Patholology and Pharmacology*, 8(1878), 68–101.

R Bone and E Elpern. "Honoring Patient Preferences and Rationing Intensive Care," *Archives of Internal Medicine*, 151(1991), 1061–1063.

D Brahams. "Euthanasia: Doctor Convicted of Attempted Murder," *Lancet*, 340(1992), 782–783.

L Brenner. "Whose Life Is It Anyway?" *Financial Planner*, (1994), 64–65.

J Bullar. "Chloroform in Dying," *British Medical Journal*, 2(1866), 10–12.

PV Caralis, B Davis, K Wright, and E Marcial. "The Influence of Ethnicity and Race on Attitudes toward Advance Directives, Life-Prolonging Treatments, and Euthanasia," *Journal of Clinical Ethics*, 4(1993), 155–165.

P Carrick. *Medical Ethics in Antiquity: Philosophical Perspectives on Abortion and Euthanasia*. (Boston: Dordrecht, 1985).

CK Cassel and De Meier. "Morals and Moralism in the Debate over Euthanasia and Assisted Suicide," *New England Journal of Medicine*, 323(1990), 750–752.

Clinical Care Committee of the Massachusetts General Hospital, "Optimum Care for Hopelessly Ill Patients." *New England Journal of Medicine*, 7(1976), 362–364.

JS Cohen, SD Fihn, EJ Boyko, AR Jonsen, and RW Wood. "Attitudes toward Assisted Suicide and Euthanasia among Physicians in Washington State," *New England Journal of Medicine*, 331(1994), 89–94.

P Cotton. "Rational Suicide: No Longer 'Crazy'?" *Journal of the American Medical Association*, 270(1993), 797.

B Dawson. "Voters Approve of Assisted Suicide," *Detroit Free Press* (March 18, 1993), p. 3B.

CJ Dougherty. "The Common Good, Terminal Illness, and Euthanasia," *Issues in Law and Medicine*, 9(1993), 151–166.

W Drozdiak. "Dutch Pass Euthanasia Measure: Doctors Granted Prosecution Immunity," *Washington Post* (February 10, 1993), p. A1.

MS Ewer. "The Suicide Device: Does It Really Matter Who Pushes the Button?" *Internal Medicine World Report*, 5(13)(1990), 7.

R Gillon. "Suicide and Voluntary Euthanasia; Historical Perspective," In: *Euthanasia and the Right to Death: The Case for Voluntary Euthanasia*. AB Downing, ed. (London: Peter Owen, 1969).

H Goddard. "'Voluntary Euthanasia Declaration' Goes Step Beyond Living Will," *Canadian Medical Association Journal*, 139(3)(1988), 246.

D Gourevitch. "Suicide among the Sick in Classical Antiquity," *Bulletin of the History of Medicine*, 43(1969), 501–518.

M Gunderson and DJ Mayo. "Altruism and Physician Assisted Death," *Journal of Medicine and Philosophy*, 18(1993), 281–295.

JC Harvey and ED Pellegrino. "A Response to Euthanasia Initiatives," *Health Progress*, 53(1994), 36–39, 53.

D Humphry. "Hemlock Founder Humphry on Hospice," *Free Inquiry*, (Winter 1991/92), 26.

D Humphry. *Final Exit: The Practicalities of Self-Deliverance and Assisted Suicide for the Dying*. (Eugene, OR: The Hemlock Society, 1991).

P Jacobs. "Outcome of Death Measure May Rest on 11th-Hour Ads," *Los Angeles Times* (October 28, 1992), p. A3.

A Japenga. "Should You Help a Patient Die?" *Hypocrites*, (November/December, 1994), 39–44.

AR Jonsen. "Living with Euthanasia: A Futuristic Scenario," *Journal of Medicine and Philosophy*, 18(1993), 241–251.

Y Kamisar. "Are Laws against Assisted Suicide Unconstitutional?" *Hastings Center Report*, 23(1993), 32–41.

F Koenig. *Lehrbuch der allgemeinen Chirugie*. (Gottingen, Germany, 1883), pp. 60–61.

HC Leake. "Active Euthanasia with Parental Consent," In: *Death and Dying—Cases in Biolaw* (Besthesda, MD: University Publications of America, 1993).

RJ Lifton. *The Nazi Doctors: Medical Killing and the Psychology of Genocide*. (New York: Basic Books, 1986).

Editorial. "May the Physician Ever End Life?" *British Medical Journal*, 1(1987), 934.

J McMahan. "Killing, Letting Die, and Withdrawing Aid," *Ethics*, 103 (1993), 250–279.

G Meilaender. "Human Equality and Assistance in Suicide," *Second Opinion*, 19(1994), 7–25.

Name Withheld. "It's Over Debbie," *Journal of the American Medical Association*, 259(2)(1988), 2142–2143.

D Orentliche. "Physician-Assisted Dying: The Conflict with Fundamental Principles of American Law." In: *Medicine Unbound: The Human Body and the Limitations of Medical Intervention*. RH Blank and AL Bonnicksen, eds. (New York: Columbia University Press, 1994), pp. 256–268.

D Orentlicher. "Physician Participation in Assisted Suicide," *Journal of the American Medical Association*, 262(1989), 1844–1845.

L Pijnenborg, PJ van der Maas, JJM van Delden, and CWN Looman. "Life-Terminating Acts without Explicit Request of Patient," *Lancet*, 341 (1993), 1196–1199.

L Pijnenborg, PJ van der Maas, PF Kardaun, JJ Glerum, JM van Delden, and CW Looman. "Withdrawal or Withholding of Treatment at the End of Life, Results of a Nationwide Study," *Archives of Internal Medicine*, 155(13)(1995), 286–292.

F Pfafflin. "The Connections between Eugenics, Sterilization, and Mass Murder in Germany from 1933 to 1945," *Medical Law*, 5(1986), 1–10.

Planned Parenthood v. Casey, (US 114 S. Court. 909 911, 1994).

R Proctor. *Racial Hygiene: Medicine under the Nazis*. (Cambridge, MS: Harvard University Press, 1988).

TE Quill. *Death and Dignity: Making Choices and Taking Charge*. (New York: Norton, 1993).

W Reichel and AJ Dyck. "Euthanasia: A Contemporary Moral Quandary," *Lancet*, 94(1989), 1321–1323.

C Saunders. "Hospice Founder Saunders on Voluntary Euthanasia," *Free Inquiry*, (Winter 1991/1992), 26.

M Simons. "Dutch Move to Enact Law Making Euthanasia Easier," *New York Times* (February 9, 1993), p. A1.

M Simons. "Dutch Parliament Approves Law Permitting Euthanasia," *New York Times* (February 10, 1993), p. A10.

PA Singer and M Siegler. "Euthanasia—A Critique," *New England Journal of Medicine*, 322(1990), 1881–1883.

T Spell. "Kevorkian Vows to Defy New Law Banning 'Assisted Suicide' in Michigan," *National Right to Life News* (December 14, 1992), p. 11.

JF Tuohey. "Mercy: An Insufficient Motive for Euthanasia," *Health Progress*, (October, 1993), 51–53.

PJ van der Maas, JJM van Delden, L Pijnenborg, and CWN Looman. "Euthanasia and Other Medical Decisions Concerning the End of Life," *Lancet*, 338(1991), 669–674.

PJ van der Maas, JJM van Delden, and L Pijnenborg. *Euthanasia and*

Other Medical Decisions Concerning the End of Life. (Amsterdam: Elsevier Science, 1992).

RA Ward. "Age and Acceptance of Euthanasia," *Journal of Gerontology*, 34(1980), 421–431.

J Wilson, D Zeman. "Judge Rules People Have Right to Die," *Detroit Free Press* (December 14, 1993), p. 1A.

K Yale. "Some Non-Religious Views Against Proposed 'Mercy Killing' Legislation," *Minnesota Law Review*, 42(1958), 969–1042.

"A Jury's Sympathy for Suicide," *New York Times* (May 6, 1994), p. A28.

"Aid in Dying Is Humane," *Los Angeles Times* (October 18, 1992), p. M5.

Compassion in Dying v. Washington, (Washington, DC: 850 F Supplemental 1454, 1994).

"Doctor in Michigan Helps a 6th Person to Commit Suicide," *New York Times* (November 24, 1992), p. A10.

"Dying Well? A Colloquy on Euthanasia and Assisted Suicide," *Hastings Center Report*, 22(1992), 6–55.

"Euthanasia Guidelines," *Washington Post* (February 17, 1993), p. A23.

Final Report of the Michigan Commission on Death and Dying. (Lansing: Michigan Death and Dying Commission, 1994). Special edition of *Biolaw* (Bethesda, MD: University Publications of America).

"Kevorkian Aids in 2 More Suicides: Total Is at 15," *New York Times* (February 9, 1993), p. A10.

"Kevorkian Helps 3rd Patient in a Week to Commit Suicide," *New York Times* (February 10, 1993), p. A16.

Law Reform Commission of Canada: Aiding Suicide and Cessation of Treatment. (1982).

"New York State Task Force on Life and the Law. When Death Is Sought: Assisted Suicide and Euthanasia in the Medical Context," *New York Times* (September 24, 1993).

"Seattle Group Aids Suicides," *The Oregonian* (June 13, 1993), p. A23.

CHAPTER 7

HJ Aaron. "Lessons from the United Kingdom." In: *Brookings Dialogues on Public Policy*. MA Strosberg, IA Fein, and JD Carroll, eds. (Washington, DC: Brookings Institute, 1986), pp. 24–31.

M Angell. "After Quinlan: The Dilemma of the Persistent Vegetative State," *New England Journal of Medicine*, 330(1994), 1524–1525.

GJ Annas. "Asking the Courts to Set the Standard of Emergency Care—

The Case of Baby K," *New England Journal of Medicine*, 330(1994), 1542–1545.

S Atkinson, D Bihari, M Smithies, K Daly, R Mason, and I McColli. "Identification of Futility in Intensive Care," *Lancet*, 344(1994), 1203–1206.

LL Basta. *Ethical and Legal Dilemmas in Medical Care near the End of Life*. Paper presented at the American College of Legal Medicine Annual Meeting, March 1994, Anaheim, CA.

LL Basta and J Tauth. "Controlling High Technology at the End of Life: How Should It Be Approached?" (1995).

R Bayer, D Callahan, J Fletcher, et al. "The Care of the Terminally Ill: Mortality and Economics," *New England Journal of Medicine*, 309 (1983), 1490–1494.

LJ Blackhall. "Must We Always Use CPR?" *New England Journal of Medicine*, 317(1987), 1281–1285.

LJ Blackhall, J Cobb, and MA Moskowitz. "Discussions Regarding Aggressive Care with Critically Ill Patients," *Journal of General Internal Medicine*, 4(1989), 399–402.

RC Bone, EC Rackow, JG Weg, and members of the ACCP/SCCM Consensus Panel. "Ethical and Moral Guidelines for the Initiation, Continuation, and Withdrawal of Intensive Care," *Chest*, 97(1990), 949–958.

R Bone and E Elpern. "Honoring Patient Preferences and Rationing Intensive Care," *Archives of Internal Medicine*, 151(1991), 1061–1063.

NK Brown and DJ Thompson. "Nontreatment of Fever in Extended-Care Facilities," *New England Journal of Medicine*, 300(1979), 1246–1250.

ST Burner, DR Waldo, and DR McKusick. "National Health Expenditures Projections through 2030," *Health Care Financing Review*, 14(1993), 1–29.

D Callahan. "Families as Caregivers: The Limits of Morality," *Archives of Medical Rehabilitation*, 69(5)(1988), 3.

D Callahan. "Medical Futility, Medical Necessity: The Problem-Without-a-Name," *Hastings Center Report*, 21(July 1991), 30–35.

AI Caplan. "Straight Talk about Rationing," *Annals of Internal Medicine*, 122(1995), 795–796.

FB Cerra, H Champion, and M Chulay. *Critical Care in the United States: Coordinating Intensive Care Resources for Positive and Cost-Efficient Patient Outcomes*. (Anaheim, CA: Society of Critical Care Medicine, 1992).

NA Christakis and DA Asch. "Biases in How Physicians Choose to Withdraw Life Support," *Lancet*, 342(1993), 642–646.

L Cohn. "The Paradox of High-Tech Health Care: Has Our Technology Outstripped Our Ability to Be Ethical, Cost-Effective and Timely in Its Delivery?" *Chest*, 93(1988), 864–867.

Council on Scientific Affairs and Council on Ethical and Judicial Affairs, American Medical Association. "Persistent Vegetative State and the Decision to Withdraw or Withhold Life Support," *Journal of the American Medical Association*, 263(1990), 426–430.

RE Cranford. "Medical Futility: Transforming a Clinical Concept into Legal and Social Policies," *Journal of the American Geriatrics Society*, 42(1994), 894–898.

M Danis, J Garrett, R Harris, and DL Patrick. "Stability of Choices about Life-Sustaining Treatments," *Annals of Internal Medicine*, 120(1994), 567–573.

JC Dougherty. "The Common Good, Terminal Illness, and Euthanasia," *Issues in Law and Medicine*, 9(1993), 151–166.

JF Drane and JL Coulehan. "The Concept of Futility: Patients Do Not Have a Right to Demand Medically Useless Treatment," *Health Progress*, 74(10)(1993), 28–32.

K Faber-Langendoen. "The Clinical Management of Dying Patients Receiving Mechanical Ventilation: A Survey of Physician Practice," *Chest*, 106(1994), 880–888.

JF Fries, CE Koop, CE Beadle, and the Health Project Consortium. "Reducing Health Care Costs by Reducing the Need and Demand for Medical Services," *New England Journal of Medicine*, 329(1993), 321–325.

JA Ginsburg and HD Scott. "A National Health Work Force Policy," American College of Physicians. *Annals of Internal Medicine*, 121(1994), 542–546.

MS Gode. "Your Final 30 Days—Free," *Washington Post* (May 2, 1993), p. C3.

SD Goold, RM Arnold, and LA Siminoff. "Discussion about Limiting Treatment in a Geriatric Clinic," *Journal of the American Geriatrics Society*, 39(1991), 277–281.

WD Gradison. "Federal Policy and Intensive Care." In: *Brookings Dialogues on Public Policy*. MA Strosberg, IA Fein, and JD Carroll, eds. (Washington, DC: Brookings Institute, 1986), pp. 37–40.

MA Grodin. "Religious Advance Directives: The Convergence of Law, Religion, Medicine, and Public Health," *American Journal of Public Health*, 83(1993), 899–903.

DC Hadorn. "Setting Health Care Priorities in Oregon: Cost-Effectiveness

Meets the Rule of Rescue," *Journal of the American Medical Association*, 265(1991), 2218–2225.

LC Hanson and M Danis. "Use of Life-Sustaining Care for the Elderly," *Journal of the American Geriatrics Society*, 39(1991), 772–777.

D Hilifiker. "Allowing the Debilitated to Die," *New England Journal of Medicine*, 308(1983), 716–719.

L Holmes, K Loughead, T Treasure, and S Gallivan. "Which Patients Will Not Benefit from Further Intensive Care after Cardiac Surgery?" *Lancet*, 344(1994), 1200–1202.

JK Iglehart. "Health Policy Report: Rapid Changes for Academic Medical Centers," *New England Journal of Medicine*, 331(1994), 1391–1395.

NS Jecker. "Appeals to Nature in Theories of Age-Group Justice." In: *Aging and Ethics*, (Totowa, NJ: Humana Press, 1991), pp. 269–283.

PE Kalb and DH Miller, "Utilization Strategies for Intensive Care Units," *Journal of the American Medical Association*, 261(1989), 2389–2395.

D Kidder. "The Effects of Hospice Coverage on Medicare Expenditures," *Health Services Research*, 27(1992), 195–217.

J Klessig. "The Effect of Values and Culture on Life-Support Decision," *Western Journal of Medicine*, 157(1992), 316–322.

WA Knaus. "Criteria for Admission to Intensive Care Units." In: *Brookings Dialogues on Public Policy*. MA Strosberg, IA Fein, and JD Carroll, eds. (Washington, DC: Brookings Institute, 1986), pp. 44–51.

WA Knaus, A Rauss, A Alperovitch, et al. "Do Objective Estimates of Chances for Survival Influence Decisions to Withhold or Withdraw Treatment?" *Medical Decision Making*, 10(1990), 163–171.

RA Knox. "Study: Americans Rethinking Effects to Prolong Life," *Boston Globe* (May 21, 1994), p. 1.

SM Kohn and G Menon. "Life Prolongation: Views of Elderly Outpatients and Health Care Professionals," *Journal of the American Geriatrics Society*, 36(9)(1988), 840–844.

AM Kramer. "Health Care for Elderly Persons: Myths and Realities," *New England Journal of Medicine*, 332(1995), 1027–1029.

S Lemeshow and J Le Gall. "Modeling the Severity of Illness of ICU Patients: A Systems Update." *Journal of the American Medical Association*, 272(1994), 1049–1055.

S Lemeshow, D Teres, J Klar, JS Avrunin, SH Gehlbach, and J Rapoport. "Mortality Probability Models (MPH II) Based on an International Cohort of Intensive Care Unit Patients," *Journal of the American Medical Association*, 270(1993), 2478–2486.

M Levetown, MM Pollac, TT Cuerdon, UE Ruttimann, and JJ Glover. "Limitations and Withdrawals of Medical Intervention in Pediatric Critical Care," *Journal of the American Medical Association*, 272(16) (1994), 1271–1275.

KR Levit, HC Lazenby, CA Cowan, and SW Letsch. "National Health Expenditures, 1990," *Health Care Financing Review*, 13(1)(1991), 51.

J Lubitz, J Beebe, and C Baker. "Longevity and Medicare Expenditures," *New England Journal of Medicine*, 332(1995), 999–1003.

J Lubitz and R Prihoda. "The Use and Costs of Medicare Services in the Last 2 Years of Life," *Health Care Financing Review*, 5(3)(1984), 117–131.

JD Lubitz and GF Riley. Trends in Medicare Payments in the Last Year of Life," *New England Journal of Medicine*, 328(1993), 1092–1096.

GD Lundberg. "American Health Care System Management Objectives: The Aura of Inevitability Becomes Incarnate," *Journal of the American Medical Association*, 269(1993), 2554–2555.

N McCall. "Utilization and Costs of Medicare Services by Beneficiaries in Their Last Year of Life," *Medical Care*, 22(4)(1984), 229–242.

RM McCann, WJ Hall, and A Groth-Juncker. "Comfort Care for Terminally Ill Patients: The Appropriate Use of Nutrition and Hydration," *Journal of the American Medical Association*, 272(1994), 1263–1266.

KM McIntyre. "Failure of 'Predictors' of Cardiopulmonary Resuscitation Outcomes to Predict Cardiopulmonary Resuscitation Outcomes: Implications for Do-Not-Resuscitate Policy and Advance Directives," *Archives of Internal Medicine*, 153(1993), 1293–1296.

A Maksoud, DW Jahnigen, and CI Skibinski. "Do-Not-Resuscitate Orders and the Cost of Death," *Archives of Internal Medicine*, 153(1993), 1249–1253.

KG Manton, E Stallard, and HD Tolly. "Limits to Human-Life Expectancy: Evidence, Prospects, and Implications," *POPUP Developmental Review*, 17(1991), 603–637.

A Menotti and S Giampaoli. "Health and Social Consequences of Prolonging Life, with Special Reference to Cardiovascular Diseases: The Italian Situation," *American Journal of Geriatric Cardiology*, (May/June 1994), 13–19.

V Mor and D Kidder. "Cost Savings in Hospice: Final Results of the National Hospice Study," *Health Services Review*, 20(1985), 407–422.

EH Morreim. "Fiscal Scarcity and the Inevitability of Bedside Budget Balancing," *Archives of Internal Medicine*, 149(1989), 1012–1015.

JS Morris. "Ethics and Scarcity." In: *Brookings Dialogues on Public Policy*.

MA Strosberg, IA Fein, and JD Carroll, eds. (Washington, DC: Brookings Institute, 1986), pp. 11–16.

DJ Murphy. "Can We Set Futile Care Policies? Institutional and Systemic Challenges," *Journal of the American Geriatrics Society*, 42(1994), 890–893.

National Center for Health Statistics. *1986 Summary. National Hospital Discharge Survey. Advance Data from Vital and Health Statistics* (Hyattsville, MD: Public Health Service. DHHS Publication No. 145 PHS 87-1250, 1987), pp. 1–16.

JL Nelson and HL Nelson. "Guided by Intimates," *Hastings Center Report*, 23(1993), 14–15.

D Orentlicher. "From the Office of the General Counsel: Denying Treatment to the Noncompliant Patient," *Journal of the American Medical Association*, 265(1991), 1579–1582.

JJ Paris, MD Schreiber, M Statter, R Arensman, and M Siegler. "Beyond Autonomy—Physicians' Refusal to Use Life-Prolonging Extracorporeal Membrane Oxygenation," *New England Journal of Medicine*, 329(1993), 354–357.

RA Pearlman. "Medical Futility: Where Do We Go from Here?" *Journal of the American Geriatrics Society*, 42(1994), 904–905

JD Porterfield, et al. "Optimal Criteria for Care of Heart Disease Patients. Heart Disease Advisory Committee," *Journal of the American Medical Association*, 226(11)(1973), 1340–1344.

DP Rice, "Cost-of-Illness Studies: Fact or Fiction?" *Lancet*, 344(1994), 1519–1520.

B Riddick and I Schneiderman. "Distinguishing between Effect and Benefit," *Journal of Clinical Ethics*, 5(1994), 41–43.

S Ridley, R Jackson, J Findlay, and P Wallace. "Long-Term Survival after Intensive Care," *British Medical Journal*, 301(1990), 1127–1130.

L Robinson. "A Third-Party Perspective on Reimbursement Policy." In: *Brookings Dialogues on Public Policy*. MA Strosberg, IA Fein, and JD Carroll, eds. (Washington, DC: Brookings Institute, 1986), pp. 64–69.

KM Rowan, JH Kerr, E Major, K McPherson, A Short, and MP Vessey. "Intensive Care Society's APACHE II Study in Britain and Ireland: I. Variations in Case Mix of Adult Admissions to General Intensive Care Units and Impact on Outcome," *British Medical Journal*, 307 (1993), 972–977.

KM Rowan, J Kerr, EMK McPherson, A Short, and MP Vessey. "Intensive Care Society's APACHE II Study in Britain and Ireland: II. Outcome

Comparisons of Intensive Care Units after Adjustment for Case Mix by the American APACHE II Method," *British Medical Journal*, 307 (1993), 977–981.

JE Ruark and TA Raffin. "Initiating and Withdrawing Life Support: Principles and Practice in Adult Medicine," *New England Journal of Medicine*, 318(1988), 25–30.

LJ Schneiderman and N Jecker. "Futility in Practice," *Archives of Internal Medicine*, 153(1993), 437–441.

AA Scitovsky. "The High Cost of Dying: What Do the Data Show?" *Milbank Memorial Fund Quarterly, Health and Society*, 62(1984), 591–608.

AA Scitovsky. "Medical Care in the Last Twelve Months of Life: The Relation between Age, Functional Status, and Medical Care Expenditures," *Milbank Memorial Fund Quarterly*, 66(1988), 640–660.

AA Scitovsky and AM Caporon. "Medical Care at the End of Life: The Interaction of Economics and Ethics," *Annual Revision of Public Health*, 7(1986), 59–75.

PA Singer and FH Lowy. "Rationing Patient Preferences and Cost of Care at the End of Life," *Archives of Internal Medicine*, 152(1992), 478–480.

MN Smithies, JD Bihari, and RWS Chang. "Scoring Systems and the Measurement of ICU Cost Effectiveness," *Reanimation Urgencies*, 3(1994), 495–497.

P Starr. *The Logic of Health Care Reform Transforming American Medicine for the Better*. (Knoxville, TN: Whittle Direct Books, 1992).

MS Strosberg. "Introduction: Rationing of Medical Care for the Critically Ill," In: *Brookings Dialogues on Public Policy*. MA Strosberg, IA Fein, and JD Carroll, eds. (Washington, DC: Brookings Institute, 1986), pp. 1–10.

T Tomlinson and H Brody. "Futility and the Ethics of Resuscitation," *Journal of the American Medical Association*, 264(1990), 1276–1280.

MJ Trau. "Futility, Autonomy, and Informed Consent," *Health Progress*, 72(1994), 40–46.

RD Truog, AS Brett, and J Frader. "The Problem with Futility," *New England Journal of Medicine*, 326(1992), 1560–1564.

RM Veatch and CM Spicer. "Futile Care: Physicians Should Not Be Allowed to Refuse to Treat," *Health Progress*, 74(1993), D:22–23.

W Ventres, M Nichter, R Reed, and R Frankel. "Limitation of Medical Care: An Ethnographic Analysis," *Journal of Clinical Ethics*, 4(1993), 134–145.

EH Wagner. "The Cost-Quality Relationship: Do We Always Get What We Pay For?" *Journal of the American Medical Association*, 272(1994), 1951–1952.

MH Waymack. "Old Age and the Rationing of Scarce Health Care Resources." In: *Aging and Ethics*. (Totowa, NJ: Humana Press, 1991), pp. 247–267.

WB Weeks, LL Kofoed, AE Wallace, and HG Welch. "Advance Directives and the Cost of Terminal Hospitalization," *Archives of Internal Medicine*, 154(1994), 2077–2083.

LJ White. "Clinical Uncertainty, Medical Futility, and Practice Guidelines," *Journal of the American Geriatrics Society*, 42(1994), 899–901.

MR Wicclair. "Life Sustaining Medical Care: Elderly Patients without Decision- Making Capacity," *Ethics and the Elderly*. (New York: Oxford University Press, 1993), 55.

SJ Youngner. "Applying Futility: Saying No Is Not Enough," *Journal of the American Geriatrics Society*, 42(1994), 887–889.

SJ Youngner. "Futility in Context," *Journal of the American Medical Association*, 264(10)(1989), 1295–1296.

SJ Youngner. "Who Defines Futility?" *Journal of the American Medical Association*, 260(1988), 2094–2095.

"Hospital Appeals Decision on Treating Anencephalic Baby," *Hospital Ethics*, 9(1993), 6–7.

"What Do We Owe the Elderly? Allocating Social and Health Care Resources: Recommendations of the Joint International Research Group of the Institute for Bioethics," Masstricht, the Netherlands, and the Hastings Center, Briarcliff Manor, NY. *Hastings Center Report*, 24 (1994), S1–S12 (supplemental).

CHAPTER 8

HJ Aaron. "Lessons from the United Kingdom," *Brookings Dialogues on Public Policy*. MA Strosberg, IA Fein, and JD Carroll, eds. (Washington, DC: Brookings Institute, 1986), pp. 24–31.

N Ainslie and AE Beisecker. "Changes in Decisions by Elderly Persons Based on Treatment Description," *Archives of Internal Medicine*, 154 (1994), 2225–2233.

D Avila. "Saying No to Life: Reflections on Death and Justice," *Issues in Law and Medicine*, 9(1993), 227–254.

LL Basta. *Ethical and Legal Dilemmas in Medical Care near the End of Life.* Paper presented at the American College of Legal Medicine Annual Meeting, March 1994, Anaheim, CA.

DS Bedell, TL Delbanco, EF Cook, and FH Epstein. "Survival after Cardiopulmonary Resuscitation in the Hospital," *New England Journal of Medicine,* 309(1983), 569–576.

LJ Blackhall, J Cobb, and MA Moskowitz. "Discussions Regarding Aggressive Care with Critically Ill Patients," *Journal of General Internal Medicine,* 4(1989), 399–402.

H Brady. "The Physicians Role in Determining Futility," *Journal of the American Geriatrics Society,* 42(1994), 875–878.

D Callahan. "Families as Caregivers: The Limits of Morality," *Archives of Medical Rehabilitation,* 6(5)(1988), 155–169.

D Callahan. "Limiting Health Care for the Old." In: *Aging and Ethics.* N Jecker, ed. (Totowa, NJ: Humana Press, 1991), pp. 219–226.

PL Carlen and M Gordon. "Cardiopulmonary Resuscitation and Neurological Complications in the Elderly," *Lancet,* 345(1995), 1253–1254.

L Chelluri, A Grenvik, and M Silverman. "Intensive Care for Critically Ill Elderly: Mortality, Costs, and Quality of Life," *Archives of Internal Medicine,* 155(1995), 1013–1022.

L Chelluri, MR Pinsky, MP Donahoe, and A Grenvik. "Long-Term Outcome of Critically Ill Elderly Patients Requiring Intensive Care." *Journal of the American Medical Association,* 269(24)(1993), 3119–3123.

NA Christakis and DA Asch. "Biases in How Physicians Choose to Withdraw Life Support," *Archives of Medical Rehabilitation,* 342(1993), 642–645.

N Daniels. *Just Health Care.* (New York: Cambridge University Press, 1985).

M Devor, A Wang, M Renvall, D Feigal, and J Ramsdell. "Compliance with Social and Safety Recommendations in an Outpatient Comprehensive Geriatric Assessment Program," *Journal of Gerontology, 49* (1994), M168–M173.

LL Emanuel and EJ Emanuel. "Decisions at the End of Life: Guided by Communities of Patients, *Hastings Center Report,* 23(1993), 6–14.

TE Finucane, JM Shumway, RL Powers, and RM D'Alessandri. "Planning with Elderly Outpatients for Contingencies of Severe Illness: A Survey and Clinical Trial," *Journal of General Internal Medicine,* 3(1988), 322–325.

LJ Fitten, R Lusky, and C Hamann. "Assessing Treatment Decision-

Making Capacity in Elderly Nursing Home Residents," *Journal of the American Geriatrics Society*, 38(1990), 1097–1104.

D Frankl, R Oye, and PE Bellamy. "Attitudes of Hospitalized Patients toward Life-Support: A Survey of 200 In-Patients," *American Journal of Medicine*, 86(1989), 645–658.

MD Godkin and EL Toth. "Cardiopulmonary Resuscitation and Older Adults' Expectations," *Gerontologist*, 34(1994), 797–802.

L Goldman. "Cost-Effectiveness Perspectives in Coronary Artery Disease," *American Heart Journal*, 119(1990), 733–740.

S Goold, R Arnold, and LA Siminoff. "Discussion about Limiting Treatment in a Geriatric Clinic," *Journal of the American Geriatrics Society*, 41(1993), 277–281.

LC Hanson and M Danis. "Use of Life-Sustaining Care for the Elderly," *Journal of the American Geriatrics Society*, 39(1991), 772–777.

W Harmon (ed.). *The Top 500 Poems*. (New York: Columbia University Press, 1992).

Hastings Center. *Guidelines on the Termination of Life-Sustaining Treatment and the Care of the Dying*. (Bloomington: Indiana University Press, 1987).

DM High. "Why Are Elderly People Not Using Advance Directives?" *Journal of Aging and Health*, 5(1993), 497–515.

Hippocrates. *Hippocrates*. 6 Vol. Trans. by WHS Jones, Loeb Classical Library. (Cambridge, MA: Harvard University Press, 1923/1988).

NS Jecker (ed.). "Appeals to Nature in Theories of Age-Group Justice," In: *Aging and Ethics*. (Totowa, NJ: Humana Press, 1991), pp. 269–283.

NS Jecker. "Being a Burden on Others," *Journal of Clinical Ethics*, 4(1993), 16–20.

M Kohn and G Menon. "Life Prolongation: Views of Elderly Outpatients and Health Care Professionals," *Journal of the American Geriatrics Society*, 36(1988), 840–844.

AM Kramer. "Health Care for Elderly Persons: Myths and Realities," *New England Journal of Medicine*, 332(1995), 1027–1029.

PJ Lawson-Mathew and KS Channer. "Reporting on Reports—Cardiological Intervention in Elderly Patients," *Journal of the Royal College of Physician of London*, 29(1955), 11–14.

A Leaf. "Medicine and the Aged," *New England Journal of Medicine*, 297(1977), 887–890.

PJ Liacos. "Dilemmas of Dying," *Medicolegal News*, 7(3)(1979), 4–7.

"Mercy for the Dying," *New York Times* (May 28, 1994), p. 18.

DL Miller, DW Jahnigen, and M Gorbien. "Cardiopulmonary Resuscitation: How Useful? Attitudes and Knowledge of an Elderly Population," *Archives of Internal Medicine*, 152(3)(1992), 578–582.

DJ Murphy. "Can We Set Futile Care Policies? Institutional and Systemic Challenges," *Journal of the American Geriatrics Society*, 42(1994), 890–893.

DJ Murphy, AM Murray, BE Robinson, and EW Campion. "Outcomes of Cardiopulmonary Resuscitation in the Elderly," *Annals of Internal Medicine*, 111(1989), 199–205.

D Niemira. "Life on the Slippery Slope: A Bedside View of Treating Incompetent Elderly Patients," *Hastings Center Report*, 23(1993), 14–17.

J Newald. "Right-to-Life Issues Further Clouded by Aging Population," *Hospitals*, 60(24)(1986), 72.

D Northridge and RJC Hall. "Cardiological Services for the Elderly," *Journal of the Royal College of Physicians of London*, 29(1995), 9–10.

JG Ouslander, AJ Tynchuk, and B Rahbar. "Health Care Decisions among Elderly Long-Term Care Residents and Their Potential Proxies," *Archives of Internal Medicine*, 149(1989), 1367–1372.

RB Reilly, TA Teasdale, and LB McCullough. "Projecting Patients' Preferences from Living Wills: An Invalid Strategy for Management of Dementias with Life-Threatening Illness," *Journal of the American Geriatrics Society*, 42(1994), 997–1003.

B Riddick and L Schneiderman. "Distinguishing between Effect and Benefit," *Journal of Clinical Ethics*, 5(1994), 41–43.

G Sachs, C Stocking, and S Miles. "Empowerment of the Older Patients: A Randomized, Controlled Trial to Increase Discussion and Use of Advance Directives," *Journal of the American Geriatrics Society*, 40(1992), 269–273.

RH Schmerling, SE Bedell, A Lillifield, and TL Delbanco. "Discussing Cardiopulmonary Resuscitation: A Study of Elderly Outpatients," *Journal of General Internal Medicine*, 3(1988), 317–321.

R Schonwetter, S Teasdale, G Taffer, BE Robinson, and RJ Luchi. "Educating the Elderly: Cardiopulmonary Resuscitation Decisions before and after Intervention," *Journal of the American Geriatrics Society*, 39(1991), 372–377.

Z Schostak. "Jewish Ethical Guidelines for Resuscitation and Artificial Nutrition and Hydration of the Dying Elderly," *Journal of Medical Ethics*, 20(1994), 93–100.

SA Schroeder, JA Showstack, and J Schwartz. "Survival of Adult High-Cost Patients. Report of a Follow-up Study from Nine Acute-Care Hospitals," *Journal of the American Medical Association*, 245(1981), 1446–1449.

JS Tobias and RL Soulami. "Fully Informed Consent Can Be Needlessly Cruel," *British Medical Journal*, 397(1993), 1199–1201.

T Tomlinson, K Howe, M Notman, and D Rossmiller. "An Empirical Study of Proxy Consent for Elderly Persons," *Gerontologist*, 30(1990), 54–64.

RT Uhlmann, RA Pearlman, and KC Cain. "Physicians' and Spouses' Predictions of Elderly Patients' Resuscitation Preferences," *Journal of Gerontology*, 43(1988), M115–M121.

RT Uhlmann, RA Pearlman, and KC Cain. "Understanding of Elderly Patients' Resuscitation Preferences by Physicians and Nurses," *Western Journal of Medicine*, 150(1989), 705–707.

RM Walker, RS Schonwetter, DR Kramer, and BE Robinson. "Living Wills and Resuscitation Preferences in an Elderly Population," *Archives of Internal Medicine*, 155(1995), 171–175.

MH Waymack. "Old Age and the Rationing of Scarce Health Care Resources." In: *Aging and Ethics*. N Jecker, ed. (Totowa, NJ: Humana Press, 1991), pp. 247–267.

"What Do We Owe the Elderly? Allocating Social and Health Care Resources: Recommendations of the Joint International Research Group of the Institute for Bioethics," Masstricht, the Netherlands, and the Hastings Center, Briarcliff Manor, NY. *Hastings Center Report*, 24 (1994), S1–S12 (Supplemental).

MR Wicclair (ed.). "Life Sustaining Medical Care: Elderly Patients without Decision-Making Capacity," In: *Ethics and the Elderly*. (New York: Oxford University Press, 1993), 55.

NR Zweibel and CK Cassel. "Treatment Choices at the End of Life: A Comparison of Decisions by Older Patients and Their Physician-Selected Proxies," *Gerontologist*, 29(1989), 615–621.

CHAPTER 9

American Thoracic Society. "Withholding and Withdrawing Life-Sustaining Therapy," *American Review of Respiratory Disease*, 144(1991), 726–731.

Aristotle. Ethica Nicomachea: *Masterpieces of World Philosophy*. FN Magill, ed. (New York: Harper Collins, 1990), p. 73.

Aristotle. *The Basic Works of Aristotle*. M McKeon, ed. (New York: Random House, 1941).

S Atkinson, D Bihari, M Smithies, K Daly, R Mason, and I McColl. "Identification of Futility in Intensive Care," *Lancet*, 344(1994), 1203–1206.

D Avila. "Saying No to Life: Reflections on Death and Justice," *Issues in Law and Medicine*, 227(1993), 227–254.

WJ Bennett (ed.). *The Book of Virtues: A Treasury of Great Moral Stories*. (New York: Simon & Schuster, 1993), p. 21.

RC Bone, EC Rackow, JG Weg, and members of ACCP/SCCM Consensus Panel. "Ethical and Moral Guidelines for the Initiation, Continuation, and Withdrawal of Intensive Care," *Chest*, 97(1990), 949–958.

H Brady. "The Physicians Role in Determining Futility," *Journal of the American Geriatrics Society*, 42(1994), 875–878.

D Callahan. "*Ad Hominem* Run Amok: A Response to John Lachs," *Journal of Clinical Ethics*, 5(1994), 13–15.

Camp v. White, 510 So. 2d 166, 168 (Ala. 1987).

NA Christakis and DA Asch. "Biases in How Physicians Choose to Withdraw Life Support," *Lancet*, 342(1993), 642–645.

RE Cranford. "Commentary," *Cambridge Quarterly of Healthcare Ethics*, 2(1993), 343–346.

JR Curtis, DR Park, MR Krone, and RA Pearlman. "Use of the Medical Futility Rationale in Do-Not-Attempt-Resuscitation Orders," *Journal of the American Medical Association*, 273(2)(1995), 124–128.

JF Drane and JL Coulehan. "The Concept of Futility: Patients Do Not Have a Right to Demand Medically Useless Treatment," *Health Progress*, 74(1993), 28–32.

L Edelstein. "The Hippocratic Oath: Text, Translation, and Interpretation." In: *Ancient Medicine: Selected Papers of Ludwig Edelstein*. O Temkin and CL Temkin, eds. (Baltimore: Johns Hopkins Press, 1967).

EJ Emanuel. "A Constitutional Right to Refuse Unwanted Care," *Medical Ethics*, 5(1990), 15–16.

G Evans. "The Texas Natural Death Act," *Texas Medicine*, 84(2)(1988), 37–41.

K Faber-Langendoen and DM Bartles. "Process of Forgoing Life-Sustaining Treatment in a University Hospital: An Empirical Study," *Critical Care Medicine*, 20(1992), 570–577.

DR Field, EA Gates, RK Creasy, AR Jonsen, and R Laros. "Maternal Brain

Death during Pregnancy: Medical and Ethical Issues," *Journal of the American Medical Association*, 260(1988), 816–822.

M Jurback. "Preventive Ethics: Expanding the Horizons of Clinical Ethics," *Journal of Clinical Ethics*, 5(5)(1993), 174–175.

D Frankl, R Oye, and PE Bellamy. "Attitudes of Hospitalized Patients toward Life-Support: A Survey of 200 Inpatients," *American Journal of Medicine*, 86(1989), 645–658.

DM Gianelli. "High Court: States Can Regulate Food Withdrawal," *American Medical News*, 6/13 July, 1990), 1.

GR Gillett. "Learning to Do No Harm," *Journal of Medicine and Philosophy*, 18(1993), 253–268.

WD Gradison. "Federal Policy and Intensive Care," In: *Brookings Dialogues on Public Policy*. MA Strosberg, IA Fein, and JD Carroll, eds. (Washington, DC: Brookings Institute, 1986), pp. 37–40.

TE Hill, *Autonomy and Self-Respect*. (Cambridge: Cambridge University Press, 1991).

TP Hill. "Commentary," *Cambridge Quarterly of Healthcare Ethics*, 2(1993), 346–349.

Hippocrates. *Hippocrates* (6 vol.). Translated by WHS Jones, Loeb Classical Library. (Cambridge, MA: Harvard University Press), pp. 1923–1988.

PK Hitti. *Islam—A Way of Life*. (South Bend, IN: Regnery/Gateway, 1970).

T Hobbes. "Leviathan, Parts I and II," In: *The Library of Liberal Arts*. HW Schneider ed. (Indianapolis, IN: Bobbs-Merrill, 1958).

S Hook. "It Didn't Have to Be. In: *Living Philosophies: The Reflections of Some Eminent Men Women of Our Time*. C Fadiman, ed. (New York: Doubleday, 1990), pp. 245–263.

IM Kennedy. "Treat Me Right," *Essays in Medical Law and Ethics*, 360(1988), 360–361.

J Lachs. "When Abstract Moralizing Runs Amok," *Journal of Clinical Ethics*, 5(1994), 10–13.

RD Lamm. "Columbus and Copernicus: New Wine in Old Wineskins," *Mount Sinai Journal of Medicine*, 56(1989), 1–10.

JD Lantos, PA Singer, RM Walker, et al. "The Illusion of Futility in Clinical Practice," *American Journal of Medicine*, 87(1989), 81–84.

EH Loewy and RA Carlson. "Futility and Its Wider Implications: A Concept for Further Examination," *Archives of Internal Medicine*, 153(1993), 429–431.

RS Loewy. "Commentary," *Cambridge Quarterly of Healthcare Ethics*, 2 (1993), 349–352.

JM Luce and C Fink. "Communicating with Families about Withholding and Withdrawal of Life Support," *Chest*, 101(1992), 1185–1186.

RM McCann, WJ Hall, and A Groth-Juncker. "Comfort Care for Terminally Ill Patients: The Appropriate Use of Nutrition and Hydration," *Journal of the American Medical Association*, 272(1994), 1263–1266.

BJ McNeil, SG Panker, HC Sox, Jr., and A Tversky. "On the Elicitation of Preferences for Alternative Therapies," *New England Journal of Medicine*, 306(1982), 1259–1262.

CM Mangione and B Lo. "Beyond Fear: Resolving Ethical Dilemmas Regarding HIV Infection," *Chest*, 95(1989), 1100–1106.

A Meisel. "Legal Myths about Terminating Life Support," *Archives of Internal Medicine*, 151(1991), 1497–1502.

SH Miles. "Medical Futility," *Law, Medicine, and Health Care*, 20(1993), 310–315.

JE Munoz-Silva and CM Kjellstrand. "Withdrawing Life Support: Do Families and Physicians Decide as Patients Do?" *Nephron*, 48(1988), 201–205.

S Neu and CM Kjellstrand. "Stopping Long-Term Dialysis: An Empirical Study of Withdrawal of Life-Supporting Treatment," *New England Journal of Medicine*, 314(1986), 14–20.

LJ O'Connell. "Commentary," *Cambridge Quarterly of Healthcare Ethics*, 2(1993), 342–343.

"Optimum Care for Hopelessly Ill Patients: A Report of the Clinical Care Committee of the Massachusetts General Hospital," *New England Journal of Medicine*, 295(1976), 362–364.

D Orentlicher. "The Illusion of Patient Choice in End-of-Life Decisions," *Journal of the American Medical Association*, 267(1992), 2101–2104.

RA Pearlman. "Foregoing Medical Nutrition and Hydration: An Area for Fine-Tuning Clinical Skills," *Journal of General Internal Medicine*, 8(1993), 225–227.

RA Pearlman. "Medical Futility: Where Do We Go from Here?" *Journal of the American Geriatrics Society*, 42(1994), 904–905.

RA Pearlman, SH Miles, and RM Arnold. "Contributions of Empirical Research to Medical Ethics," *Theoretical Medicine*, 14(1993), 197–210.

ED Pellegrino. "Compassion Needs Reason Too," *Journal of the American Medical Association*, 270(1993), 874–875.

ED Pellegrino. "Ethics," *Journal of the American Medical Association*, 270 (1993), 202–203.

JD Porterfield and the Heart Disease Advisory Committee. "Optimal

Criteria for Care of Heart Disease Patients. Heart Disease Advisory Committee," *Journal of the American Medical Association*, 226(11)(1973), 1340–1344.

RA Sedler. "The Constitution and Hastening Inevitable Death," *Hastings Center Report*, 23(1993), 20–25.

NG Smedira, BH Evans, LS Grais, et al. "Withholding and Withdrawal of Life Support from the Critically Ill," *New England Journal of Medicine*, 322(1990), 309–315.

MZ Solomon, L O'Donnell, B Jennings, et al. "Decisions near the End of Life: Professional Views on Life-Sustaining Treatments," *American Journal of Public Health*, 83(1993), 14–23.

R Steinbrook, B Lo, J Moulton, G Saika, H Hollander, and PA Volberding. "Preferences of Homosexual Men with AIDS for Life-Sustaining Treatment," *New England Journal of Medicine*, 314(1986), 457–460.

P Steinfels. "Help for the Helping Hands in Death," *New York Times* (February 14, 1993), p. D1.

CJ Stolman. "Should Medical Encounters Be Studied Using Ethnographic Techniques? *Journal of Clinical Ethics*, 4(1993), 183–185.

RJ Sullivan. "Accepting Death without Artificial Nutrition and Hydration," *Journal of General Internal Medicine*, 8(1993), 220–224.

Task Force on Ethics of the Society of Critical Care Medicine. "Consensus Report on the Ethics of Foregoing Life-Sustaining Treatments in the Critically Ill," *Critical Care Medicine*, 18(1990), 1435–1439.

Task Force on Pain Management, Catholic Health Association. "Pain Management: Theological and Ethical Principles Governing the Use of Pain Relief for Dying Patients," *Health Progress*, (Jan./Feb. 1993), 30–39.

JS Tobias and RL Soulami. "Fully Informed Consent Can Be Needlessly Cruel," *British Medical Journal*, 307(1993), 1199–1201.

"The United States Bishops' Committee Statement on Nutrition and Hydration," *Cambridge Quarterly of Healthcare Ethics*, 2(1993), 341–342, Discussion 342-52.

LJ White. "Clinical Uncertainty, Medical Futility, and Practice Guidelines," *Journal of the American Geriatrics Society*, 42(1994), 899–901.

D Wilson. "New Insights into the Old Controversy over Long-Term Tube Feeding," *Bioethics Bulletin*, 5(1993), 1–8.

N Wray, B Brody, T Bayer, et al. "Withholding Medical Treatment from the Severely Demented Patient: Decisional Processes and Cost Implications," *Archives of Internal Medicine*, 148(1988), 1980–1984.

SJ Youngner. "Futility in Context," *Journal of the American Medical Association*, 264(10)(1989), 1295–1296.

SJ Youngner. "Who Defines Futility?" *Journal of the American Medical Association*, 60(1988), 2094–2095.

"Mas-ala 5," *Koran*.

CHAPTER 10

GJ Annas. "The Health Care Proxy and the Living Will," *New England Journal of Medicine*, 324(1991), 1210–1213.

"Behind a Boy's Decision to Forego Treatment," *New York Times* (June 13, 1994), p. A12.

L Brenner. "Whose Life Is It Anyway?" *Financial Planner*, (1994), 64–65.

A Brett. "Limitations of Listing Specific Medical Interventions in Advance Directives," *Journal of the American Medical Association*, 266(1991), 825–828.

DW Brock. "Advance Directives: What Is Reasonable to Expect from Them?" *Journal of Clinical Ethics*, 5(1994), 57–60.

DW Brock and SA Wartman. "When Competent Patients Make Irrational Choices," *New England Journal of Medicine*, 322(1990), 1595–1599.

H Brody. "The Physician's Role in Determining Futility," *Journal of the American Geriatrics Society*, 42(1994), 875–878.

LL Bunetti, SD Carperos, and RE Westlund. "Physicians' Attitudes toward Living Wills and Cardiopulmonary Resuscitation," *Journal of General Internal Medicine*, 6(1991), 323–329.

ED Caine and YC Conwell. "Self-Determined Death, the Physician, and Medical Priorities: Is There Time to Talk?" *Journal of the American Medical Association*, 270(1993), 875–876.

PV Caralis, B Davis, K Wright, and E Marcial. "The Influence of Ethnicity and Race on Attitudes toward Advance Directives, Life-Prolonging Treatments, and Euthanasia," *Journal of Clinical Ethics*, 4(1993), 155–165.

CV Chambers, JJ Diamond, RL Perkel, and LA Lasch. "Relationship of Advance Directives to Hospital Charges in a Medicare Population," *Archives of Internal Medicine*, 154(1994), 541–547.

NA Christakis and DA Asch. "Biases in How Physicians Choose to Withdraw Life Support," *Lancet*, 342(1993), 642–645.

R Cogen, B Patterson, S Chavin, J Cogen, L Landsberg, and J Posner.

"Surrogate Decision-Maker Preferences for Medical Care of Severely Demented Nursing Home Patients," *Archives of Internal Medicine*, 152(Sept. 1992), 1885–1888.

CB Cohen and PJ Cohen. "Do-Not-Resuscitate Orders in the Operating Room," *New England Journal of Medicine*, 325(1991), 1879–1882.

LL Emanuel and MJ Barry. "Advance Directives for Medical Care: A Case for Greater Use," *New England Journal of Medicine*, 324(1991), 889–895.

EL Diamond, JA Jernigan, RA Moseley, V Messina, and RA McKeown. "Decision-Making Ability and Advance Directive Preferences in Nursing Home Patients and Proxies," *Gerontologist*, 29(5)(1989), 622–626.

DJ Doukas and DW Gorenflo. "Analyzing the Values History: An Evaluation of Patient Medical Values and Advance Directives," *Journal of Clinical Ethics*, 4(1993), 41–45.

EJ Emanuel and LL Emanuel. "Proxy Decision Making for Incompetent Patients: An Ethical and Empirical Analysis," *Journal of the American Medical Association*, 267(1992), 2067–2071.

LL Emanuel. "Advance Directives: What Have We Learned So Far?" *Journal of Clinical Ethics*, 4(1993), 8–16.

LL Emanuel, MJ Barry, and JD Stoeckle. "Advance Directives: Can Patients' Stated Treatment Choices Be Used to Infer Unstated Choices?" *Medical Care*, 32(1994), 95–105.

LL Emanuel, JJ Barry, JD Stoeckle, LM Ettelson, and EJ Emanuel. "Advance Directives for Medical Care: A Case for Greater Use," *New England Journal of Medicine*, 324(1991), 889–895.

LL Emanuel and EJ Emanuel. "The Medical Directive: A New Comprehensive Advance Care Document," *Journal of the American Medical Association*, 261(1989), 3288–3293.

LJ Fitten, R Lusky, and C Hamann. "Assessing Treatment Decision-Making Capacity in Elderly Nursing Home Residents," *Journal of the American Geriatrics Society*, 38(1990), 1097–1104.

ER Gamble, PJ McDonald, and PR Lichstein. "Knowledge, Attitudes, and Behavior of Elderly Persons Regarding Living Wills," *Archives of Internal Medicine*, 151(1991), 277–280.

G Gordon and P Dunn. "Advance Directives and Patient's Self-Determination Act," *Hospital Practice*, 27(1992), 39–40, 42.

PJ Greco, KA Schulman, R Lavizzo-Mourey, and J Hansen-Flashen. "The Patient Self- Determination Act and the Future of Advance Directives," *Annals of Internal Medicine*, 115(1991), 639–643.

J Hare and C Nelson. "Will Outpatients Complete Living Wills? A Comparison of Two Interventions," *Journal of General Internal Medicine*, 6(1991), 41–46.

DM High. "Advance Directives and the Elderly: A Study of Interventional Strategies to Increase Their Use," *Gerontologist*, 33(1993), 342–349.

DM High. "All in the Family: Extended Autonomy and Expectations in Surrogate Health Care Decision-Making," *Gerontologist*, 28(Suppl.) (1988), 46–51.

DM High. "Standards for Surrogate Decision-Making: What the Elderly Want," *Journal of Long-Term Care Administration*, 17(1989), 8–13.

DM High. "Why Are Elderly People Not Using Advance Directives?" *Journal of Aging and Health*, 5(1993), 497–515.

S Hook. "It Didn't Have to Be." In: *Living Philosophies: The Reflections of Some Eminent Men and Women of Our Time*. C Fadiman, ed. (New York: Doubleday, 1990), pp. 245–263.

CB Klem. "Attitudes of Direct Care Staff in Home Health Care toward Advance Directives," *Home Health Nurse*, 12(3)(1994), 55–59.

J LaPuma, D Orentlicher, and RJ Moss. "Advance Directives on Admission: Clinical Implications and Analysis of the (Patient Self-Determination Act) PSDA of 1990," *Journal of the American Medical Association*, 266(1991), 402–405.

B Lo, GA McLeod, and G Saika. "Patient Attitudes to Discussing Life-Sustaining Treatment," *Archives of Internal Medicine*, 146(1986), 1613–1615.

MK Luptak and C Boult. "A Method for Increasing Elders Use of Advance Directives," *Gerontologist*, 34(1994), 409–412.

N Lurie, AM Pheley, SH Miles, and S Bannick-Mohrland. "Attitudes toward Discussing Life-Sustaining Treatments in Extended Care Facility Patients," *Journal of the American Geriatrics Society*, 40(1992), 1205–1208.

D Lush. "Advance Directives and Living Wills," *Journal of the Royal College of Physicians of London*, 27(3)(1993), 274–277.

J Lynn and JM Teno. "After the Patient Self-Determination Act: The Need for Empirical Research on Formal Advance Directives," *Hastings Center Report*, 23(1)(1993), 20–24.

DJ Mazur and JF Merz. "How the Manner of Presentation of Data Influences Older Patients in Determining Their Treatment Preferences," *Journal of the American Geriatrics Society*, 41(1993), 223–228.

JA Menikoff, GA Sachs, and M Siegler. "Beyond Advance Directives—Health Care Surrogate Laws," *New England Journal of Medicine*, 327(1992), 1165–1169.

W Modell. "A 'Will' to Live," *New England Journal of Medicine*, 290(1974), 907–908.

DW Molloy and GH Guyat. "A Comprehensive Health Care Directive in a Home for the Aged," *Canadian Medical Association Journal*, 145(1991), 307–311.

Oklahoma Natural Death Act. Oklahoma H.B. 1482, July 1, 1990.

Omnibus Budget Reconciliation Act. 1990, Pub L No. 101-508, 4206, 4751.

D Orentlicher. "Advance Medical Directives," *Journal of the American Medical Association*, 263(1990), 2365–2367.

JG Oushlander, AJ Tynchuk, and B Rahbar. "Health Care Decisions among Elderly Long-Term Care Residents and Their Potential Proxies," *Archives of Internal Medicine*, 149(1989), 1367–1372.

RA Pearlman, RF Uhlmann, and NS Jecker. "Spousal Understanding of Patient Quality of Life: Implications for Surrogate Decision," *Journal of Clinical Ethics*, 3(1992), 114–121. (discussions 121–123).

President's Commission for the Study of Ethical Problems in Medicine and Biomedical and Behavioral Research. *Deciding to Forego Life-Sustaining Treatment*. (Washington, DC: U.S. Government Printing Office, 1983).

RB Reilly, TA Teasdale, and LB McCullough. "Projecting Patients' Preferences from Living Wills: An Invalid Strategy for Management of Dementis with Life-Threatening Illness," *Journal of the American Geriatrics Society*, 42(1994), 997–1003.

M Renders and PA Singer. "Comparing Patients' Satisfaction with Two Different Advance Directives," *Clinical Research*, 40(1992), 617A.

JM Roe, MK Goldstein, K Massey, and D Pascoe. "Durable Power of Attorney for Health Care: A Survey of Senior Center Participants," *Archives of Internal Medicine*, 152(1992), 292–296.

SM Rubin, WM Strull, MF Fialkow, SJ Weiss, and B Lo. "Increasing the Completion of the Durable Power of Attorney for Health Care: A Randomized, Controlled Trial," *Journal of the American Medical Association*, 271(1994), 209–212.

DE Saunders. "The Physician and the Living Will," *Journal of the South Carolina Medical Association*, 84(3)(1988), 114–118.

LJ Schneiderman, R Kronick, RM Kaplan, JP Anderson, and RD Langer. "Effects of Offering Advance Directives on Medical Treatments and Costs," *Annals of Internal Medicine*, 117G(October 1, 1992), 599–606.

AB Seckler, DE Meier, M Mulvihill, M Cammer, and BE Paris. "Substituted Judgment: How Accurate Are Proxy Predictions?" *Annals of Internal Medicine*, 115(1991), 92–98.

C Shawler, DM High, KK Moore, and C Velotta. "Clinical Considerations: Surrogate Decision-Making for Hospitalized Elders," *Journal of Gerontological Nursing*, 18(1992), 5–11.

A Shegal, A Galbraith, M Chesney, P Schoenfeld, G Charles, and B Lo. "How Strictly Do Dialysis Patients Want Their Advance Directives Followed?" *Journal of the American Medical Association*, 267(1992), 59–63.

E Siegert, L Beauchamp, P Mulhausen, and G Kochersberger. "Advance Directives Education Survey," *Journal of the American Geriatrics Society*, 40(1992), P172.

S Silverman, S Fry, and N Armistead. "Nurses' Perspectives on Implementation of the Patient Self-Determination Act," *Journal of Clinical Ethics*, 5(1994), 30–37.

MD Silverstein, CB Stocking, JP Antel, J Beckwith, RP Roos, and M Siegler. "Amyotrophic Lateral Sclerosis and Life-Sustaining Therapy: Patients' Desires for Information, Participation in Decision-Making, and Life-Sustaining Therapy," *Mayo Clinics Proceedings*, 66(1991), 906–913.

WD Smucker, PH Ditto, KA Moore, JA Druley, JH Danks, and A Townsend. "Elderly Outpatients Respond Favorably to a Physician-Limited Advance Directive Discussion," *Journal of the American Board of Family Practice*, 6(1993), 473–482.

R Spears, PJ Drinka, and SK Voeks. "Obtaining a Durable Power of Attorney for Health Care from Nursing Home Residents," *Journal of Family Practice*, 36(1993), 409.

KL Steltler, BA Elliott, and CA Bruno. "Living Will Completion in Older Adults," *Archives of Internal Medicine*, 152(1992), 954–959.

RD Swartz and E Perry. "Advance Directives Are Associated with 'Good Deaths' in Chronic Dialysis Patients," *Journal of the American Society of Nephrology*, 3(1993), 1623–1630.

Teno, J Fleishman, DW Brock, and V Mor. "The Use of Formal Prior Directives among Patients with HIV-Related Diseases," *Journal of General Internal Medicine*, 5(1990), 490–494.

Tomlinson, K Howe, M Notman, and D Rossmiller. "An Empirical Study of Proxy Consent for Elderly Persons," *Gerontologist*, 30(1990), 54–64.

M Walker, RS Schonwetter, DR Kramer, and BE Robinson. "Living Wills and Resuscitation Preferences in an Elderly Population," *Archives of Internal Medicine*, 155(1995), 175.

WB Weeks, LL Kofoed, AE Wallace, and HG Welch. "Advance Directives and the Cost of Terminal Hospitalization," *Archives of Internal Medicine*, 154(1994), 2077–2083.

SM Wolf, P Boyle, D Calahan, JJ Fins, B Jennings, JL Nelson, et al. "Sources of Concern about the Patient Self-Determination Act," *New England Journal of Medicine*, 325(1991), 1666–1671.

NR Zweibel and CK Cassel. "Treatment Choices at the End of Life: A Comparison of Decisions by Older Patients and Their Physician-Selected Proxies," *Gerontologist*, 29(1989), 615–621.

UV Zyl. "The Right to Die: A South African Perspective," *Medical Law*, 7(1989), 417–422.

Oklahoma Directive to Physicians (before 1980).

Florida Registry Living Will Registry of America, Incorporated. (Adm. LS Driggers, 1988).

"Florida's Health Care Surrogate Act 1990, section 745-746: 'A health care surrogate may not provide consent for ... experimental treatments or therapies, except as recommended by federally approved institutional review boards.'"

"Uniform Health-Care Decisions Act drafted by the National Conference of Commissioners on Uniform State Laws and by it—approved and recommended for enactment in all states at its Annual Conference Meeting in its 102nd year in Charleston, SC, July 3–August 6, 1993. Uniform Law Commissioners approved by the American Bar Association, Kansas City, MO, February 7, 1994."

CHAPTER 11

A Brett. "Limitations of Listing Specific Medical Interventions in Advance Directives," *Journal of the American Medical Association*, 266(1991), 825–828.

LL Bunetti, SD Carperos, and RE Westlund. "Physicians' Attitudes toward Living Wills and Cardiopulmonary Resuscitation," *Journal of General Internal Medicine*, 6(1991), 323–329.

M Danis, LI Southerland, JM Garrett, et al. "A Prospective Study of Advance Directives for Life-Sustaining Care," *New England Journal of Medicine*, 324(1991), 882–888.

KW Davidson, C Hackler, DR Caradine, and RS McCord. "Physicians' Attitudes on Advance Directives," *Journal of the American Medical Association*, 262(1989), 262:2415–2419.

LL Emanuel and MJ Barry. "Advance Directives for Medical Care: Patients' and Families' Preference for Medical Care: A Case for Greater Use," *New England Journal of Medicine*, 324(1991), 889–895.

EL Diamond, JA Jernigan, RA Moseley, V Messina, and RA McKeown. "Decision-Making Ability and Advance Directive Preferences in Nursing Home Patients and Proxies," *Gerontologist*, 29(5)(1989), 622–626.

RD Dresser. "Confronting the 'Near Irrelevance' of Advance Directives," *Journal of Clinical Ethics*, 5(1994), 55–56.

MH Ebell, MA Smith, KG Seifert, and K Poisinelli. "The Do-Not-Resuscitate Order: Outpatient Experience and Decision-Making Preferences," *Journal of Family Practice*, 31(1990), 630–634.

MA Everhart and RA Pearlman. "Stability of Patient Preferences Regarding Life-Sustaining Treatments," *Chest*, 97(1990), 159–164.

ER Gamble, PJ McDonald, and RP Lichstein. "Knowledge, Attitudes, and Behavior of Elderly Persons Regarding Living Wills," *Archives of Internal Medicine*, 151(1991), 277–280.

D Greaves, "The Future Prospects for Living Wills," *Journal of Medical Ethics*, 12(1989), 179–182.

J Hare and C Nelson. "Will Outpatients Complete Living Wills? A Comparison of Two Interventions," *Journal of General Internal Medicine*, 6(1991), 41–46.

J Hare, C Pratt, and C Nelson. "Agreement between Patients and Their Self-Selected Surrogates on Difficult Medical Decision," *Archives of Internal Medicine*, 152(1992), 1049–1054.

SC Johnston, MP Pfeifer, R McNutt, and the End-of-Life Study Group. "The Discussion about Advance Directives: Patient and Physician Opinions Regarding When and How It Should Be Conducted," *Archives of Internal Medicine*, 155(May 22, 1995), 1025–1030.

PE Kalb and DH Mille. "Utilization Strategies for Intensive Care Units," *Journal of the American Medical Association*, 261(1989), 2389–2395.

R Kielstein and HM Sass. "Using Stories to Assess Values and Establish Medical Directives," *Kennedy Institute of Ethics Journal*, 303(1993), 303–325.

T Malloy, RS Wington, J Meeske, and TG Tape. "The Influence of Treatment Descriptions on Advance Medical Treatment Decisions," *Journal of the American Geriatrics Society*, 40(1992), 1255–1260.

DJ Mazur and JF Merz. "How the Manner of Presentation of Data Influences Older Patients in Determining Their Treatment Preferences," *Journal of the American Geriatrics Society*, 41(1993), 223–228.

LJ Schneiderman, RA Pearlman, RM Kaplan, JP Anderson, and EM Rosenberg. "Relationship of General Advance Directive Instructions to Specific Life-Sustaining Treatment Preferences in Patients with Serious Illness," *Annals of Internal Medicine*, 152(1992), 2114–2122.

J Sugerman. "Outcomes Research and Advance Directives," *Journal of Clinical Ethics*, 5(1994), 60–61.

J Sugerman, M Weinberger, and G Samsas. "Factors Associated with Veterans' Decisions about Living Wills," *Archives of Internal Medicine*, 152(1992), 343–347.

JM Teno, J Lynn, RS Phillips, et al. "Do Formal Advance Directives Affect Resuscitation Decisions and the Use of Resources for Seriously Ill Patients?" *Journal of Clinical Ethics*, 5(1994), 23–30.

JM Teno, HL Nelson, and J Lynn. "Advance Care Planning: Priorities for Ethical and Empirical Research," *Hastings Center Report*, 24(1994), S32–S36.

J Tsevat, EF Cook, DB Matcher, NV Dawson, SK Broste, AW Wu, RS Phillips, RK Oye, and L Goldman for the SUPPORT Investigators. "Health Values of the Seriously Ill." *Annals of Internal Medicine*, 122(1995), 514–520.

SB Yellen, LA Burton, and E Elpern. "Communication about Advance Directives: Are Patients Sharing Information with Physicians?" *Cambridge Quarterly of Healthcare Ethics*, 1(1992), 377–387.

SJ Youngner. "Applying Futility: Saying No Is Not Enough," *Journal of the American Geriatrics Society*, 42(1994), 887–889.

NR Zweibel and CK Cassel. "Treatment Choices at the End of Life: A Comparison of Decisions by Older Patients and Their Physician-Selected Proxies," *Gerontologist*, (1989), 615–621.

CHAPTER 12

N Ainslie and AE Beisecker. "Changes in Decisions by Elderly Persons Based on Treatment Description," *Archives of Internal Medicine*, 154 (1994), 2225–2233.

GJ Annas. "Asking the Courts to Set the Standard of Emergency Care—The Case of Baby K," *New England Journal of Medicine*, 330(1994), 1542–1545.

GJ Annas. "Reframing the Debate on Health Care Reform by Replacing Our Metaphors," *New England Journal of Medicine*, 332(11)(1995), 744–747.

H Brody. "The Physician's Role in Determining Futility," *Journal of the American Geriatrics Society*, 42(1994), 875–878.

ED Caine and YC Conwell. "Self-Determined Death, the Physician, and Medical Priorities: Is There Time to Talk?" *Journal of the American Medical Association*, 270(1993), 875–876.

AL Caplan. "Straight Talk about Rationing," *Annals of Internal Medicine*, 122(1995), 795–796.

CK Cassel and DE Meier. "Morals and Moralism in the Debate over Euthanasia and Assisted Suicide," *New England Journal of Medicine*, 323(1990), 750–752.

Council on Ethical and Judicial Affairs, American Medical Association. "Ethical Issues in Health Care System Reform: The Provision of Adequate Health Care," *Journal of the American Medical Association*, 272(1994), 1056–1062.

N Daniels. *Just Health Care*. (New York: Cambridge University Press, 1985).

M Danis, J Garrett, R Harris, and DL Patrick. "Stability of Choices about Life-Sustaining Treatments," *Annals of Internal Medicine*, 120(1994), 567–573.

CJ Dougherty. "Ethical Values at Stake in Health Care Reform," *Journal of the American Medical Association*, 268(1992), 2409–2412.

Editorial. "Who Owns Medical Technology," *Lancet*, 345(1995), 1125–1126.

K Faber-Langendoen. "The Clinical Management of Dying Patients Receiving Mechanical Ventilation: A Survey of Physician Practice," *Chest*, 106(1994), 880–888.

LJ Fitten, R Lusky, and C Hamann. "Assessing Treatment Decision-Making Capacity in Elderly Nursing Home Residents," *Journal of the American Geriatrics Society*, 38(1990), 1097–1104.

TR Fried, MD Stein, PS O'Sullivan, DW Brock, and DH Novack. "Limits of Patient Autonomy: Physician Attitudes and Practices Regarding Life-Sustaining Treatments and Euthanasia," *Archives of Internal Medicine*, 153(1993), 722–728.

JF Fries, CE Koop, CE Beadle, and the Health Project Consortium. "Reducing Health Care Costs by Reducing the Need and Demand for Medical Services," *New England Journal of Medicine*, 329(1993), 321–325.

GR Gillett. "Learning to Do No Harm," *Journal of Medicine and Philosophy*, 18(1993), 253–268.

JA Ginsburg and HD Scott. "A National Health Workforce Policy," *Annals of Internal Medicine*, 121(1994), 542–546.

M Gunderson and DJ Mayo. "Altruism and Physician Assisted Death," *Journal of Medicine and Philosophy*, 18(1993), 281–295.

DC Hadorn. "Setting Health Care Priorities in Oregon: Cost-Effectiveness Meets the Rule of Rescue," *Journal of the American Medical Association*, 265(1991), 2218–2225.

L Holmes, K Loughead, T Treasure, and S Galliuam. "Which Patients Will Not Benefit from Further Intensive Care after Cardiac Surgery?" *Lancet*, 344(1994), 1200–1202.

JK Inglehart. "Health Policy Report: The American Health Care System: Managed Care," *New England Journal of Medicine*, 327(1992), 742–748.

WA Knaus. "Criteria for Admission to Intensive Care Units." *Brookings Dialogues on Public Policy*. MA Strosberg, IA Fein, and JD Carroll, eds. (Washington, DC: Brookings Institute, 1986), pp. 44–51.

JD Lantos, PA Singer, RM Walker, et al. "The Illusion of Futility in Clinical Practice," *American Journal of Medicine*, 87(1989), 81–84.

LL Leape. "Error in Medicine," *Journal of the American Medical Association*, 272(1994), 1851–1857.

JR LeGall, S Memeshow, and F Saulnier. "A New Simplified Acute Physiology Score (SAPS II) Based on a European/North American Multicenter Study," *Journal of the American Medical Association*, 270(24) (1993), 2957–2963.

S Lemeshow and J Le Gall. "Modeling the Severity of Illness of ICU Patients: A Systems Update," *Journal of the American Medical Association*, 272(1994), 1049–1055.

S Lemeshow, D Teres, J Lalar, JS Avrunin, SH Gehlbach, and J Rapoport. "Mortality Probability Models (MPH II) Based on an International Cohort of Intensive Care Unit Patients," *Journal of the American Medical Association*, 270(1993), 2478–2486.

M Levetown, MM Pollac, TT Cuerdon, UE Ruttimann, and JJ Glove. "Limitations Withdrawals of Medical Intervention in Pediatric Critical Care," *Journal of the American Medical Association*, 272(16)(1994), 1271–1275.

KR Levit, HC Lazenby, CA Cowan, and SW Letsch. "National Health Expenditures, 1990," *Health Care Finance Review*, 13(1)(1991), 29–54.

DW Light. "The Practice and Ethics of Risk-Rated Health Insurance," *Journal of the American Medical Association*, 267(1992), 2503–2508.

B Lo, GA McLeod, and G Saika. "Patient Attitudes to Discussing Life-Sustaining Treatment," *Archives of Internal Medicine*, 146(1986), 1613–1615.

GD Lunberg. "American Health Care System Management Objectives: The Aura of Inevitability Becomes Incarnate," *Journal of the American Medical Association*, 269(1993), 2554–2555.

T Malloy, RS Wington, J Meeske, and TG Tape. "The Influence of Treatment Descriptions on Advance Medical Treatment Decisions," *Journal of the American Geriatrics Society*, 40(1992), 1255–1260.

CM Mangione and B Lo. "Beyond Fear: Resolving Ethical Dilemmas Regarding HIV Infection," *Chest*, 95(1989), 1100–1106.

A Meisel. "Legal Myths about Terminating Life Support," *Archives of Internal Medicine*, 151(1991), 1497–1502.

SH Miles. "Nourishment and the Ethics of Lament," *Linacre Quarterly*, 56(1989), 64–69.

DJ Murphy. "Can We Set Futile Care Policies? Institutional and Systemic Challenges," *Journal of the American Geriatrics Society*, 42(1994), 890–893.

JL Nelson. "Families and Futility," *Journal of the American Geriatrics Society*, 42(1994), 879–882.

Plato. *The Dialogs of Plato*. B Jowett, ed., 4th ed., rev. by DJ Allen and HE Dole. (London: Oxford University Press, 1953).

RM Poses, C Bekes, FJ Copare, and WE Scott. "The Answer to 'What Are My Chances, Doctor?' Depends on Who Is Asked: Prognostic Disagreement and Inaccuracy for Critically Ill Patients," *Critical Care Medicine*, 17(1989), 827–833.

TE Quill. "The Ambiguity of Clinical Intentions," *New England Journal of Medicine*, (Sept. 30, 1993), 1039–1040.

MC Rogers, R Snyderman, and EL Rogers. "Sounding Board: Cultural and Organizational Implications of Academic Managed-Care Networks," *New England Journal of Medicine*, 331(1994), 1374–1377.

LJ Schneiderman, RM Kaplan, RL Pearlman, and H Teetzel. "Do Physicians' Own Preferences for Life-Sustaining Treatment Influence Their Perceptions of Patients' Preferences?" *Journal of Clinical Ethics*, 4 (1993), 28–33.

MG Secundy. "Balancing Communication Skills and Clinical Assessment," *Journal of Clinical Ethics*, 4(1993), 185–186.

R Smith. "Medicine's Core Values: Summit Meeting Agrees on Several, but Others Need Further Debate," *British Medical Journal*, 309(1994), 1247–1248.

B Starfield. "Is Primary Care Essential?" *Lancet* 344(1994), 1129–1133.

JS Tabias and RL Soulami. "Fully Informed Consent Can Be Needlessly Cruel," *British Medical Journal*, 307(1993), 1199–1201.

T Tomlinson and H Brody. "Ethics and Communication and Do-Not-Resuscitate Orders," *New England Journal of Medicine*, 318(1988), 43–46.

DJ Ullyot. "President's Page: What Concerns Us about Managed Care?" *Journal of the American College of Cardiology*, 25(1995), 549–550.

J Virmani, LJ Schneiderman, and RM Kaplan. "Relationship of Advance Directives to Physician–Patient Communication," *Archives of Internal Medicine*, 154(1994), 909–913.

GS Wagner, B Cebe, MP Rozear, and EA Stead. *What This Patient Needs Is a Doctor*. (Durham, NC: Carolina Academic Press, 1978).

SH Wanzer, DD Federman, SJ Adelstein, et al. "The Physician's Responsibility toward Hopelessly Ill Patients: A Second Look," *New England Journal of Medicine*, 320(1989), 844–849.

G Weissmann. *The Doctor Dilemma: Squaring the Old Values with the New Economy*. (Knoxville, TN: Whittle Direct Books, 1992), p. 69.

SH Woolf. "Practice Guidelines: A New Reality in Medicine: Impact on Patient Care," *Archives of Internal Medicine*, 153(1993), 2646–2655.

"Hospital Appeals Decision on Treating Anencephalic Baby," *Hospital Ethics*, 9(1993), 6–7.

"Tomorrow's Doctoring: Patient Heal Thyself," *Economist*, (Feb. 1995), 19–21.

CHAPTER 13

LL Basta and M Davis. "Does the Living Will Deserve to Live? Lessons from Denmark" (in press).

DW Brock. "Advance Directives: What Is Reasonable to Expect from Them?" *Journal of Clinical Ethics*, 5(1994), 57–60.

Council on Scientific Affairs and Council on Ethical and Judicial Affairs, American Medical Association. "Persistent Vegetative State and the Decision to Withdraw or Withhold Life Support," *Journal of the American Medical Association*, 263(1990), 426–430.

P Juul-Jensen and M von Magnus. "Vejledning om laegers forpligtelser i relation til indholdet af livestestamenter mv," (Til landets laeger). *Sundhedsstyrelsens Vejledning*, Denmark. 22(Sept. 1992), 1300.

Biomedical Ethics, *Biolaw*, (Bethesda, MD: University Publications of America, 1994), S110–S150.

CHAPTER 14

LL Basta. *Can Medical Ethics Exist in an Economic Vacuum*. Paper presented at the annual meeting of the International Medical Society, Miami, FL (April, 1995).

LL Basta. "'The Universal Living Will,' A Third Generation Advance Directive," Copyright, Library of Congress No TXU 685-553, January 9, 1995.

L Cohn. "The Paradox of High-Tech Health Care: Has Our Technology Outstripped Our Ability to Be Ethical, Cost-Effective and Timely in Its Delivery?" *Chest*, 93(1988), 864–867.

A de Tocqueville. "Consequences of the Three Preceding Chapters." *Democracy in America*. (New York: Vintage Books), pp. 185–186.

DM English and A Meisel. "Uniform Health-Care Decisions Act Gives New Guidance," *Estate Planning*, (Nov.–Dec. 1994), 355–362.

G Grisez. "Should Nutrition and Hydration Be Provided to Permanently Comatose and Other Mentally Disabled Persons?" *Linacre Quarterly*, 57(1990), 30–43.

"Guidelines for Withholding Food and Water: Sustenance Discussed," *Medical Tribune* (October 4, 1990).

LC Hanson and M Danis. "Use of Life-Sustaining Care for the Elderly," *Journal of the American Geriatrics Society*, 39(1991), 772–777.

S Hook. "It Didn't Have to Be." *Living Philosophies: The Reflections of Some Eminent Men and Women of Our Time*. C Fadiman, ed. (New York: Doubleday, 1990), pp. 245–263.

NS Jecker. "Being a Burden on Others," *Journal of Clinical Ethics*, 4(1993), 16–20.

S Lemeshow and J Le Gall. "Modeling the Severity of Illness of ICU Patients: A Systems Update." *Journal of the American Medical Association*, 272(1994), 1049–1055.

RM McCann, WJ Hall, and A Groth-Juncker. "Comfort Care for Terminally Ill Patients: The Appropriate Use of Nutrition and Hydration," *Journal of the American Medical Association*, 272(1994), 1263–1266.

KM McIntyre. "Loosening Criteria for Withholding Prehospital Cardiopulmonary Resuscitation," *Archives of Internal Medicine*, 153(1993), 2189–2192.

T Malloy, RS Wington, J Meeske, and TG Tape. "The Influence of Treatment Descriptions on Advance Medical Treatment Decisions," *Journal of the American Geriatrics Society*, 40(1992), 1255–1260.

DJ Mazur and JF Merz. "How the Manner of Presentation of Data Influences Older Patients in Determining Their Treatment Preferences," *Journal of the American Geriatrics Society*, 41(1993), 223–228.

A Meisel. "Legal Myths about Terminating Life Support," *Archives of Internal Medicine*, 151(1991), 1497–1502.

A Meisel. "The Legal Consensus about Foregoing Life-Sustaining Treatment: Its Status and Its Prospects," *Kennedy Institute of Ethics Journal*, (1992), 309–345.

"Mercy for the Dying," *New York Times* (May 28, 1994), p. 18.

RA Pearlman, KC Cain, DL Patrick, et al. "Insights Pertaining to Patient Assessments of States Worse Than Death," *Journal of Clinical Ethics*, 4(1993), 33–41.

JE Ruark and TA Raffin. "Initiating and Withdrawing Life Support: Principles and Practice in Adult Medicine," *New England Journal of Medicine*, 318(1)(1988), 25–30.

NG Smedira, BH Evans, LS Grais, et al. "Withholding and Withdrawal of Life Support from the Critically Ill," *New England Journal of Medicine*, 322(5)(1990), 309–315.

RJ Sullivan. "Accepting Death without Artificial Nutrition and Hydration," *Journal of General Internal Medicine*, 8(1993), 220–224.

D Wilson. "New Insights into the Old Controversy over Long-Term Tube Feeding," *Bioethics Bulletin*, 5(1993), 1–8.

N Wray, B Brody, T Bayer, et al. "Withholding Medical Treatment from the Severely Demented Patient: Decisional Processes and Cost Implications," *Archives of Internal Medicine*, 148(1988), 1980–1984.

NR Zweibel. "Why Don't More People Have a Living Will?" *Medical Ethics*, 5(1990), 1–2.

Glossary

Active euthanasia Administering a medicine in a large enough dose with the intent to cause death and end suffering.

Advanced dementia The patient is generally awake and able to respond but is confused as far as time, place, and names are concerned because of deterioration of brain function not due to medication or a transient or reversible condition.

Assisted suicide Assisting patient to take his or her own life by providing a prescription or medicine in a dose sufficient to cause death.

Autonomy The principle of autonomy gives to the adult competent individual the right of self-determination and to have full control over decisions related to invasion of the body.

Beneficence The physician should be the patient's advocate under all circumstances. The patient's well-being should be placed above the physician's self-interest.

Central registry A computer-based data bank in which the names and identification of patients executing a Living Will is stored and can be readily retrieved.

Coma Total unawareness of self and environment with no periods of awakening; could be deep with total lack of response or less deep when some reflex response could be evoked with stimulation.

Competence to make medical treatment decisions Not necessarily equivalent to legal competence. It stipulates that the patient is able to understand, evaluate, and choose a treatment.

CPR Cardiopulmonary resuscitation by electric shock to the heart and artificial ventilation with or without external chest compressions. This is employed in the treatment of cessation of heart or lung function.

DNR Do-not-resuscitate order: indicates that for medical reasons or a terminal condition CPR is inappropriate in the event of cessation of the heartbeat or breathing.

High brain death Loss of high brain functions that define a person: decision making, passions, and reason.

Informed consent The patient agrees to a certain medical intervention based on his or her evaluation of all relevant information about the procedure, alternatives, and the competence of the treating team.

Living Will A legal document by which the patient states his/her preference to forgo life-sustaining treatment during terminal illness or a terminal state of unconsciousness.

Nonmaleficence "First do no harm" is the first law in the practice of medicine.

Passive euthanasia To terminate artificial means of life support in order to allow the natural process of death to take its course.

Paternalism Forced decision making without adequate information or consent from the patient.

Patient best-interest standard To apply treatment as judged to be in the patient's best interests in accordance to competent medical standards and rational prevailing societal sentiments.

Patient Self-Determination Act (Part of Budget Reconciliation Act of 1990, PL 101-508, sections 4206, 4751): A federal law, implemented in December 1991, that requires institutions to notify patients about the availability of formal advance directives.

Permanent vegetative state Irreversible vegetative state due to severe injury or acute oxygen deprivation to progressive degenerative metabolic or developmental brain disorder.

Persistent vegetative state A vegetative state that has persisted for a period of time (three months when caused by disease and twelve months after head injury).

Proxy for health-care decisions Many Living Will legislations allow for the appointment of a proxy decision maker to make health-care decisions when the patient is no longer competent to make them.

Shared decision making An adult, competent individual has the ultimate right to accept or refuse medical treatment even if that decision is deemed irrational or harmful.

Subjective standard There is clear and convincing evidence that the medical decision to be implemented is exactly what an incompetent or unconscious patient would have chosen for himself/herself.

Substitute judgment standard To implement the recommendation of an appointed guardian or family member as a substitute for the patient's own judgment.

Universal Living Will A new, comprehensive Living Will document written in plain English with a work booklet explaining various scenarios covered in the Will.

Vegetative state Unawareness of self and environment with sleep–wake cycles and with either complete or partial preservation of brain-stem autonomic functions.

Whole brain death Disappearance of all brain functions including the primitive autonomic functions of the brain stem. The brain produces no spontaneous electric activity.

Index

0 2117 0048628 8
W & J College Library